*May you have magic
and joy through the
seasons!*

Eight Extraordinary Days:
Celebrations, Mythology, Magic, and
Divination for the Witches' Wheel of the Year

KIKI DOMBROWSKI

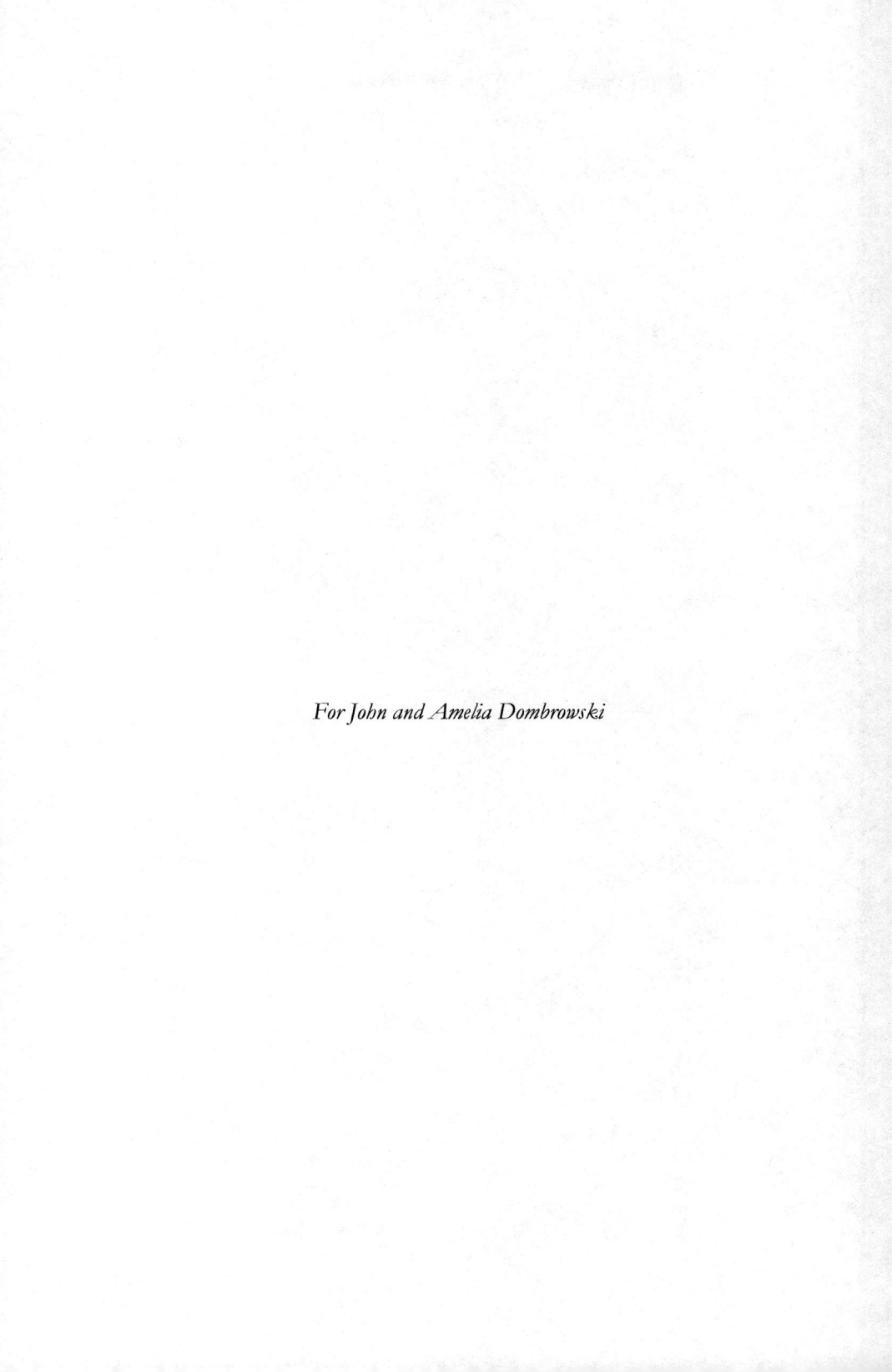

For John and Amelia Dombrowski

All photographs were taken from Public Domain websites.
The cover photograph is by Robert Lukeman.
A gracious thank you to Gregory Hamilton-White for designing my book cover for
me. You can find out more information about what he does at
www.aromagregory.com

CONTENTS

ACKNOWLEDGMENTS

This book wouldn't have been completed without the support and supervision of the following people. Thank you to Kyndyll Lackey for taking the time to help me with editing this book. Thank Tonya Brown at *Witch Way Magazine*, who has been an incredible support during the writing of this book. She has become a dear friend and I am so grateful. To the staff of AromaGregory: Greg, Roy, and Charity: thank you for pushing me to finally get my book completed. Thank you to my closest circle of friends: Joy, Brit, Morgan, Aurelien, Heidi, Kristin, and Robert, who listened to me talk about this project with enthusiasm. To Professor Parrish and Professor Mock: thank you for having faith in me as a writer. And to my family: thank you for accepting me for who I am and giving me a variety of titles, such as "the Mother Earth Child," and "the Alchemist." Your help throughout the years has allowed me to grow into the creative and eccentric person I am happy to be today.

INTRODUCTION

Think about the way you feel at different points of the year. How do you feel emotionally in the winter? What are you excited to do during the summer? What do you crave to eat or drink in the autumn? It seems like the usual progression of things: the changing of the seasons affects us on every single level: physical, mental, and spiritual. As nature evolves over the course of the seasons, our frame of mind and spiritual focus follow as well. Perhaps this explains the great volume of work available on holidays, pagan and otherwise. Visit any store and its shop will mirror the holiday of the season. At Halloween/Samhain we see spooky decorations; at Christmas/Yule we find evergreen trees and wreaths; in the spring we see all the necessary items to craft a garden and rest comfortably outdoors. In the summer we look forward to being outdoors, playing sports, hiking, camping, and having outdoor parties. In the autumn we look forward to large and comforting meals, campfires, and ghost stories. Mainstream magazines feature recipes and crafts to celebrate various holidays year-round. It seems that we've been programmed to feel a certain way at certain holidays, or as I like to believe, the seasons have programmed us to feel a certain way at certain holidays.

The Witches' Wheel of the Year encompasses the holidays that witches, modern pagans, and Wiccans celebrate. The Wheel of the Year represents the cycle of the seasons, following nature's birth, growth, decline, death, and rebirth. These eight holidays, also known as Sabbats, follow the cycles of nature and are meant to reconnect with pre-Christian traditions that celebrated agricultural and seasonal holidays. The word Sabbat comes from the French word s'ebattre, which means "to rejoice, frolic, and revel."

The book has a collective feel of information that you can reference and study at any time of the year, much like you would with an almanac. In this book I strive to weave together a few of my favorite things: mythology, ancient history, green magic, domestic witchcraft, meditations, and divination, all in the form of collected articles and research. In addition to this, I paired each holiday with a form of divination I believe to be compatible with the traditions and celebrations of the specific Sabbat. However, these forms of divination can be studied and practiced whenever you feel inspired.

For the most part you will find this book to be focused on Celtic and Norse mythology as well as Arthurian legend. I have branched out where I felt I could, but you should keep in mind that seasonal/agricultural holidays are not just limited to those regions. Additionally, modern pagans from varying traditions may have different ways of celebrating these holidays. I have attempted to offer methods for celebrating the holidays regardless of background, though my own areas of expertise are in mythology and green witchcraft. I have been a student of witchcraft since I was 13, and I share with you accumulated research and practice from over twenty years. This, however, is by no means the only information out there.

My hope is that no matter what your spirituality is, no matter how you choose to worship or what you believe in, you can enjoy the natural and magical progression of the seasons as written in this book. Allow this book to inspire you to find new ways to celebrate the Wheel of the Year or incorporate new traditions into your established ones. However you decide to read this book, see it as a springboard for deepening your appreciation for the natural cycle of life on Earth and gaining divine insight through mythology and magic.

CHAPTER ONE:

SAMHAIN

OVERVIEW, MAGIC, ACTIVITIES, AND CORRESPONDENCES

The history of Samhain takes us back to a time predating Christianity: a time of powerful and archetypal gods and goddesses, where life was not lost in a whirlwind of social media, where food had to be grown at home, honor had to be earned, knowledge of divinity was respected, and health and wellbeing were a fragile state for many. The passage of the season was observed with intensity, concern, and anticipation. Many pinpoint the Celtic celebration of Samhain as the origin from which Halloween would evolve, and its namesake has been resurrected for modern day pagans, witches, and Wiccans who celebrate the Old Ways.

A Brief Look at Celtic Samhain

Most information we have about Samhain was written down by missionaries visiting Ireland between 400 CE and 1100 CE. Samhain was the beginning of the New Year to the Celts. It was a liminal festival marking the time between the Autumn Equinox and the Winter Solstice. They celebrated the end of the harvest season, acknowledged the inevitable death of nature, and prepared for

transition into colder, darker months. The absolute last crop had to be harvested by Samhain and animals were tended to in preparation for colder months. Those animals that could not last the winter would be slaughtered: the meats would be enjoyed at great feasts along with the bounty from the final harvest, which included barley, apples, oats, nuts, wheat, and turnips.

The best known gathering of Samhain took place at the Hill of Tara in County Meath, Ireland. The Hill of Tara is an ancient sacred site, a place that was believed to be the entrance to the Otherworld. It was also a place where Irish kings held their royal reign. Almost 500 feet high, this prehistoric hill fort hosted a week-long Samhain celebration, beginning three days prior and lasting three days after Samhain. The feast hosted a gathering of tribes from all over Ireland. For the week there was feasting and drinking, sport competitions, horse racing, diplomatic discussion, and law regulation.

Additional archeological evidence suggests that massive bonfires were lit at the nearby Hill of Ward (or Tlachtga). It is believed all local hearth fires were extinguished at Samhain. Druids then ritualistically rekindled a new fire at the Hill of Ward. Embers from this fire were distributed to each home to initiate new fires for the new year. Ceremonies at the Hill of Ward are said to date all the way back to 1450 BCE, and to this day bonfires are still lit at Halloween in honor of the ancient traditions.

Samhain was not all regulations, agricultural work, and harvest. Samhain, perhaps most famously, also contained a mystical and supernatural element, as well. The ancient Celts believed Samhain was a time immersed in magic. As a day heralding the death of nature and final harvest, Samhain was shared with the realm of ancestors, spirits of the dead, and faeries. Celts believed the boundary between our world and the Otherworld -- that is the realm which shadows ours and is home to spirits and faeries -- was thinnest at Samhain. Access to the Otherworld was granted to (and often feared by) humans on Samhain. Likewise, residents of the Otherworld could easily visit our mortal world.

There are instances in Irish myth that show the magical and mystical nature of Samhain. Faeries were believed to travel from their summer homes in the hill mounds to their winter homes in the hill barrows on Samhain. Caer, a swan-girl in Irish legend, took her bird form on Samhain and met with Oenghus, god of love. God Dagda and Goddess Morrigan were said to mate on this day to ensure crop and animal fertility in the coming year. The goblin Aillen was burned at the Hill of Tara each Samhain until he was finally killed by Irish hero Finn. Another Irish hero, Cuchulain, is said to have gone on a faerie hunt on Samhain, where he killed birds that were actually shape-shifted goddesses.

Apples and Samhain

Apples hold a special place in Celtic mythology, where they are connected to otherworldly magic and considered to be the fruit of the dead. They are a symbol of magic, beauty, and immortality. The Celtic god Dagda lived in a kingdom with always-fruited and abundant apple trees. Apples are harvested in the autumn and were likely a staple item in Samhain feasts. They've played an important role in food, games, and fortune telling on Halloween, thus making them a key ingredient in Samhain celebrations. Over time, many forms of fortune telling involving apples became fun party games. Bobbing for apples was originally a marriage divination: the first person to bite into the apple would be the first person to marry in the upcoming year. Although there is no concrete evidence, bobbing for apples may actually have its roots dating all the way back to Celtic times. There is evidence, however, that it was in practice during medieval times, which we could conclude from manuscript illustrations, the first from the 14th century showing servants bobbing for apples.

Apple divination is a fun activity to try out on Samhain. Many of these divinations come to us from Victorian America, where colonists carried their traditions from Ireland and Britain. A simple apple divination to see your future romantic interest is as follows. Peel an apple, creating one long, unbroken peel. Take the apple peel and throw it over your shoulder. Next, examine the shape of the peel and see if it looks like a letter. This letter will be the first initial of your future romantic partner. An alternative way of doing this is to throw the peel into a bowl of water and see the letter shape it takes. Next, you can slice your apple and count the number of seeds. If there an even number of seeds you will find a romantic mate within the year. If there are an odd number of seeds you may have to wait a little longer.

Apples are said to have magical powers of enhancing beauty,

HALLOWE'EN PLEASURES

Bobbing. bobbing everywhere Apples in a tub.

assisting in healing, and being a special addition to a love spell. Samhain is also an excellent time to pay attention to messages in dreams. Taking note of images and messages from dreams can bring insight into your waking life. On Samhain take an apple and slice it in half, horizontally. Carve a topic you wish to know the future about in the flesh of the apple -- for example, money, health, love, or a symbol that represents one of these things. Anoint the apple with one drop of sandalwood oil and one drop of jasmine oil. Hold the apple back together in your hands and recite the following: "May this apple bring to me dreams of prophecy. This Samhain give me dreams with fortune's view, allow me to see the future true." Place the apple by your bedside and see if your Samhain dreams hold any messages about the future. The next morning, write your dreams down in a journal and follow up with the notes to see if they come true or resonate with you. Take the apple outside and leave it as an offering to the faeries.

Jack-o'-Lantern's History and Pumpkin Magic

It is believed that jack-o'-lanterns date back to Celtic times. At Samhain, turnips were hollowed out, lit, and carried or hung to ward off wandering spirits and mischievous faeries. But the most common tale of the jack-o'-lantern is the tale of the blacksmith Jack, who was rejected from Heaven and too evil to be welcomed to Hell. It is said that Jack won a bet against the devil and was thrown out of Hell. When he was thrown out of Hell and back to Earth, a burning coal followed him. Jack happened upon a turnip patch, and picked one and ate it as a snack. He placed the burning coal inside the hollowed out turnip and used it as a lantern to guide his eternal stroll around Earth. In the British Isles, turnips were customarily used to create jack-o'-lanterns. However, once immigrants settled in America, the jack-o'-lantern received an upgrade. Pumpkins are a common autumn fruit in America, abundant and ready for picking around Halloween. Immigrants in the New World also found the pumpkin to be much easier to carve than the stubborn turnip.

The pumpkin is a staple in the Halloween collection, but it also contains magical potency that can be used in Samhain magic as well. The pumpkin is associated with abundance, fertility, good health, and transformation. It is easy to see why it would be a wonderful fruit associated with fertility. Its round shape is reminiscent of a full, pregnant belly. It's full of seeds, which create life and abundance, connecting it to growth and prosperity. During Samhain collect pumpkin seeds and add them to prosperity mojo pouches. Or, hold a seed, make a wish, and plant it in the earth, asking to have the wish grow with the pumpkin in due time.

Bonfire Magic

Samhain is a time of transition; it is an excellent time to rid yourself of negativity and lifestyles that you have outgrown. Banishment magic is a tool for releasing all that no longer applies to you. This banishment spell is in honor of the bonfire traditions of

Celtic Samhain and can be done if you are attending a fire during the Samhain season. Prior to the bonfire, search for three small sticks. While looking, contemplate three things you want to banish from your life: perhaps it is financial debt, anxiety, an unhealthy diet, loneliness, or so on. When you have collected the sticks, write what you want to banish on them, or assign one thing you wish to banish to each stick. When you attend the bonfire, bring the sticks with you. When you feel the opportunity is right, take one stick at a time and throw it into the fire. Visualize the negativity leaving you, and imagine how good it would feel for that thing to be banished from your life. Finally, imagine what positive thing will replace the negative thing you banished. For example, without anxiety, imagine seeing yourself in a space of peace and quiet. How does it feel to have the obstacle or challenge removed from your life? How does it impact your life? Once you're confident with that banishment, repeat the process with the other sticks.

Samhain Spell Bottle

Witch Bottles have quite a place in the history of witchcraft. Spell bottles dating back to medieval times have been found in houses across the British Isles, mostly found buried on properties, hidden in chimneys, or stowed away in walls. It is believed that the contents were used to protect a home from evil and witchcraft, and the contents were not for the faint of heart. Nail clippings, thorns, hair, and even urine have been some of the contents found in medieval spell bottles. Although these may be a little antiquated or intense for some modern day crafters and practitioners, spell bottles are still created for various magical intentions. For example, if you would like to bring protection to your property you can add rosemary, nails, black crystals, and salt to a bottle and bury it on your property.

At Samhain, consider collecting items from nature that you associate with the season. For example, if you go on a hike, pick up an acorn, pine cone, pine needles, juniper berries, etc. In addition to what you find in nature, consider adding small tokens from ancestors, pumpkin seeds, apple seeds, black crystals, pure tobacco, dried chrysanthemums, angelica, or sprigs of yew. Decorate the bottle with orange, black, or purple designs if you're creative. You can keep this bottle on your altar when you want to reconnect with the energy of

Samhain, or wish to bring in the excitement, love, and otherworldly nature of October into your life.

Otherworld Incense Blend
Use this incense for lifting the veil between our world and the Otherworld. This is a loose leaf blend to burn on top of a charcoal disc. Mix equal parts of the following: rosemary, copal, myrrh, mugwort, calendula, and cinnamon. If you would like, add pure tobacco. This is a potent, smokey blend – you only need a pinch!

Samhain Journaling
- When was a time you felt you had to visit the underworld and examine your shadow side?
- Have you ever seen a ghost? What was the experience like?
- Tell a story about someone special from your life who has passed away.
- How did you celebrate Halloween as a child?
- What do you want to banish from your life? How would your life improve as a result of the banishment?
- What makes you feel like a witch? When did you know you were a witch?
- If you could speak to ancient ancestors, what would you ask them?

Correspondences:
- Names: Samhain, Halloween, All Hallow's Eve, Witches' New Year
- Date of Celebration: November 1st (or October 31st)
- Deities Honored: Anubis, Arawn, Baba Yaga, Cailleach, Cerridwen, Hecate, Inanna, Kali, Morrigan, Osiris, Persephone
- Magical Focus: divination, banishment, protection
- Activities: astral travel, bobbing for apples, carving pumpkins or turnips, contacting the spirit world, divination, dressing up, hay rides, honoring ancestors, visiting corn mazes
- Altar Decorations: acorns, apples, bells, black and orange candles, cauldron, fall leaves, jack-'o-lantern, masks, mementos from ancestors, pomegranates, pumpkins, scrying mirrors

- Food and Beverages: apple, candy, corn, mulled cider, nuts, pomegranate, pumpkin, roasted meats (especially pork), squash, turnips
- Plants, Herbs, Incense: allspice, calendula, catnip, chamomile, cinnamon, copal, dragon's blood, mugwort, myrrh, nutmeg, patchouli, rosemary, valerian, wormwood
- Crystals: black onyx, jet, obsidian, red jasper
- Colors: red, rusts, black, bronze, orange, yellow

HECATE AND THE CROSSROADS MEDITATION

Hecate is an ancient Greek Goddess of the crossroads, death, regeneration, and magic. She was once revered as a moon goddess in Greece, ruling over the three phases of the moon. As Hecate Thrice, she ruled over sky, sea, and earth. Under the darkness of the new moon, it is said she would roam the ancient roads with her dogs. Hecate was said to be skilled in divination. She was able to give visions for insight and guidance to humans. Offerings of dogs, black lambs, and honey were left for her at crossroads on full moons when divination was performed as well as rites to commune with the dead. In *Medea* by Eurpides, we see a once powerful goddess being demoted to a crone goddess of the underworld and servant to Persephone. By the Middle Ages she was known as the "Queen of Witches."

In *Pure Magic: A Complete Source in Spellcasting,* Judika Illes notes the natural connection witches have with Hecate: "midwives, herbalists, and magical practitioners consider themselves among Hecate's initiates."[1] Many witches today have reclaimed the magic and power of Hecate, looking to her in times of personal transition as well as seasonal transition, making her underworldly citizenship and magical powers a perfect fit for Samhain. Samhain is a special time to connect with Hecate and ask for her wisdom. Use this meditation to help you make a decision and choice between two options.

Before beginning the meditation consider what the two options you have. Clearly understand the two options and how it would benefit you to decide on one of them. Purify your body before the meditation with smudge, purifying bath, or oils. Bring yourself into a meditative state with whichever method you prefer. I recommend Laurie Cabbot's "Alpha State Meditation" in her book *Power of the Witch.* You can also try mindful breathing, a method which utilizes listening to your breathing and focusing solely on the action of your breathing, or listening to a recording of binaural beats, which are said to help ease the brain into a meditative state. You can also begin the meditation by visualizing a place you love and feel safe in. However you decide to move towards a state of meditation, follow the script below to connect with Hecate.

Visualize yourself on a quiet country road on Samhain Eve; it is dusk and the air is cool and crisp. You are on this road to find answers about what direction to take in the future. You are moving along the road to a sacred space ahead where Hecate is said to help wanderers find their way.

You begin to walk down the unpaved and dusty dirt road. It is by faint light and intuition that you are able to move towards the crossroads. You are holding a basket in your hand with offerings for Hecate. What are you giving to Hecate as an offering for her guidance? Honey? Wine? Garlic? An antique? A special jewel or trinket? Once you look at the offerings continue down the dirt road towards the crossroads.

As you move down the road, there are lanterns lit along each side of it as you approach a fork ahead. You see a special statue at the crossroads -- a silvery, beautiful woman with three busts: one facing forward, one facing down the left path, and one facing down the right path. She is the Triple Hecate. There are flowers, candles, decorations, and offerings displayed at the base of the Hecate statue. Many have come before you to seek the same wisdom and guidance, and many will come after you. But now is the special time for you to receive the guidance you need from Hecate.

Move towards the statue and place the offerings down. Greet Hecate in the manner you wish to. Thank her for helping you find clarity in your decision.

Begin by explaining your situation to Hecate. Ask her to show you the most benevolent outcome for choosing the first option. After a pause, Hecate responds to you, the bust to the left awakening and gesturing to the left road. She tells you there is nothing to be afraid of and asks you to walk down the left road to see your first option. Follow down the path and see what visions, wisdom, or intuitive hits you get out of the exploration. When you are done, return to Hecate at the crossroads.

Ask Hecate to show you the most benevolent outcome for the second option. The right bust comes to life and gestures towards the right road. Walk down this road to see what visions, wisdom, or intuitive hits you get out of exploring the second option. When you are done, return to Hecate at the crossroads.

Thank Hecate for the wisdom she shared with you. Ask her if there is anything else you need to know before you leave. Listen to anything she has to share: she may show you an event, give you something, or tell you something. Thank her when you are done and walk back down the path to where you started, taking with you the sacred advice and divine wisdom needed to make the best decision for yourself.

THE FANTASTIC TOAD

The image of the witch is all around us at the time of Halloween and Samhain. Whether she's posing sweetly in a vintage card or in displayed as a crone in a store's window, she usually is in the company of her familiars: the cat and the toad. Even though today's society has embraced the sweet and precious kitty, the same cannot be said for the fantastic toad.

During Medieval Times, the toad was said to be a demon in disguise. In England, they were a symbol of misfortune, and the fear of getting warts from touching a toad prevailed. Because of these misconceptions, sadly, our society has been turned off to the proud nature of the toad. However, if we look at the toad's many faces, perhaps we can learn to embrace his charm and magic.

Toad's Connection to Earth, Fortune and Fertility

The toad's closeness to the soil and nature truly makes him a cherished child of Mother Earth. In ancient Mexican cultures, he was a symbol of Earth. He is one of the animals you want to have in your garden. This amphibian thrives on bugs that would normally do damage to crops and flowers. His song varies from species to species, yet its soothing voice lets us know that nature is blossoming. His presence, surprisingly, has historically been a symbol of fortune and fertility.

In parts of Central Europe, it was believed that toads were guardians of great treasures. Therefore, to treat a toad kindly could potentially mean being rewarded with a gift from his hoard. In Estonia, it was believed that house spirits or faeries took the form of a toad. As a result, they were well respected as signs of good fortune and wealth. Feng Shui pays tribute to the Chinese legend of the three-legged toad of the moon in the form of figurines, which are said to bring money and prosperity. Tin miners in Cornwall believed the sight of the toad while mining signaled a lucky strike.

Toads were a symbol of luck in love and fertility as well. Perhaps this is in part due to the many eggs it releases and the toad's birth and metamorphosis in water. One folk medicine remedy suggested that the blood of a toad was a powerful aphrodisiac. In Scotland, it was believed to be good luck if a toad crossed a bride's path. Votives and offerings in the shape of toads would be left in central European churches by the Mother Mary for conception and smooth pregnancy.

Toad's Connection to Witches

It was during the Burning Times that the confessions and legends of toads began to intermingle with the world of the witch. In one confession, a witch said that she gathered toads to bring with her for Sabbat celebration. Oddly, she dressed them in small black or scarlet colored velvet robes, fashioning some with bells. Another sorcerer confessed that his toad familiar gave him the ability to be invisible, transport to different places, and shape-shift into the form of any animal.

The toad's appeal in magic is most likely in part to its natural toxic secretions, called Bufotenine, which comes from glands behind their ears. This poison was allegedly used in potions, flying ointments, and in alchemy. Specifically, the skin of the toad was used in flying ointments, and in alchemy toads were considered to symbols the dark side of nature. Toads even received a small role in Macbeth as an ingredient in the witches' "charmed pot." Furthermore, many shamanic cultures revered the secretions of the toad for hallucinogenic experiences.

Toad's Connection to the Otherworld

In ancient Germanic regions, it was unlucky to kill toads because it was believed that human souls resided in them. The belief that human souls were inside the toad progressed into the idea that toads were actually sinners who passed over and were undergoing penance. As a result, toads were to be treated with sympathy and pity. A story from Godfrey-Leland states that one toad would crawl to the altar of "Saint Michael in Schwatz" on the evenings before festivals to pray and weep.

Toads even served as guardians for those who passed over. In Lithuania, there are grave markers in the shape of toads. Toad's magic also assisted in divination and amulets. In Ancient Egypt, small amulets of toads were worn as symbols of creation, birth, and rebirth. One object from the Late Dynasty of Egypt is most fascinating: it is a magic rod with small figurines of toads, frogs, and turtles, which were believed to be helpers to the Sun God. The object was used as part of a burial to guarantee rebirth and triumph over evil forces. In *Natural History*, Pliny explains that the bones of a toad had the ability to soothe quarrels and acts as an aphrodisiac. This could be the foundation for the lore of the "toad stone, " the precious stones in the toad's head that could bring great happiness and detect poison. Many an amulet bears the shape the toad, with the wish of drawing their magic and good fortune into the wearer's life.

The Toad as an Animal Totem

Welcoming the toad into your life will bring grounding energy. He represents strength, pride, and nature. If you are looking for a way to connect with the elements of earth and water as an amphibian does, the toad is able to traverse and master both of these. Much like the frog, the toad also expresses the ability to transform, as he does through his life. He can help gain the ability to see people and nature through keen observation, as well as turn inwards for a deeper understanding of the self. More than anything, it is the toad's quiet pride and patience that allows it to prosper and bring luck and magic into the lives of those he touches.

A Toad Stone Alternative

On Samhain, you can perform a small spell to create your own toad stone. This gentle approach to creating a toad stone does not involve the harm of any animals, although you will need to get your hands dirty in the soil. You will need a piece of moss agate, a green candle, and vetivert oil. On the morning before Samhain, bring the moss agate to a place where you know toads reside. This could be in your garden, by a local pond, or if you are fortunate enough to have a toad as a pet, in your toad's tank. If you do not believe you have toads in your neighborhood, simply find a natural place in your garden or yard where you can place a figurine of a toad. Or, find a small pot and fill it with soil from outdoors, bring it indoors and place it by an image or figurine of a toad. Take the clean stone (don't anoint with oils- this could harm the toad) and bury it in the soil at this location. Recite the following incantation:

Precious toad, spirit of the Earth:
I ask you to bless this stone,
so I may have fortune and love in my life.
And in return, I will revere you this Samhain Eve.

On Samhain Eve, anoint the green candle with vetiver oil, and light it in reverence to the toad spirit. Take a moment to envision the toad, giving thanks to its presence in your life. If there is a specific magic you would like from the toad stone, whether it be for fertility, prosperity, divination, transformation, love, luck, or self-examination, envision yourself receiving the magic's end result. The following morning, retrieve the stone and carry it with you to bring good luck and fortune. If you wish to bring the good fortune of the toad into your life, consider getting (or creating) a toad house in your garden. This way, you can enjoy the presence of the toad as a familiar.

FLYING WITCHES' OINTMENT: A POISON HISTORY AND A MODERN RECIPE

Astral Projection is a term used to describe the psychic experience of seemingly leaving the body to visit other places and times. It is when our spiritual or astral essence is said to leave the physical constraints of the human body. The history of trying to become psychically charged, finding spiritual nexus through trance, and experience the out-of-body sensation of astral travel goes back to the earliest tribes. Singing, dancing, and using substances that caused hallucinations were methods of trying to access astral travel and divine prophecy.

There is a long, historical tradition of ancient civilizations using hallucinatory substances to have a drug-induced state, feeling it was a spiritual experience drawing them closer to divinity and deeper understanding of themselves and the world around them. The Oracle at Delphi inhaled the gases and vapors said to give them their sight, though some archaeologists believe their water was tainted with mind-altering, naturally occurring chemicals. In Peru, Ayahuasca is a drink created for highly powerful hallucinatory experiences. In her blog, "On Flying Witches Ointments," Sarah Anne Lawless points out that remains of belladonna, marijuana, and henbane have been discovered in Northern Europe all the way back to the Neolithic Period. It is no surprise that flying witches' ointment would have been created to mimic these same out-of-body experiences.

The witches' experience with hallucinatory trance manifested in the concoction of flying witches' ointment, which was said to help the witch leave the human realm and transcend to magical heights, metaphorically flying on her broom to locations of her pleasing. During the witch trials between the 15th and 17th centuries, people accused of witchcraft were said to possess the strange ointment, or said to tell wild tales of the flights they experienced while under its influence. Many academics, philosophers, scientists, and alchemists studied the ointments, Sir Francis Bacon being one of the few notables to study the concoction.

There are only a dozen or so recipes recorded, most of which appear incomplete or confusing. The cryptic recipes may have actually served as a means to protect non-practitioners from accidentally poisoning themselves, as ingredients were given nicknames and measurements were not recorded. The secrets of the ingredients, measurements, and preparations are lost with those who crafted the ointments originally.

It appears that the historical witches' ointment was made from a base of animal fat. Tinctures and herbs with hallucinatory or sedative effects were added to the ointment – this possibly included poisonous herbs such as hemlock, belladonna, henbane, nightshade, and mandrake. These herbs can be dangerous and can cause serious illness, hallucinations, paralysis, blindness, and death. The witch was said to anoint herself with the ointment. It has been suggested that the ointment was applied to a porous membrane (i.e. inside the nose or vagina) for quick absorption into the body, though this is most likely a myth. The effects of the plants and herbs would make the user feel as if s/he were flying.

Due to the poisonous, volatile, and unpredictable nature of most of the herbs associated with the flying witches' ointment recipes, it is not recommended to brew or use. The use of potentially illegal and harmful drugs is not justified in today's world by many. Those who misuse them may end up in humiliating binds, as one lady high on belladonna found out after she stole a boat and road it through a UK canal. The risk of death is too severe to bother experimenting with incomplete historical recipes. Flying is best left for the birds (or on Southwest), and astral projection is best practiced in a safe setting with professionals, meditation, psychic exercises, and/or gentler concoctions. That being said: it is not beyond the scope of a witch to create an ointment with safe herbs associated with astral projection and psychic enhancement. Some will go further to have hallucinatory experiences, though that will not be recommended here.

I created a safer and friendly modern version of a Flying Witches' Ointment. This is a topical ointment only and not to be ingested. Please keep in mind that some of the ingredients can still aggravate gentle skin and sinuses. Read up on the herbs and understand what they are for, or try a test patch of the ointment. Do not use anything that you think would be harmful to you, and if you have any questions consult your doctor or an herbalist. It should also be noted that there are some practitioners who do not bother using "modernized" Flying Witches' Ointment, as it does not have the same psychotropic effects as powerful (and poisonous) recipes have. Decide what practice is best for you, and keep your safety and wellness the top priority. If you are willing to work with aromatherapy and herbs with magical properties associated with astral projection and psychic abilities, enjoy the recipe below!

Kiki's Flying Witches' Ointment
>   8 ounces Shea or Cocoa Butter
>   3 Hazelnuts
>   3 Star Anise
>   3 Cinnamon sticks
>   1 tablespoon Mugwort
>   1 tablespoon Ditany of Crete
>   1 tablespoon Cinquefoil
>   ½ teaspoon ground Nutmeg
>   (optional, can be irritant) ½ teaspoon Scullcap
>   (optional, can be irritant) ½ teaspoon Wormwood
>   9 drops Benzoin essential oil
>   9 drops Jasmine essential oil
>   9 drops Sandalwood essential oil

Bring water to a boil and then reduce to a simmer using a double boiler. If you do not have a double boiler, bring water to a boil in a pot and fit a metal mixing bowl on top of the pot to create a double boiler. Slowly melt the base until it is completely liquid. Add the herbal ingredients (all but the oils) and simmer for at least thirty minutes, stirring frequently. At the end of the thirty minutes, turn off the heat and stir in the oils. Pour the concoction through a mesh strainer or cheesecloth into a measuring cup. Then, transfer the still-liquid ointment to selected containers. Allow it to cool and solidify before use.

DIVINATION HIGHLIGHT: SCRYING

Scrying is a form of divination that utilizes the art of gazing. Scrying involves gazing into a reflective surface to try and gain psychic impressions. For some, scrying can help shift the mind into a trance-like state where psychic messages are easily received in the form of images, symbols, and feelings. It is a form of divination that is commonly associated with Samhain, perhaps in part due to the Victorian divination that requires gazing into a mirror to see images of future lovers.

History of Scrying

The history of scrying is a vast one: cultures from around the world used scrying as a means of gaining psychic information. Ancient societies such as Mesopotamia, Greece, Rome, and Celtic Ireland practiced scrying. It is a practice that continued through history, influencing some of the greatest esoteric minds. Dr. John Dee used a crystal ball to communicate with angels in the late 16th century, as a result of his practice he gained knowledge of the Enochian alphabet and language. Nostradamus was said to have used scrying to predict future lineage of the kings of France for Queen Catherine de'Medici.

What to Use for Scrying

Many scryers have depended on a crystal ball or blackened mirror to scry. Crystal spheres and mirrors are a staple item at metaphysical shops; obsidian or jet are favored crystals for scrying because of their dark and shiny surfaces. You can however practice scrying without a store bought item if you would prefer. Some people choose to carefully stare into the flame of a small spell candle. Some like to use a reflective surface of water to scry into. To do this at home, fill a dark shallow bowl with water. One option to make the water darker is to add a few drops of black ink into the water.

Preparation for Scrying and How to Scry

People have different methods for setting up an area in which to scry. Be sure that you will not be disturbed by outside distractions in this space. Prepare a clean, comfortable, and darkened space to scry in – the room can have a traditional protective circle of salt, be decorated with crystals, and have incense burning, if those are things you would like to add to your space. You may want to smudge before and after your sessions to clear energy.

The method I have found most functional is as follows: Set up your scrying instrument (crystal ball, bowl, or mirror) on a table in front of you. Use two candles on the sides of the instrument. Some people prefer just one candle -- play around with this to see what works best for you. Arrange the candles so the surface has a glow of light, but does not reflect back a mirror reflection of yourself (you do not want to be staring at yourself for the entire scrying session). Close your eyes for a moment to ground and center yourself. Use this time to say a mantra or prayer, connect with spirit guides, and/or focus your intentions on a question you would like to examine during your scrying session. When you open your eyes, gaze into the surface of the scrying instrument. "Unfocus" your eyes, and lean into the feeling of "staring into space." Quiet your mind by focusing on your breath. Scrying sessions generally are between 5 and 20 minutes long. When you first begin, keep your sessions shorter, and continually increase the amount of time you scry.

What to Expect from Scrying

The big question is: what are you going to experience when you scry? Results differ from scryer to scryer, and from session to session. Some scryers say they will see actual images in the surface -- perhaps their eyes have a moment of "matrixing" where a shape seen in the surface is reclassified in their mind as something they're already familiar with. Some say they will see nothing at all, but instead experience a very calming and meditative session where they are able to escape the "hamster's running wheel" feeling in their mind, coming out of the session feeling refreshed, zen, or inspired. Others have said they've seen the scrying tool's surface fill with what appears to be clouds or smoke. Instead of looking for something, perhaps it is worth noticing how you feel or what you hear. Much like dream interpretations, scrying interpretations tend to be personal, based on personal experiences and associations with certain symbols and images. Through practice and journaling you can start to develop a sense of what certain images, sounds, and feelings indicate and represent. Journaling also will allow you to the valuable opportunity to reflect on past sessions to see if anything has come to pass.

Scrying Exercises in Nature for Samhain

Scrying doesn't need to be confined to indoor spaces. It can be experimented with in a natural setting as well. One traditional method of scrying uses the surface of water. Consider visiting a natural body of water during the night hours and using the water's surface and moon's reflection as a means for scrying. I know for me personally one of the more powerful scrying experiences I had was with water; during a supermoon full moon, I went to the bank of the Connecticut River and had a profound scrying experience with memorable images that left me feeling spiritually attuned. Another option for scrying with water could be visiting a stream or the ocean during the day, and watching the light play with the moving water. Perhaps the sound of the crashing waves or a bubbling brook will put you in a trance-like state where you feel inspired to receive or even hear messages from spirit. According to Cassandra Eason in *Scrying the Secrets of the Future*, ancient Druids would go behind a waterfall and look through the falling water to scry.[2]

As Samhain is considered a fire festival, scrying can be done (cautiously) with fire as well. Fire ceremonies are an ancient practice, and gazing into the flame for wisdom may hold messages as ancient as they are sacred.

During a Samhain bonfire take a moment to quietly enjoy the dancing flames, asking Spirit to give you lasting spiritual and psychic impressions for the upcoming new year. Enjoy the power, light, and warmth of the fire for both its energizing connection to Samhain and its sacred and ancient ability to drift into a spiritual trance so essential for initiating a scrying session. You may want to focus on the shape of the flame, the glowing of the coals and the wood, the noise the fire makes, or even the way the smoke moves. Contemplate what different events would mean to you: what would the message be if the smoke kept smothering you? What if you were debating something and there was a sudden loud pop in the fire?

If you wish to examine more fire divination you may also read about Pyromancy in the Imbolc chapter.

HONORING QUIET TIME IN NOVEMBER

For many witches, the month of October is a monumental one: it is a month of anticipation culminating in the celebration of Samhain. For witches, October can feel like a hectic time of juggling a busy schedule of leading workshops on witchcraft or reading tarot. For the partying witch, Halloween isn't just an evening affair; it is a month-long celebration of Haunted Hayrides, costume parties, and guided walks through cemeteries and paranormal hotspots. And for those who love a good cozy feeling, October is the welcoming tide of everything pumpkin flavored as well as the right time to bust out sweaters from the closet.

Let's face it: we had a really good October, but we are wiped out! November is the true time of reflection and relaxation, as it heralds in the blank slate weekends, restful time alone, and the joyous return to honoring life inside the home. For many, October is so much fun there is barely space for peace and quiet. Allow the crisp air of November and the quietness of the evening sky to ask you the opportunistic question of "Now What?"

Creating a Sacred Space and Honoring Introspection

November through February (or March or April, depending on where you live) is a darker, colder time, when the notion of spending more than twenty minutes outdoors can incite whimpering and whining. With the exception of snow shoe hiking enthusiasts and ice skaters, it is not the best feeling when you look out the window and see a cold, damp, dark day outside. Fold to the temptation to spend time inside. Make November a time when you can create a sacred space inside your home, where you feel comfortable and can explore your spirituality. While indoors, it is a great time to take up hobbies and activities that allow you the opportunity to spend time with the most important person in your life: yourself. Contemplate what aspects of yourself you have been neglecting and use the downtime of the indoor months accordingly.

Candles, incense, crystals, inspiring artwork, books, and house plants all seem to create an inviting space. However, it is important to consider what is most important to your own comfort. What is your favorite room of the house? What is it you would like to accomplish in there? If you are an avid reader, do you have a bright book nook where you can curl up for time with your favorite heroines on a Sunday afternoon? If you need more rest, how is your bedroom set up? Is the artwork soothing and calming? How do you invite magic into each room of the house? Is it with crystals, amulets, antiques, or trinkets from travel? Personalize and spiritualize your space. Light incense in the living room. Put potted plants in the window. Diffuse lavender essential oil in your bedroom. Decorate with candles and crystals. Take time to clean, organize, and create an area where you can spend hours cultivating rejuvenation, creativity, and spirituality. And when all else fails, build a blanket fort.

Holiday Fund Spell and Prosperity Magick with Lakshmi

No matter what holiday you enjoy at the end of December, there tends to be a good deal of gift exchanging involved in the process. Although there are many ways to be a frugal shopper, the holiday season can certainly create a drain on prosperity. November is a great time to do some prosperity work to fortify your bank account for all that spending. This "Holiday Fund Spell" is adapted from "Lakshmi Bank" in the wonderful book *A Goddess is a Girl's Best Friend* by Laurie Sue Brockway. In her book, Brockway suggests making a bank to the Hindu goddess of prosperity, wealth, and good fortune in order to increase the flow of money in your life. Find a glass jar or container and place a picture of Lakshmi on it. In the bottom of the container place a piece of green jade, aventurine, or other crystal associated with money. The first money to place in the jar should be four new quarters, which you can anoint with patchouli oil or money-attracting oil if you would like. Place money into the jar each day, no matter how large or small the amount is. When it is time to empty the jar and access your holiday funds, be sure to put aside a small amount of the wealth you've attracted to donate to charity.

Turn Towards Creativity

Allow the quiet and reflective energies of November to open up your creative side. Everyone is creative: from cooking, to writing, to tap dancing, to knitting scarves, you have a creative talent that can be explored further! Let Pinterest be your map on the quest for making the most impressive of holiday goods. Let your Book of Shadows help you add a bit of magic to each creation. When making food consider the magical properties and see if you can create jams and jellies with the intentions of a kitchen witch. "Persephone's Pomegranate and Cranberry Jam," or "Sugar Plum Faerie Food" can offer a slice of spirit with spice. Make oatmeal cookies with raisins for prosperity or dark chocolate truffles with cherries for love.

For writers, November is synonymous with NaNoWriMo, which stands for National Novel Writing Month. If you are a writer, NaNoWriMo is an online platform through which people try to reach a goal of writing 50,000 words within the month of November. Though the task seems daunting, it is a great support system for authors trying to push through the novel-writing project. Although it is an online group, many cities have local meet-ups known as write-ins. If you are not a JK Rowling or George Martin in the making, consider if writing in other capacities can be of service to you. Dream journaling is an excellent means of recalling messages and symbols from your dreams. Poetry writing is the perfect opportunity to express those feelings and emotions you have had trouble vocalizing. And list writing is a chance to organize thoughts and create plans and goals towards a more fulfilling life. Pick up a pen and see what magic can come from it.

SAMHAIN CHAPTER NOTES

[1] Illes, Judika. *Pure Magic: A Complete Source in Spellcasting.* San Francisco, CA: Weiser Books, 2007. P. 39.

[2] Eason, Cassandra. *Scrying the Secrets of the Future.* Franklin, NJ: New Page Books, 2007.

CHAPTER TWO:
YULE

OVERVIEW, MAGIC, ACTIVITIES, AND CORRESPONDENCES

Yule may fall at one of the coldest times of the year, but it is still a time of hope. This is the shortest day of the year, and it signifies that every day after this until the Summer Solstice will grow longer. We need celebrations this time of year to get us through the cold and dark days. The sun will grow stronger, and life will eventually return to nature. At Yule we come together with our loved ones to have feasts and exchange presents. We take comfort in the warmth of each other's company. We give thanks for our families, find peace with others, rest, and review the year.

History of Yule and Winter Solstice Celebrations

Many Wiccans, Pagans, and witches always have a good chuckle when they ask how Yule is celebrated. Why? Many of the customs are those people would usually associate with Christmas, because Christians adapted old pagan customs to fit their holiday. This is not so unusual: many cultures adapt and change things to fit new needs and beliefs. Just look at how the Romans borrowed from the Greeks. In the same way, you will find that Yule has similar traditions to those enjoyed at Christmastime.

Yule itself was a winter festival celebrated by Scandinavian and Germanic tribes, though the celebration of the winter solstice is something that cultures around the world took part in. The word "Yule" comes from the Icelandic word "jol" and the Old English word "geol," meaning "wheel." Yule was a 12-day festival of celebration with drinking and feasting. At this time of the year, Odin would be known as "Jolnir," the Lord of Yule, who would give gifts to people in the countryside, much like our modern-day Santa gives gifts to well-behaved children.

In Rome, Saturnalia was celebrated to honor the god Saturn, who was said to help the return of spring and the growing season. Festivities began at the Temple of Saturn, candles were lit to keep away evil spirits, and bonfires were built to celebrate the return of the sun. Offerings of wax dolls and clay masks were left to Saturn, replacing earlier traditions of human sacrifice. Saturnalia is most widely recognized as being a wild holiday, when masters and slaves traded places. On this holiday mischief was at hand, as slaves and masters exchanged their roles, and the king of slaves was known as the Lord of Misrule. There was plenty of gambling, feasting, and  drinking to be had at this roguish time of the year, where all pretenses and societal norms were thrown to the wayside.

Western Europe was not the only place where the Winter Solstice was celebrated. In Ancient Egypt, the birth of the sun god Horus was also celebrated at the Winter Solstice, also during a twelve-day festival. According to Dorothy Morrison in *Yule: A Celebration of Warmth and Light*, buildings were decorated with twelve-fronded palm branches: "Because palm branches put out one shoot each month, the twelve-fronded branch formed a type of calendar. This made them a great representation of the entire birth, death, and rebirth cycle of the Sun; using them to honor the Sun was believed to speed His growth and strength, and encourage Him to stay in the sky longer."[1]

Mistletoe Magic

Mistletoe is native to Europe and Great Britain; it grows on host trees such as oak or apple. As Frank Tainter observes in his article "What does Mistletoe have to do with Xmas?", "Mistletoes are flowering plants (angiosperms) that obtain their nutrition by living on and parasitizing other plants. This relationship was observed across the European continent by ancient peoples who were so impressed with these plants that the mistletoe became interwoven into legends, myths, and religious beliefs."[2]

According to Roman historians, Pliny the Elder wrote about his observations of Celt tribes in *The Natural History*, noting that mistletoe was a revered plant to the Druids. Mistletoe was hardy enough to stay green in the coldest part of the year, showing its virility and endurance. The Druids believed that mistletoe that grew on oak was the most sacred of all. n the *The Secret of Mistletoe*, A.R. Bane shares a story about faeries' connection to the plant: "Faeries lived in the folds of the green mistletoe leaves during the winter...its magical powers protected them from the elements."[3]

Druids believed that mistletoe had healing powers, representing life, endurance, and hope during the coldest months of the year. Mistletoe was collected in a special ceremony by Druid priests, cut with a golden sickle during a specific phase of the moon. Pliny said that the Druids made a potion from the mistletoe to help protect against illness, though this is not recommended today, as mistletoe is toxic to ingest.

Mistletoe has been linked to lightning and thunder and has been considered protective against stormy weather. In Germany, mistletoe was known as ghost stick, and anyone who held it was said to be able to see ghosts. Mistletoe berries grow in bunches of three, connecting it to the triskele symbol and sacred triad. Mistletoe returns to the spotlight at the Summer Solstice as well, when it is said that having it under your pillow on Midsummer's Eve will lead to psychic dreams.

Mistletoe is connected to fertility magic and can be hung in bedrooms to help promote conception. At Yule we are all familiar with the tradition of being kissed if found standing under mistletoe, and perhaps this connects back to the idea that it is a plant that assists in fertility. Decorate your Yule tree with mistletoe to bring energies of love, good health, and hope into your home.

Holly Magic

Holly is a protective herb and said to promote luck when it is carried. Hang holly around the house at Yule for good luck. In *Cunningham's Encyclopedia of Magical Herbs*, Scott Cunningham suggests the following ritual with holly: "After midnight on a Friday, without making a sound, gather nine holly leaves, preferably from a non-spiny plant. Wrap these up in a white cloth using nine knots to tie the ends together. Place this beneath your pillow and your dream will come true."[4] You can also create a wreath with holly woven into it as a good luck charm for your home.

Yule Log

Traditionally, a Yule log would be collected and carved to fit into the fireplace. The log would be lit on the Winter Solstice, and if it stayed lit until morning, the home would be blessed with luck and fortune. Before the log was lit, it would be decorated with evergreens, sometimes also sprinkled with offerings of grain or cider. It was also said that while the log burns, people would gather around the fire to tell stories and sing songs. A piece of the Yule log would be preserved to be used as kindling for the following year's Yule log fire. If you light a Yule log, make a wish anytime the wood pops or sparks. You can also scatter the ashes from the Yule log in the garden to ensure an abundant crop in the spring.

If you are more of a kitchen witch, or just enjoy a reason to eat sweets, there are chocolate cake recipes made to like a Yule Log as well. Bake and decorate this, and light candles in it.

Yule Tree Ornaments

One of the most fun activities of the holiday season is decorating a tree for the house. An evergreen Yule tree would be brought into the home and decorated as a symbol of green life in the darkest time of the year. Decorations would be put on it for good luck and to celebrate the return of the sun. There are many homemade decorations that can be made to incorporate magic into them:

- Cinnamon Star for Prosperity: You will need five cinnamon sticks and various herbs for decoration. With a hot glue gun, gently glue together the sticks, one at a time, to form a star. You may want to wrap ribbon or decorative twine at the corners to cover the glue. Decorate the star with bay leaves, moss, and seeds for prosperity.
- Orange Slices for Sunlight: Take an orange and carefully slice it thin. Cover a baking sheet with aluminum foil and lay the orange slices on them. Cover the slices with a generous amount of confectioner's sugar and bake at 200 degrees for two to three hours, flipping over halfway through. This will dry out the oranges, though you may want to hang them to dry afterwards as well. These orange slices make beautiful, natural ornaments, or string them together with dried apple slices to make a garland, celebrating the brightness of the sun and the warmth and love of home.
- Ornaments with Intention: You can find empty, clear ornaments at most hobby stores that are meant to be filled with whatever decorations you wish. To create ornaments that have magical properties for specific intentions, consider using the following decorations/ingredients:
    - For health and wellness: Incorporate lavender, eucalyptus, rosemary, thyme, peppermint, crystal quartz, lemon and lime peels, and blue or white colored decorations.
    - For money and prosperity: Incorporate chamomile, basil leaves, dill weed, coins, pine needles, seeds, green rice, beans, jade, green calcite, lode stone, and green or gold colored decorations .
    - For love: incorporate rose buds, dried apple pieces, violets, tonka beans, vanilla beans, rose quartz, rhodochrosite, ruby, garnet, and pink or gold colored decorations.
    - For wisdom and creativity: use acorns, hazelnuts, almonds, and yellow or orange colored decorations.
    - For magic and psychic abilities: include star anise, amethyst, moonstone, and purple colored decorations.

- For a Yule themed ornament: use mistletoe, holly, evergreen, ivy, birch, pine cones, pyrite, bloodstone, and red and green colored decorations.

Three Candles, Three Wishes Spell

At this time of joy and light, cast this spell to manifest three wishes. Each candle brings you Yuletide gifts: red for love, green for prosperity, and gold for hope.

Light the red candle the night before Yule, contemplating how you want to see love manifested in your life. Light the red candle and recite: "With this red candle on Yule, I draw love close and dear to me. My wish for love shall be granted, the most benevolent outcome to be fulfilled. So mote it be."

Light the green candle the night of Yule, contemplating how you want to see prosperity manifested in your life. "Light the green candle and recite: "With this green candle on Yule, I draw prosperity close and dear to me. My wish for prosperity shall be granted, the most benevolent outcome to be fulfilled. So mote it be."

Light the gold candle the night after Yule, contemplating what you are hopeful for in your life. What are you thankful for? Where do you need to make peace? Light the gold candle and recite: "With this gold candle on Yule, I draw hope close and dear to me. My wish for hope shall be granted, the most benevolent outcome to be fulfilled. So mote it be."

Yule Present Meditation

We often equate December holidays with exchanging gifts with our loved ones. We give gifts to show our gratitude and love, and to spread comfort and joy. For this meditation we will look at the presents under the Yule tree to better understand what gifts have come into your life, what you are most thankful for, and what magical gifts you can carry with you and focus on whenever you need to.

Begin by moving into a comfortable, seated position. You may want to do this in a room in your home that is decorated for the holidays or by a warm winter fire. If you choose to, light candles that smell like fir or pine, or burn frankincense and myrrh incense. Close your eyes and center yourself, moving into a meditative state in the way you choose.

With your mind's eye visualize yourself in a cozy, beautifully decorated living room. In this room there are various holiday decorations, perhaps some that you recognize from your youth, perhaps some that you have in your home currently, perhaps lavish and luxurious ones that you hope to have in your home someday. You feel at peace here: the room smells like the holidays: you smell the pine from the holiday tree, and coming from a nearby kitchen are the sweet smells of baked goods cooking in the oven. There is a warm fire place with a fire crackling, stockings hanging over the hearth and decorations of wreaths with holly and mistletoe in the room. Take a moment to enjoy your surroundings, taking in the comfort and joy of the holiday spirit.

There are three presents in front of you. What do the boxes look like? Which one are you drawn to the most?

Choose your first present and pick up the box. The first present represents a reward from your work during the past year. Is it small or large? Heavy or light? How is it wrapped and decorated? Is there a label on it saying who it is from? Take a moment to open it up. What is inside? What does it represent to you and how do you feel. If you ever need a reminder of your accomplishments, think of this gift that you have received.

Choose your second present and pick up the box. The second present is something that you need to help you succeed in the next year. Is it small or large? Heavy or light? How is it wrapped and decorated? Is there a label on it saying who it is from? Take a moment to open it up. What is inside? What does it represent to you and how do you feel. If you ever need motivation to move towards reaching your goals, think of this gift you have received.

Now, pick up the third box. The third present is a magical token representing your personal magical gifts and skills. Is it small or large? Heavy or light? How is it wrapped and decorated? Is there a label on it saying who it is from? Take a moment to open it up. What is inside? What does it represent to you and how do you feel. If you ever need to conjure motivation or connect with your spiritual practice, think of this gift you have received.

Next take a moment to go over to the Yule tree. Under the tree there are two gifts that you found to give to two people who are dear and close to you. Who are these gifts for, and how have you connected with these special people in their waking lives? What are the gifts that you are giving to them? Think about what these gifts are, and why you are thankful for these people in your life.

Before ending the meditation, look out the window of the room you are in. What does the weather like? Look to the fireplace and see the Yule Log burning, bringing warmth and comfort to the holiday scene in front of you. Feel hope moving forward, knowing that the sun will rise, the days will become longer and the sun will become stronger. There is hope, warmth, and growth in the days ahead.

Yule Journaling
- What can you forgive yourself for?
- What are ways that you find peace within yourself?
- What was a major lesson or wisdom shared with you recently?
- What promises or oaths do you want to make for the coming year?
- How do you show love to your friends and family? How do they show love in return?

- If you could get any present for someone special in your life, what would you get and for whom?

Correspondences
- Names: Yule, Winter Solstice, Alban Arthan
- Date of Celebration: Winter Solstice, which usually falls between December 20th and December 23rd.
- Deities Honored: Attis, Cailleach, Dumuzi, Holly King, Horned God, Father Winter, Lord of Misrule, Mithris, Odin, Horus, Saturn
- Magical Focus: Gratitude, Health, Peace, Rebirth, Transformation, Wisdom
- Activities: Baking Cookies, burning a Yule Log, caroling, decorating a tree, exchanging gifts, feasting, forgiveness, rest and recuperation, sharing stories, spending time with family and friends
- Altar Decorations: cinnamon sticks, frankincense and myrrh, gold decorations, holly, mistletoe, pine cones, pomanders
- Food and Beverages: apple cider, brussel sprouts, chicken pot pie, chili, cranberries, eggnog, nuts, oranges, pears, pork, shepherd's pie, stuffed cabbage, traditional holiday cookies (such as shortbread, snowball, caraway, ginger snaps), turkey, wassail, winter greens, winter squash
- Plants, Herbs, Incense: bay leaves, bayberry, birch, cedar, cinnamon, cloves, evergreens, frankincense, garlic, ginger, holly, ivy, juniper, mistletoe, myrrh, nutmeg, oak, peppermint, rosemary, sage, yew
- Crystals: bloodstone, diamond, emerald, garnet, ruby
- Colors: red and green; also blue, gold, silver, white.

DIY HOLIDAY PRESENTS FOR YULE
Holiday presents can be a fun way to spend an afternoon at home crafting original, unique, and magical gifts to share with family and friends. This list contains some of the crafts and ornaments I have created, though the list is truly endless.

Bookmarks and Book of Shadows Pages
If you enjoy scrapbooking, then consider creating Book of Shadows pages and bookmarks for friends and coven members. I

made bookmarks out of old tarot cards by punching a hole in the top of the card and lacing decorative ribbon through it. Book of Shadows pages can be made with simple typed out lists, or creative drawings and colorful paper. Use your imagination: knowledge is a gift that keeps giving.

Homemade Divination Kit

If you are handy with making crafts, a homemade divination kit is a unique and special gift for someone who likes to read the future. From making homemade oracle cards, to carving runes or ogham on wood, or stringing crystals to make pendulums, homemade divination kits can be simple or complex. At the end of this chapter I have included lithomancy as the divination focus, as it is a divination kit of crystals that would be easy to collect for a gift.

Bath and Body Products

No matter who is on your holiday list, bath and body products are always a fun present to add to anyone's gift basket, witch or muggle. These recipes come from my own Book of Shadows – I hope you enjoy them and share them at Yule!

Kiki's Love-Attracting Coffee Sugar Scrub

This sugar scrub is a hit every holiday season, and smells warm and inviting. The ingredients added will draw loving energies into your life, attracting romance, love, care, and comfort. In addition, it is very moisturizing for your skin: the sugar scrubs away dry skin, the coffee is said to help with circulation and brightness, and the oils will add additional moisture during the winter season.

1½ Cup White Sugar
1½ Cup Brown Sugar
½ Cup Ground Coffee[5]
Pinch of crushed Cardamom Seeds[6]
Pinch of crushed Rose Petals
One or two vanilla beans[7]
½ cup Coconut Oil
½ cup Sweet Almond or Jojoba Oil
Vanilla Absolute Oil or a high-quality vanilla fragrance oil[8]

Rose essential oil or rose water

Melt the coconut oil at a low heat. Remove from heat, allow to cool for a few minutes, and add in the sweet almond or jojoba oil. In a large bowl, blend the white sugar, brown sugar, and coffee, cardamom, rose petals, and vanilla bean. Slowly blend in the oils, until everything is blended. Blend in rose water and vanilla oils, a little at a time, until desired fragrance has been reached.

Priestess Body Butter
    ¾ cup shea butter
    ½ cup cocoa butter
    ½ cup coconut oil (organic, cold pressed, unrefined)
    ¼ cup sweet almond oil or jojoba oil
    10-20 drops amber essential oil
    10-20 drops sandalwood oil

Melt and blend the shea butter, cocoa butter and coconut oil in a double boiler. Remove from the heat and allow it to cool for a few minutes. Blend in the sweet almond or jojoba oil. Slowly start to add in the essential oils, a few drops at a time, blending until desired fragrance is reached. Place blended butters and oils into the refrigerator for at least an hour, at which point everything will be solidified. Whip with an electric beater until smooth and store in a glass jar. A little goes a long way: you won't need much for moisturizing skin, otherwise it'll feel a little too greasy.

I use fragrance oils to align with the properties of the spirituality and wisdom in this recipe. I also try and use oils that I know are a little gentler on skin types. Please keep in mind that some people are sensitive to oils. But some other oils to consider:
    *Earthy fragrance: cedarwood and patchouli
    *Floral fragrance: jasmine and gardenia
    *Romance fragrance: dragon's blood and rose
    *Healing fragrance: lavender and lemon balm

Soaps
These are simple recipes for melt-and-pour soap blends. You can get soap kits at hobby stores and online, and they can be nicely wrapped for holiday presents. Melt the soap base in a double boiler,

then slowly stir in the ingredients listed below. The ingredient lists below are designed to produce one bar of soap each, though you are welcome to add drops slowly and to your desired fragrance. Once everything is well blended, pour the soap into soap molds.

Rosy Love Soap
For enhancing loving energies around you and attracting romance into your life.
> 9 drops red dye
> 2 drops rose oil
> 2 drops frangipani oil
> 2 drops vanilla oil
> 2 drops ylang ylang oil
> Add rose petals if desired.

Prosperity Soap
For bringing luck, abundance, prosperity, and money into your life. A great soap to have on hand at your place of business. Cinnamon oil is strong, please keep this in mind and only use this soap on your hands!
> 6 drops green dye
> 5 drops patchouli oil
> 3 drops orange oil
> 1 drop cinnamon oil
> Add chamomile herbs or honeysuckle petals if desired.

Master Healer Soap
This is one of my absolute favorite soap recipes of all time, a special one to share and try out. You will need to infuse sweet almond oil with calendula, which is a process that takes a while. To do this, fill a glass jar with dried calendula herbs. Pour sweet almond oil over it, tightly close, and store in a dark and cool place for two to three weeks. Run the oil through a mesh strainer, taking out the old calendula, squeezing the oil out of the petals. Put new calendula petals in the jar, and return the oil to the jar, repeating this process for another month or two if you would like. Remember that carrier oils have a shelf life: they go stale after some time, so it is recommended to use within a year.
> ½ tsp. calendula-infused oil

½ tsp. coconut oil
6 drops amber oil
3 drops frankincense oil
3 drops cedarwood oil
3 drops tea tree oil

Egyptian Sun Soap
An excellent soap for greeting the returning sun. Also used for empowerment, magickal enhancement, wisdom, and growth.

8 drops yellow dye
1 drop orange dye
9 drops Egyptian Musk oil
3 drops Sandalwood oil
3 drops High John the Conqueror oil

Winter Solstice Oil Blends
There are multiple sources that list various oil blends that align with the winter solstice. The essential oils that correspond with Yule include orange, cedarwood, frankincense, sandalwood, myrrh, fir, and cinnamon.

Kiki's Winter Solstice Oil
I personally think this smells like the sky before it snows in New England. In a 2 dram oil bottle combine:

12 drops myrrh oil (Essential myrrh is thick and sticky; I prefer a high grade fragrance oil. If you use essential myrrh, it'll need to be warmed so it isn't as thick. Or, substitute frankincense oil.)
12 drops peppermint oil
12 drops juniper berry oil
12 drops vanilla oil
12 drops anise oil
Blend well, and fill the remainder of the bottle with a carrier oil, such as jojoba.

A favorite oil blend from another source, which just uses essential oils, comes from *The Enchanted Formulary* by Eve LeFey and Lady

Rhea:

> 2 parts allspice oil
> 2 parts vanilla oil
> 1 part orange
> 1 part cedarwood
> 1 part frankincense
> 1 part sandalwood
> Add bay leaf, frankincense resin, myrrh resin, and gold glitter.

My friend Lori, the Holistic Wellness Witch, makes an incredible body butter using frankincense and vanilla together. The fragrance has a citrus touch to it, and has inspired me to suggest to you to blend frankincense, vanilla, and orange essential oils for a good winter solstice blend. Or, you can contact Lori through her Facebook page, and get a batch of the good stuff from her directly: https://www.facebook.com/pg/holisticwellnesscoach.org

THE CAILLEACH APPROACHES: REFLECTIONS WITH THE GODDESS OF WINTER

The Cailleach is an ancient goddess of the land: she is a dark goddess of winter who carries the wisdom of age. She is the most powerful during the winter months, and as Rachel Patterson notes in *The Cailleach*, "Towards the end of the autumn when the weather starts to get that clear, fresh and chilly air you can feel her draw near."[9]

There are theories about her origin dating her back to Neolithic Britain and Celtic tribes. Some theories even link her to the Hindu goddess Kali. Her name translates to "hag" or "crone," though the prefix "Caill" means "covering," suggesting that she is a veiled older woman. Patricia Monaghan describes Cailleach in *The New Book of Goddesses and Heroines* as an important and ancient deity: "She controlled the seasons and the weather; she was the cosmic goddess of earth and sky, moon and sun. Because she does not appear in the written myths of Ireland and Scotland, but only in ancient tales and place-names, it is presumed that she was the goddess of the pre-Celtic settlers off the islands of Europe. She was so powerful and beloved that even when newcomers imported divinities like Brigid, the Cailleach was remembered."[10]

The Cailleach goes by varying names, dependent on the region where her legends are being told. Some portray her as being a giant with a blue face, red teeth, and white hair. There is a Scottish tale that says she is dressed in plaid and carries a staff. Often portrayed as a giant, she is said to have created mountains from boulders that dropped from her apron. She is a guardian of wild animals, streams, and wells. Owls, deer, and wild boars are sacred to her, and her places are cairns and mounds in the countryside hills.

The Cailleach is very much connected to the cold winter and the changing of the weather. There are tales that say she rides a wolf across the sky, bringing with her howling cold winds and snow. She is said to carry a staff or hammer, and when she hits the ground with it, grass turns to ice. In Ireland, it is believed that on February 1st, Cailleach's commands portend the remainder of winter: if winter will be long and difficult, Cailleach will make the weather sunny and mild so people can go outside to collect more firewood. If the weather is bad on that day, it can be assumed that winter is soon to draw to an end. There is another story about the Cailleach searching for water in the forest at the beginning of February. She comes across a well of youth, drinks from it, and transforms into Brigid.

Cailleach is a powerful goddess who may be portrayed in a terrifying light, but also has a caring side as well. She has wisdom of the land and the endurance to survive the cold weather. She is said to be of comfort and support in times of transition, guiding those who ask into new beginnings. In her article "The Cailleach, the Old Woman of Winter," Danu Forest considers the mystical powers of Cailleach's wintery magic and ancient wisdom: "The Cailleach's great age signifies her position as a keeper of mysteries, and as gateway to the infinite. She serves as midwife for the dying year as tenderly as she holds the seeds of the new, warm and safe in her lap beneath the earth, whilst her cauldron bubbles, hinting of the new life that will eventually come, after the long sleep that is winter."

Working with the Cailleach opens a gateway to wisdom, transformation, and rebirth, and will open you up to secrets and methods for growth by examining magic under the weak sun of the winter.

Cailleach and the Well of Wisdom

The Cailleach is connected with all bodies of water, but also with sacred wells. There are many wells connected to her, one being in Banffshire, Scotland, which is called "Taber Cailleach," meaning "Well of the Old Woman." People visit this well and leave her offerings, walking around the well nine times before they leave.

At the Winter Solstice, work with Cailleach to see what wisdom you need to focus on: what discoveries can you make about yourself at this time of the year? What mystical and ancient wisdom can Cailleach help you access? Light a blue candle, a silver candle, and a red candle when you are ready to connect with Cailleach. Say a prayer or incantation, do a meditation in which you visualize speaking with Cailleach at a hillmound, or write a letter to Cailleach. Ask her to help you discover this wisdom between the Winter Solstice and Imbolc, leading you deeper into yourself and the world around you.

Cailleach and the Power of Transformation

Cailleach has the power to transform herself in many ways. In one legend, she transforms herself into a large bird. Some legends say that she comes alive at Samhain but then turns to stone at Imbolc. There are also titles given to Cailleach that hint at her being veiled, suggesting that, as a veiled one, she was a keeper of ancient land mysteries and a woman of powerful magic. You can ask Cailleach to help transform an aspect of yourself that you'd like to change.

There is a special Asian tea called Butterfly Pea Flower Tea that turns blue when it is brewed. This blend is a perfect drink to have in honor of Cailleach. Brew a cup of blue tea, taking a moment to hold the cup of tea in your hands and visualizing Cailleach's veil of transformation lifting before you, ushering in a new, transformed self.

Cailleach and the Gift of Rebirth

In Glen Lyon, Scotland, there is said to be an old hut with a set of stones inside of it. Each spring the villagers take the stones out of the hut and set them up to overlook their flocks. It is believed that this has been a ritual, going on for many generations, having started with a visit from the Cailleach herself and her family one very cold winter. The Cailleach asked the villagers for shelter, and was pleased and grateful for them allowing her and her family to stay in the hut until the weather was better. Before leaving, she gave them the set of sandstones, said to be in the shape of Cailleach and each of her family members. She told the villagers that if they took care of the stones and allowed them to be outdoors each spring, she would keep the land fertile.

Cailleach is the builder of mountains: she can help you create something monumental in your life. Find a collection of stones you can associate with Cailleach and her family: these could include sandstone, hag stones, pebbles, howlite, blue limestone, kyanite, sodalite, blue quartz, or blue agate. Keep the stones in a special place during the winter, and on the first day of spring weather, put them on display, asking Cailleach to bring abundance and monumental growth to an aspect of your life.

SACRED SITES AT THE WINTER SOLSTICE

Ancient Sites around the world were built to align with astronomical events, including buildings and structures that link to solar events and significant dates in the indigenous calendars. The Winter Solstice appears to be one of the most revered holidays in this regard, with many sites highlighting the rising sun on a day that signified new hope for a growing season, renewal of life, and the return of the sun to many ancient civilizations. Although there are many sites that align with the Winter Solstice, there are a handful of spectacular places that reveal the sacred significance of this day to the ancient people of each region.

Stonehenge

Stonehenge is a popular destination for visitors who want to be enchanted by mystery and lore. The construction of this stone circle in southern England started around 2900 BCE, and there continued to be construction and activity at the site until about 1600 BCE. It is a place of legend and magic, its purpose still a collection of evolving theories as archeologists and researchers continue to make more discoveries in the area. Stonehenge's stones align with the solar calendar, and on the winter solstice it appears that the stone circle is aligned for the setting sun's rays to hit the central altar stone. There is more information on Stonehenge in the Mabon chapter.

Glastonbury Tor

Glastonbury, England is said to be a place of spiritual importance, with some linking its man-made hillmound to the legend of Avalon. The now abandoned Church of St. Michael on the top of Glastonbury Tor was once believed to be the final resting place of King Arthur and Queen Guinevere, though it has since been proven that the story was fabricated to draw more people to the church. Regardless of whether the legendary king and his queen were buried there or not, the hill offers a spectacular view on the Winter Solstice. Orion rises over the tor in the winter months, and if you watch the sun rise from the nearby Windmills Hill on the morning of the Winter Solstice, you can watch the sun climb along the slope of the mound towards the summit. There is more information on Glastonbury Tor in the Mabon chapter.

Newgrange

One of the most breathtaking of ancient monuments is the mound chamber Newgrange, located in County Meath, Ireland. This site was built around 3200 BCE, and though today it is covered in grass, it is believed that it was once decorated with white quartz. The passageway of Newgrange is a long shaft, and during the days around the Winter Solstice the light enters through this passageway to illuminate a large, round chamber in the back. The light of the Winter Solstice hits the back wall of the Newgrange chamber, illuminating a spiral carving on its back wall.

Maeshowe

Maeshowe is another ancient cairn site, though located in the northern Orkney Islands of Scotland, near the stone circles of Brodgar and Stenness. Built around 2800 BCE, the light of the Winter Solstice sunset shines through the opening, illuminating the shaft leading to the back chamber. There is evidence that the entrance to the chamber could be shut from the inside, thus the theory could be made that people could be in the back chamber and crawl out of the shaft at the sunset of the winter solstice, having a shamanic experience of rebirth. If you cannot make the journey to Maeshowe in person, you still have the opportunity to watch the sunlight in the cairn with a live WebCam at http://www.maeshowe.co.uk, which likens Maeshowe to a "Neolithic Cathedral."

Gavrinis

Gavrinis is a small island off the coast off the Brittany region of France and is the home to a megalithic burial chamber covered in beautiful spiral artwork. On the Winter Solstice the rising sun lights the passageway and illuminates the chamber. In *The Encyclopedia of Celtic Mythology and Folklore*, Patricia Monaghan remarks that, "Some have theorized that the rising sun, as it begins its rebirth toward summer on that day, may have been thought to revivify the bones places within, of which traces have been found.".[11] Gavrinis has a mystical look to it and it seems fitting that this chamber would have a magical or ritual purpose for rebirth on the Winter Solstice.

Goseck Circle

Goseck Circle in Germany may be one of the oldest astronomical observatories in the world. Constructed around 4900 BCE, this site consists of wooden fences, one mound, and ditches that may have been used for religious rituals. It is also located on the same latitude as Stonehenge, and close in latitude to the Majorville Medicine Wheel in Alberta, Canada. The Winter Solstice sun rises and sets from the southeast and southwest gates of Goseck Circle. Another fascinating find from this region is the Nebra Sky Disc, a bronze disc that was discovered near the Goseck Circle, depicting the sun, moon, and stars (including the constellation of Pleiades). The ancient people of this region not only followed the motion the sun for observation, but revered it as well.

Mnajdra Temple

On the small Mediterranean island of Malta, there is a set of Neolithic chambers, one of which was built between 4000 and 3000 BCE. The complex is made up of three buildings which show examples of stone doors and oracle holes. There are also curious structures at the site, such as a mushroom-shaped altar. These temples follow the seasons of the year, and on the Winter Solstice the light of the sunrise aligns with inner buildings in the complex.

Karnak Temple

Karnak Temple is a complex of ancient Egyptian buildings in Luxor, Egypt. Construction began around 2055 BCE, with continual construction and use until 395 CE. This region is one of the most exquisite and mysterious in the ancient worlds, a place even visited by ancient Greeks and Romans for knowledge and reverence. The sanctuary that honors the Sun God Amun is aligned to the Winter Solstice sunrise.

Great Zimbabwe

The magnificent stone city of Great Zimbabwe in Africa was built around 1200 CE. The granite stone complex at one point may have had a population of up to 18,000 people. Small soapstone artifacts carved like birds have been found at the complex's ruins. It appears that the stones of the buildings line up to the stars in Orion as they rise on the morning of the Winter Solstice.

Cahokia Mounds

The Cahokia Mounds of Illinois, United States, reveal one of the first major cities in North America. It is a 2,200 acre complex with 120 earth mounds that was occupied between 900 and 1350 CE. Mound 72 is 6 feet tall, 70 feet wide, 140 feet long, and oriented to the Winter Solstice. 300 burials have also been discovered near the site. In addition to this, a nearby sun circle made of cedar wood posts functioned as a calendar, following the solstices and equinoxes.

Offerings of wolf teeth, red ochre, and quartz have been discovered by the solstice posts.

Chankillo

The Thirteen Towers of Chankillo are at an ancient observatory in the Peruvian coastal desert. Although once thought to be a fort, there is now a theory that the line of towers appear to follow the solar calendar. From observation points the sun can be seen rising over specific towers. For Peru, the winter solstice is in June, and the sun rises over the left-most tower at this point in the year.

DIVINATION HIGHLIGHT: LITHOMANCY: DIVINATION WITH STONES

I have opted to include lithomancy in this chapter, as it is something that would be an excellent addition to the Yule gift basket. It is something that can be collected and pieced together as a unique gift. During the cold season, crystals can appear to be solid and cold as ice, so at winter we honor divination with stones and crystals.

Lithomancy comes from the Greek words "lithos" for stone and "mancy" for divination. It is the casting or scrying of stones, crystals, and gems. Stone casting divination traditionally uses 13 stones pulled from a pouch and released onto an area that is divided into various sections with different meanings. The exciting aspect of lithomancy is that you can follow a very traditional system of reading crystals and stones, or you can create your own system, depending on what works best for you.

Traditional Lithomancy

There are 13 stones in a traditional lithomancy set. They are separated into two categories: personal stones and planetary stones. The personal stones represent your life and the people in your life. The planetary stones follow astrological interpretations while the others have more broad meanings. It is recommended that you pick stones and crystals that you are drawn to; however, there are suggestions in the following list of interpretations based on the astrological correspondences of crystals. Please note that the stones names listed here come from the comprehensive book *Lithomancy: The Psychic Art of Reading Stones* by Gary L. Wimmer. Some people make variations on the "personal stones." I have seen lists that include spirit, earth, fire, water, and air while other lists have universe, news, and luck stones. I am following Wimmer's guide because it is the most extensive and descriptive.

- Life Stone: the subject's thoughts, activities, support systems, and ideas.
- Magic Stone: time and events that are happening to help you.
- Love Stone: loved ones, family, relationships, and emotional attachments.
- Commitment Stone: matters that need to be take care of and responsibilities.
- Place Stone: home, safe environments, and places of security.
- Sun Stone: identity, your unique personality, confidence, empowerment, development of courage and self-esteem, father figures. What are your ambitions? Who inspires you? Who do you inspire? How do you influence others in a positive way? (Suggestions: amber, sunstone, orange calcite, pyrite)
- Moon Stone: emotions, dreams, imagination, home, health, moods, receptivity, intuition, mother figures. What have your dreams been telling you to do? How do you rest, relax, and heal? Where do you feel safe and secure? (Suggestions: moonstone, selenite, pearl)
- Mercury Stone: communication, intellect, travel, energy, knowledge, study, flexibility, energy, information, honesty, siblings. Are you being honest with yourself and others? What do you need to study and become skilled at? What journey will lead you to a better place? (Suggestions: aventurine, bloodstone, mica, pumice)
- Venus Stone: beauty, love, fertility, sensuality, romance, partnership, culture, art, poetry, happiness, leisure, creativity, peace, forgiveness, femininity, social activity. Which relationships bring pleasure to your life? Which artistic pursuits bring you joy? How can you develop hope and kindness? (Suggestions: pink tourmaline, chrysocolla, emerald, turquoise)
- Mars Stone: ambition, determination, competition, expansion, personal power, assertion, decisions, endurance, courage, masculinity. When do you have to show courage? What aspect in your life can you be more proactive in? How do you keep anger

and jealousy in check? (Suggestions: garnet, red jasper, ruby, flint, carnelian)

- Jupiter Stone: aspirations, luck, generosity, opportunity, abundance, indulgences, expansion, morality, law. Where can you be more open minded? What are you grateful for in your life? What are your goals for growth? (Suggestions: tiger's eye, lepidolite, topaz)
- Saturn Stone: responsibility, delays, limitations, restrictions, discipline, organization, focus, perseverance, authority figures. What needs better organization and structure in your life? How do you stay focused and optimistic? How do you respond to stress? (Suggestions: jet, obsidian, hematite, coal)

Wimmer adds the additional planets (and Pluto) in to make a collection of 16 stones total.

- Uranus Stone: originality, rebellion, eccentricity, bohemianism, enlightenment, connections to the occult, mysterious, invention, friendship. Where do you feel the most free and independent? How is your uniqueness a personality strength? How do you honor your flashes of insight? (Suggestions: opal, labradorite, fluorite)
- Neptune Stone: spirituality, empathy, art, delusion, abstract ideas, introspection, psychic abilities, charisma, deception. How spiritual are you? How do you connect with Divinity? Are you trying to avoid your problems? Are you craving time alone for reflection? (Suggestions: amethyst, celestite, kyanite, lapis lazuli)
- Pluto Stone: change, transition, rebirth, purpose, values, secrets, profound thoughts or revelations, potential, redemption, psychology. How do you respond to change? What needs to be reevaluated in your life? Are you open to deeply spiritual or
- challenging revelations? (Suggestions: tourmalinated quartz, moldavite)

The traditional way of reading crystals and stones seems to have very few guidelines and is left up to the reader's interpretation. Create an area for the stones to be cast in using a long string or ribbon; throw the stones into the circle. Interpret readings based on where the stones land and where they land in relation to each other. Do you see any shapes made out of certain stones? Perhaps seeing a heart shape indicates a need to focus on love, or a line of stones indicates needing to stay on target. Are there stones pointing at each other? Perhaps these stones are important solutions or advice for each other. Are they all near each other? This could indicate very strong relationships with each other. Let your intuition help you determine which patterns have certain meanings.

You may want to consider mapping out your own "mat" or "guide" to throw the stones on. If you enjoy the astrological aspects of lithomancy, create a circular map that shows the astrological houses, basing the interpretations on where the stones land. Or, you may want to create a Wheel of the Year to use in correlation with the stones. You may wish to throw the stones on top of tarot or oracle cards to add another layer to a card reading. Get creative: lithomancy takes study, intuitive practice, and self-reflection to really get into the flow.

Creative and Alternative Lithomancy

While some people feel it necessary to follow the traditional guidelines for lithomancy, others like to create their own parameters, creating their own meanings for specific stones and crystals as well as using various numbers of crystals. You can use fancy crystals, pebbles you find on walks, or even include small trinkets that are not stones. You can create a complex or simple system of lithomancy, one that has many or few stones, one that involves casting stones onto a map or one that involves pulling a couple stones with a message. Below is

a simple lithomancy system as an example, but create your own if you are so inclined. Hold the bag and ask for insight into your day, envisioning that you will gain guidance from the chosen crystal. Pull one crystal from the bag to receive a daily message or gain insight into a question you have.

- Clear Quartz: Now is time to study and do research. What methods do you utilize to clear your mind, or do you need to figure out how to clear your mind? What needs cleansing and purification in your life?
- Amethyst: Listen to your intuition. When do you feel most connected to Divinity? How do you bring balance into your life?
- Lapis Lazuli: Pay attention to your dreams. Meditate to find your solution. Connect with Goddess energy.
- Malachite: Connection to Earth, follow your heart to happiness. What makes you feel good. Now is a time to create and manifest your goals. Express your feelings.
- Citrine: What inspires you? What makes you happy? Laughter and joy will assist you now. Connect with your creative side.
- Carnelian: Do what you are most passionate about. What excites you? Pay attention to romance and potential romance in your life.
- Tiger's Eye: Time to get grounded. Consider doing physical activity. Remember your humanity. Connect with animals, whether they are in nature, your pets, or spirit animals.
- Hematite: Now is a time for transformation. How do you react to change? Consider reordering your priorities and cutting out things that drain your energy.
- Selenite: Now is a time to connect with the universe and divinity. Ask and you shall receive.
- Rose Quartz: Now is a time for healing, self-love, and self-awareness. Comfort yourself as you comfort others.

"Yes" and "No" Stones

If you would prefer a very quick--yet effective--form of stone divination, this method only needs three small white stones and three small black stones, all similar in size and shape. Keep the six stones in a small bag and hold the bag with a question that could be answered with "yes" or "no." Pull three stones. If you pull three white stones, the answer to your question is yes. If you pull two white stones and one black stone, the answer is probably yes. If you pull two black stones and one white, the answer is probably no. If you pull three black stones, the answer to your question is no.

YULE CHAPTER NOTES

[1] Morrison, Dorothy. *Yule: A Celebration of Warmth and Light.* St. Paul, MN: Llewellyn Publications, 2000. P. 4.

[2] Tainter, Frank H. "What Does Mistletoe Have to Do With Christmas?" *The American Phytopathological Society.* http://www.apsnet.org/publications/apsnetfeatures/pages/mistletoe.aspx.

[3] Bane, A.R. *The Secret of Mistletoe.* Self-Published, 2011. P. 2.

[4] Cunningham, Scott. *Cunningham's Encyclopedia of Magical Herbs.* St. Paul, MN: Llewellyn Publications, 1987. P. 124.

[5] Please note that the coffee is very fragrant and you do not need too much in combination with the sugar, otherwise the coffee fragrance will overpower the oil scents.

[6] For this I cracked open the pods, discarded the shells, and finely crushed the seeds. They are very fragrant, add a little at a time to determine how much you want to add.

[7] Vanilla beans can be expensive, so use what you would like to add their loving properties to this blend.

[8] There is no measurement for this, as you will add a few drops at a time, to desired level of fragrance.

[9] Patterson, Rachel. *The Callieach.* Moon Books: Hants, UK, 2016.

[10] Monaghan, Patricia. *The New Book of Goddesses and Heroines.* St. Paul, MN: Llewellyn Publications, 1997. P. 65-66.

[11] Monaghan, Patricia. *The Encyclopedia of Celtic Mythology and Folklore.* New York: Facts on File, Inc., 2004. P. 208.

CHAPTER THREE:
IMBOLC

OVERVIEW, MAGIC, ACTIVITIES, AND CORRESPONDENCES

On Imbolc we find ourselves in some of the coldest times of the year, yet it is considered the first spring ritual. We start seeing the first signs of spring, even in the cold snow, and in the past this was the time when animals started to show they were healthy and able to provide life. Imbolc comes from the Irish word 'mbolg, meaning "in the belly." The name refers to the time when ewes are pregnant, begin lactating and are heavy with milk. Imbolc is the first of three fertility sabbats (the others being Ostara and Beltane), and the first of four Celtic fire festivals (the others being Beltane, Lughnasadh, and Samhain).

Imbolc has always been a quiet holiday, not only in many of its celebrations, but also because it is mellower and less well known than holidays like Samhain or Beltane. That is not to make Imbolc any less special: it's a very valuable holiday in the Wheel of the Year. At this time of the year, even in the midst of cold, wintery weather and dark days that seem to be dragging on, we start to see some of the first signs that springtime is just around the corner. I have always called

Imbolc the "Introvert's Holiday." It's a time you want to stay inside and be cozy and warm with a cup of cocoa and a good book. And so, perhaps Imbolc is quiet, but it's a wonderful time to feel inspired through reflection, hopefulness for the returning spring, and creativity.

Ancient and Modern Celebrations in February

February marked a special point in the calendar for many different ancient cultures, some of which are still revered today. Very little is known about the ancient Irish celebrations of Imbolc, though it was one of the quarter points in the calendar year. Imbolc marked the point between the Winter Solstice and the Spring Equinox. Farms were a busy scene at this time of year, as many of the animals are pregnant and producing milk. As Courtney Weber in *Brigid: History, Mystery, and Magick of the Celtic Goddess* points out: "The world was coming back to life. Through the lens of the harvest, Samhain was an end. Imbolc was a beginning."[1] Traditionally, the Celts celebrated the lengthening of light hours in the day of Imbolc with fire celebrations. Candles, fireplaces, and bonfires were all lit to honor Brigid and the returning warmth and brilliance of life.

Romans also had a holiday during February, though theirs was a rowdy fertility and purification festival. Lupercalia was celebrated on February 15th, and some modern day researchers link it to both

Valentine's Day and Candlemas. This holiday was a purification rite which honored the wolf who was said to mother the founders of Rome, twins Romulus and Remus. Lupercalia was also a fertility rite, eventually being linked with Lupercus, a god similar to the forest god Faunus. This was a time that was believed to be run by the spirits of nature. Rites were held for purification and to rid the world of the wild energy of nature spirits. Torchlight processions were held, and rituals were held for fertility. Priests were believed to sacrifice goats, their skins worn by young men through the Lupercalia celebrations. The young man lashed celebrants with pieces of the goat skin, which was said to promote fertility.

Catholics toned down their February holiday with the celebration of Candlemas, which coincides at the same time as Imbolc on February 2nd. The holiday observed Christ being brought to temple 40 days after his birth as well as the purification of Mary. Candles are blessed in churches on Candlemas. In Paris, where the holiday is known as La Chandeleur, crepes and pancakes are eaten, perhaps their round and golden shape symbolic of the sun.

Today in Ireland, February 1st also marks the celebration of St. Brigid, a saint from Ireland who was originally a goddess in earlier pagan traditions. In her Christian form she was the foster mother to Jesus. It was believed the Bridget would walk earth on St. Brigid's eve. People would hang a strip of cloth outside the door for Brigid to bless. This cloth would then be sewn into clothing to protect people from danger, or wrapped around someone in need of healing. Oat bread and corn would be left out as offerings for Brigid and her cow. Brigid's crosses would be woven to protect the home.

Today many of these traditional customs from the Feast of St. Brigid cross over into Imbolc celebrations. Brigid is a popular and well known goddess among neopagans. Modern day pagans celebrate Imbolc in Brigid's honor, and a time in the calendar to reflect on her wonderful roles as a goddess of many crafts and talents.

Imbolc: The Quiet Holiday

Imbolc is often a quiet holiday, one that focuses on rest and purification. This is an excellent time to practice divination and do meditation to let go of psychic and emotional baggage. Sometimes we discover the most productive and proactive moments once we've given ourselves the chance to be quiet and chill for a little bit first. Think of Imbolc as the opportunity to get yourself prepared in the down time before the growth spurt of spring. This is the last quiet pause in the year until the harvest festivals conclude next Samhain. Use Imbolc as a time to chill: reflect, meditate, do something comforting and warming, use a self-care activity to make you feel rested and healthy, practice purification magic, light candles, and have a nice quiet day (or weekend). It's the holiday that fully supports your craving to eat grilled cheese sandwiches in a blanket fort while you read a book. It's the holiday that is all about lighting candles and meditating in the bath instead of running around downtown on a Friday. Make Imbolc your opportunity to celebrate downtime, daydreaming, creating, and resting.

Brigid's Holiday

Imbolc is the feast celebration of the Celtic Goddess Brigid, who is the goddess of fire, healing, inspiration, transformation, iron-crafting, and the hearth. As the daughter of Dagda, she has strong powers of fertility. She is an immortal member of the Tuatha de Danaan, and a favorite goddess for poets and singers. She was born in a Druid's home and was said to have been born in the doorway (neither inside nor outside). She was also said to drink milk from Otherworldly cows.

Brigid is known as a goddess of fire and transformation, associated with iron crafters and forging. In Kildare there is a temple that was tended by 19 priestesses who cared for a never-extinguished flame. Kildare became a convent in the 5th century, but nuns continued to tend to the flame until the 11th century. In 1993, the Sisters of St. Bridget relit the flame and it has been tended ever since. In her role of hearth goddess, she overlooks the domestic realm of motherhood, healing, and fertility. She protects expecting mothers and those in childbirth. She also protects the homestead, keeping it safe from fires and lightning.

Brigid is sometimes as a triple goddess, and those three aspects show her many roles of support and inspiration. Some have categorized her three roles as "Brigid the Healer, Brigid of the Forge, and Brigid of the Poets" or "Patron of food production, goddess of war, and goddess of knowledge." In the Irish mythological Ulster Cycle her three roles are known as "Brigid the Hospitaller, Brigid of the Judgements, and Brigid the Cowless." No matter how Brigid reveals herself to you, it is apparent that she is someone who can be called upon when you are in need of blessings, support, and inspiration.

Offerings for Brigid

There was an old belief that you could leave a loaf of bread for St. Bridget and corn for her sacred white cow on Candlemas to ensure a prosperous agricultural season. If you wish, leave out the same offerings on your altar to Brigid to ensure a prosperous and fertile season. You can also share preserves and loaves of bread with friends and family as a sign of friendship and love through the last weeks of winter. You can also leave out long strips of cloth for Brigid on Imbolc eve, and collect them to use during the year when you are in need of her support and comfort. You can also put together a special Imbolc Spell Jar to leave out for Brigid's blessings. Consider filling the jar with the following:

- Salt
- Sugar
- Dried Corn Kernels
- White Rice
- Powdered Milk
- White Birch Bark or Willow wood (whatever is available in your area, please forage responsibly from fallen wood and bark).
- Tie a red ribbon around it, or use cloth that you had outside

Exploring the Outdoors and Snow Magic on Imb

Weather permitting, take a moment to go outsi nature around you. What changes do you see? Are there any sig... spring, or does it feel like the cold of winter? Imbolc would make an excellent day to honor the birds that are so sacred to Brigid and the season. Take the time to scatter birdseed, watch and listen to the birds, and enjoy their hopeful energy.

One of the first things we envision when we think of snowfall is the blanket of white outdoors. White has been considered the color of purity, innocence, spiritual awareness, and hope. Oftentimes, we envisions white light surrounding us when we want to feel protection or comfort. The color white in magic has been used for clarity, purification, happiness, truth, hope, and reverence of the Maiden Goddess. The white blanket outdoors evokes feelings of cleansing energy. Snow seems to embody the energy of transformation, renewal, purification, potential, and spiritual joy.

- Creating a Snow Altar: What better way to spend a snow day than to decorate your altar in reverence for a winter wonderland? Dress your altar in white cloth and decorate with paper snowflakes, white glitter, white candles, white roses, gamine flowers, pine cones, or winter figurines. White crystals make an incredible addition to the altar and offer energy that we can use to feel spiritually protected. In *Cunningham's Encyclopedia of Crystal, Gem, & Metal Magic*, Scott Cunningham suggests that white crystals are associated with the moon, thus lending energy to those who wish to work with psychic abilities, sleep, and dream magic. Some common white crystals to work with include howlite, white calcite, moonstone, selenite, and quartz.
- Snow Water: Collect fresh snow in a jar and combine with a small dash of sea salt. Allow it to melt on your altar or by your fireplace. Then, you can use this water for purification rituals or transformation magic. You can even save the snow water for the summer when the days are hot and balmy, and you need a splash of cooling winter energy.
- Snowfall Incense for Purification: Combine equal parts Gum Arabic, White Copal, and Benzoin resin. This makes a simple

resin incense that is white in color and can be burned for purification and spiritual awareness.

Relaxing with Brigid's Milk and Honey Bath

Take Imbolc as an opportunity to relax. Catch up on a book you've been meaning to finish. Treat yourself to a reiki or deep tissue massage session. Sleep in. Take a warm bath. If you enjoy soothing baths, try a milk and honey bath to soothe and moisturize your winter skin. Cleopatra was known for her milk and honey baths, but with Brigid taking the center stage for Imbolc, I have created a blend to put in the bath called "Brigid's Milk and Honey Bath."

2 cups milk
4 tbs honey
2 tbs coconut oil
5 drops jasmine essential oil (or another white flower oil such as neroli, gardenia, heliotrope, lily, or frangipani)
5 drops lavender essential oil

Cleaning and Smudging

Let's call Imbolc cleaning "Super Early Spring Cleaning." You may as well get a head start on making your environment clean, organized, and ready for the warmer months. Imbolc is a great time to sweep the house clean of dust from last year, and in the process, removing old energy. Burn any remaining wood from Yule to light the way for the future. Smudge your home with sage and/or palo santo, opening the windows after your home has been smudged to let out the smoke and old energy.

Consider soaking basil and lemon in warm water, and then cleaning your floors with the infused water. This will not only make your house smell amazing, but also bring loving and abundant energies into your home. Use Imbolc as a time to clean out your closet: what clothes do you use? Be honest with yourself, and remove what is not being used anymore. When you are cleaning and you come across specific objects ask yourself the following questions:
- "Do this object add value to my life?"
- "When is the last time I used this object?"
- "How do I feel when I see this object?"

- "What are the memories connected with this object, are they good for me to remember?"
- "Is there potential profit for selling this object as opposed to holding on to it?"
- "Do I know someone who could better benefit from having this object?"
- "Does this object represent me in a positive way?"
- "Does this object inspire me?"

Imbolc Journaling
Imbolc marks new beginnings, new ideas, and fresh starts.
- What projects do you wish to initiate?
- What do you want to grow in your life? See if you can create a plan, schedule, to-do list, or simply create mantras to remind yourself of what is most valuable to you.
- What are you looking forward to when spring returns?
- How does it feel to be relaxed? What can you do to be relaxed more often?
- How are you creative? How do you get inspired? What art excites you? Which creative projects need attention in your life right now?

Correspondences
- Other names for Imbolc: Oimelc, Feast of Brigid
- Date of Celebration: February 1st or February 2nd. If you wish, you can celebrate it on the exact crossquarter point between the winter solstice and the spring equinox.
- Deities honored: Aphrodite, Artemis, Brigid, Diana, Faunus, Venus, Vesta
- Magical Focus: awakening, beginnings, creativity, fertility, inspiration, purification, relaxation, wellness
- Activities: cleaning the house, clearing out old spells, creating a book of shadows, fires in hearth, hike to see first signs of spring, lighting candles, making a Bride Dolly or Brigid's Cross, meditating, planning and outlining spring goals, purification bath, reading, resting, smudging the home, writing
- Altar Decorations: bread, Bride Dolly, Brigid's Cross, flower bulbs, melted snow, silver trinkets, red and white candles, red and white ribbons, salt and sugar, white flowers

- Food and Beverages: artichoke, blackberry, cauliflower, cheese, cream, crepes, dried fruits, dried meats, eggs, lamb, milk, nuts, pancakes, pear, potato, preserves, salted meats, turnip
- Plants, Herbs, and Incenses: angelica, ash, basil, bay, birch, chamomile, coltsfoot, crocus, dragon's blood, frankincense, heather, lavender, myrrh, red sandalwood, snowdrop, vervain, witch hazel
- Crystals: citrine, crystal quartz, fire agate, moss agate, opal, rutilated quartz, sunstone
- Colors: Red and white

HONORING BRIGID ON IMBOLC THROUGH WRITING

As a goddess of transformation, Brigid overlooks creativity and inspiration; she is honored by poets and bards. Author Morgan Daimler also points out in *Pagan Portals Brigid* that Brigid can also be connected to prophecy, as it was "a skill practiced by the Irish poets and considered essential to their art." Imbolc is an excellent time to try out your writing skills. Writing can be a relaxing and cathartic practice. It is an opportunity to organize your ideas, make lists, and explore your feelings.

Poetry Writing for Brigid

Imbolc is often a time when writers take a moment to create a poem in her honor. If you are the poetic type, consider writing Brigid a poem. Below are some ideas to get you started on thinking about the contents of a good poem. There are writing prompts listed to help you start getting some words on the page as well.

What creates a vivid poem? Using strong imagery helps to create a sensory experience. Images can stimulate the senses, activating sight, sound, smell, taste, and touch. It allows the reader to picture something happening in your poem clearly.

- Describe the weather at Imbolc
- What does nature look like at Imbolc?
- Which words would you use to describe Brigid?
- What does Brigid look like?
- What does it feel like to work with metals? What are the sounds you associate with smithcrafting? What do you create with metals?
- What are the feelings you have when you are near a fire? What does it look like? What does it sound like? What does it smell like?

What adds depth to a poem? Using symbols and figurative language can add depth and thought to a piece of work. A symbol is an object, word, or action that stands for something else. Figurative language occurs when you describe something by comparing it to something else. Metaphors and similes are examples of figurative language. A metaphor uses a comparison without using "like" or "as." A simile is a comparison that uses "like" or "as."

- Which symbols do you associate with Brigid?
- Are there any omens in nature you look for as a sign of spring?

What makes a poem feel authentic? By using personal experiences and being vulnerable in your storytelling, readers will feel like they can relate to you, even if it is through a unique and personal story. Being vulnerable and revealing in a poem can also be a cathartic experience, allowing you to reflect on your emotions and feelings.

- How do you feel spiritually at Imbolc?

- Have you ever had an encounter with Brigid? What happened?
- If you had a conversation with Brigid, what would you want to talk about?
- If you asked Brigid for help with something, what would that be?
- Have you ever needed healing from grief or illness? What helped you heal?

Creating a Book of Shadows

Maybe poetry writing isn't your thing, but that shouldn't stop you from contemplating other ways to get the pen on the paper! Imbolc is an excellent time to work on your Book of Shadows. A Book of Shadows (BoS) is a compendium of a witch's magical work. Some Books of Shadows contain colorful illustrations, clips of articles, or handwritten notes. Some are neat and organized while others can only be translated by its owner/s. Some are shared within a coven, while others are for a solitary practitioner. Some are typed up notes, while others are only handwritten. Whatever your style of gathering information is, a BoS is a special place where you can collect your magical and spiritual information. A BoS takes shape over time: not only is it a fun and creative way track your studies, it can also show a timeline of your gathered knowledge and growth.

Some witches differentiate between two collections of information. A *Book of Shadows* is said to be a collection of magical workings, something special and unique to the creator. A *Grimoire* is said to be a collection of notes and resources, something that gives additional reference and information about a witch's study. In the case of two separate books, think of the BoS as something permanent and special, and the grimoire as a working space. However, many people keep all magical work and notes in the same place, preferring to keep all magical workings and notes together. It is up to you to decide what is best for your practices.

There are some covens who only share their BoS with other coven members. This is oftentimes a collection of special ceremonies and rituals that only take place within the coven. A coven BoS may also include special spells created by coven members, or a diary that tracks who comes to which ritual. For some covens, a BoS marks a passage of initiation. In this sense, members and initiates may see only certain parts of the book or have to hand-write special passages.

The following is a list of things to consider when piecing together your own BoS. It will allow you to consider the purpose, content, and layout for your book.

1. Purpose: Begin by contemplating the purpose of your BoS. It should focus on what you study, what you wish to dedicate your practice and study to, and what is most valuable to you. Do you wish to share this with your spiritual group or coven, or is this book a private collection for yourself alone? Is it something artistic, practical, or a little of both? Begin with writing a statement of intent for your BoS, and then move into outlining the content of the book.

2. Content: The content of a BoS is completely up to you. Think about the notes you have and where your studies and practices are the most important. You may want to separate your book with tabs or dividers, or just create a table of contents page at the beginning of your book. Below are some suggested themes, subjects, or divisions to consider including in your BoS:
   o Guides and Traditions within your Path
   o Journaling Section
   o Sabbat Rituals
   o Esbat Rituals
   o Special Rites and Rituals (i.e. handfasting)
   o Spellwork (you can divide further into love, money, healing, psychic, protection, and so on)
   o Sigils and Amulets
   o Elements
   o Divination (you can divide further into tarot, astrology, tea leaf readings, oracles, and so on)
   o Altar Tools/Setup
   o Wheel of the Year (you can divide further into each of the eight holidays)
   o Mythology
   o Deities/Goddesses/Gods
   o Animals and Spirit Totems
   o Faeries/Little Folk/Fae Studies
   o Supernatural/Paranormal encounters and studies

- Dreamwork and Dream Journal
- Automatic Writing/Channelled Messages
- Meditations
- Mantras, Chants or Prayers
- Holistic Healing
- Divination
- Herbal Correspondences
- Crystal Correspondences
- Aromatherapy
- History of Witchcraft
- Archaeology Studies
- Psychology Studies
- Illustrations
- Pressed flowers

3. Layout: One major thought to keep in mind is if you would like your BoS to have a more permanent feel or be something that you can actively change.

- Bound Book or Journal: If you are an artistic person, a blank journal may be the right canvas for illustrations, bullet journal pages, or scrap book art. Keep in mind that a bound book or journal is limited in its space, but can be a beautiful and creative pursuit.
- Three Ring Binder: Although a three ring binder may come off as more utilitarian, it allows for flexibility in the format and shape of your BoS. You can easily create sections with dividers, and add or take out information when you feel like it.
- Online Book: Witchcraft today has expanded to the internet in articles, blogs, graphics, and Facebook groups. If you find yourself collecting information online, consider creating an online BoS through Pinterest, Tumblr, WordPress, or a Facebook Group. One thing to keep in mind when browsing the internet is to cross check resources. There are many wonderful images, articles, graphics, and blogs with magical information online, but it is up to you to make sure the information is accurate and resonates with your own path.

o   USB of Shadows: Another thing to consider doing is maintaining all of your BoS information on your computer or a flash drive. This could be a safe way to store information that can be edited and shared easily.

4. Collecting Material: There are no deadlines for obtaining material for your Book of Shadows. You may find material immediately that you wish to add. If you are trying to find inspiration for material to add, visit some of your favorite books and write out your favorite passages or quotes. Ask your friends for spells or BoS pages to add, or print out an article that has information you want to remember and return to. Make a page with correspondences or spells you have done in the past that work well. Draw a picture of a supernatural event that has happened to you, or write out a list of goals you have for the coming year, then connect it to magic and spiritual practices that can help you get motivated. There are no limits: this is your opportunity to create your own magical and spiritual records.

SIMPLE MEDITATIONS FOR A BUSY PERSON

Meditation is a practice of quieting your mind, being still in the present moment, and being mindful of your breathing and the world around you. It is accessible for all people, from any background, who follow (or don't follow) any teaching. It is a tool to relax your mind, quiet your thoughts, and enjoy quietness and/or calmness. Whether you use meditation for spiritual or physical health, there are numerous benefits to practicing it regularly.

- Meditation helps your body. Some of the benefits of meditation include: lower blood pressure, better rest and sleeping abilities, and increased serotonin production.
- Meditation helps your mind. Some of the benefits of meditation include: increased feelings of happiness, a reduction in stress and anxiety, and an increase in attention and focus.
- Meditation helps your spirit. Some of the benefits of meditation include: feeling a deeper connection to others, development of patience and compassion, and the awakening of intuitive abilities.

If you do not think these claims are real, try meditation out. There are no negative side effects. Keep a journal and track how you are feeling before and after meditation. Reflect on how you would've reacted to something before regular meditation practice, and how that reaction has evolved after regular meditation practice.

Phone Apps for Meditation

There are numerous phone apps that allow you to follow guided meditations or listen to relaxing music while you meditate. One of my favorite meditation apps is called *Omvana*. I like this app because it allows you to mix music with various guided meditations. Some of my favorite meditations include their "3 x 3" series with author Dina Proctor, which are three minute meditations that help you focus on a given intent. I am currently working on the abundance meditation. There is also another meditation called "Growing Your Light" with Gabrielle Bernstein. It's an empowering meditation that starts the day off on the right foot, with the kind words "May you be happy. May you be healthy. May you live with ease." There are two issues with this app, however, the first being that content costs extra money, and the other being that it hasn't been updated recently. Another app that is internationally active is *Insight Timer*, which has an interactive experience. Insight Timer has a timer feature that you use while you meditate, and there are also guided meditations that you can follow. Only have a minute to meditate? No worries, there are one minute meditations that you can listen to on *Insight Timer*.

Morning Meditation

I have stopped the urge to click onto my phone first thing in the morning. I read somewhere that the first 15 minutes of your day shapes the feeling and productivity of the entire day. If this is the case, I do not want my entire day shaped by swiping a screen and staring into mindless information on social media. So, instead of doing an electronic check in, I am doing a meditation check in. This may not take 15 minutes, but I will not use my phone for the first 15 minutes of my day. Instead, I am following this simple meditation. I call it "Three Reflections Morning Meditation"

- Step One: Reflect on dreams. When I first wake up, I take a moment to reflect on my dreams, if I remember them. If I have anything to resolve in them, I do so. If I have any interpretations to make from them, I do so.

- Step Two: Reflect on three things I am thankful for. The next thing I do is take three deep, long breaths, yawning and stretching whenever I feel like it. While breathing deeply, I think of three things I am thankful for. It can be simple things: my dog, my warm bed, being in a safe place. It can be more specific things to: being able to visit the coast or the mountains whenever I'd like, having the talent of cooking, a funny conversation with a close friend. Anything you are thankful for will work: even if you cite the air you are breathing or the awesome footie pajamas you are wearing.
- Step Three: Reflect on three things I am looking forward to doing that day. I only think about things I am looking forward to. Are there any exciting events? Do I get to see anyone super special? I'm I going to have a chance to read a book? Consider what you are hopeful for during the day, those motivating factors that make you look forward to getting out of bed.

Simple Breathing Meditation

Breathing is the central focus in all meditations, long or short, and paying attention to your breathing seems to be the gateway to that calming, meditative state. Breathing meditations can be a minute long if you'd like them to be, they can be done at your office desk, while in ritual circle, or while cozying up by a campfire. Find a quiet space where you won't be disturbed when you are ready to begin mindful breathing. Sit in a comfortable position, try and sit straight up so you aren't hunched over. Close your eyes and take a deep breath in, feeling the air move through your nose and fill your chest and abdomen. Breath out slowly, feeling the air leave your body and move out your nose. And simply repeat. Keep your focus on your breath, only giving attention to the breath. If you have thoughts that enter your mind, release them with your breath.

Meditation while Walking

I am an avid hiker, and will put off many responsibilities to make time for the forest. I was more than thrilled to hear that walking meditations are a common practice, and you can use your walking (or hiking) time as your meditation time. Spiritual writer Thich Nhat Hanh said of walking: "The first thing you do is lift your foot. Breathe in. Put your foot down in front of you, first your heel and then your toes. Breathe out. Feel your feet on the solid Earth. You have already arrived. We frequently walk with the sole purpose of getting from one place to another. But where are we in between? When you walk, arrive with every step. That is walking meditation. There's nothing to it."

For a walking meditation, pick a location where you will have some privacy and silence. I prefer the woods, but perhaps you have a city park, or heck, maybe even a favorite mall that is quiet when it first opens. Walk slowly, you are in no rush. Focus on the feeling of your foot lifting from the ground: how does it feel lifted? Then, focus on the feeling of your foot returning to the ground: do you feel the earth beneath you? Focus on the motion of your body, and pay attention to your surroundings. What do you see? What do you hear? What do you smell? Is nature gifting you with any messages?

One thing I like to do is meditate with the intention of discovering something beautiful to take a picture of, and then I can just focus on the feeling of walking and discovering beauty in nature. If you find your thoughts getting distracted, simply return to the feeling of your feet touching the earth, knowing that you are planted firmly in the present moment.

Meditation while Cooking

One of my favorite activities to do is cooking: I love being able to create something that can offer sustenance and nutrition to those I love. I also think it is a creative and inspired activity. Since cooking is creative and healing, it makes sense that there are methods to making it a mindful activity by incorporating meditation into it. Meditation while cooking can be very peaceful: take a moment to be present with your soup! I say that half kiddingly, but seriously. Pause in the kitchen and really savor the skill in front of you: What if you just shut out the outside world and focused on the awesome feeling of spreading butter onto an English Muffin? How about turning your attention to the swirling of cream in coffee, listening only to the sound of the spoon hit your mug? What if you watched the oven as a batch of cookies baked, breathing in the sweet and healing smells of sugar and chocolate? Even cleaning can be a meditative moment.

While you clean your dishes, focus on the feeling of the warm water moving over your hands. Envision it washing away all the worries of the day, removing the dirt and purifying you.

Chanting Mantras in Traffic

I have to mention this, even though I do not know if it neatly fits into the category of meditation, I consider it one of the more soothing practices of my day. Mantras come from the ancient Hindu Vedic scripts, though they are also practiced in other Eastern traditions such as Buddhism and Taoism. According to Tris Thorp on Deepak Chopra's website, the word *mantra* actually is divided in two: "man" means "mind" and "tra" means transport. Furthermore, the article describes mantras as the "basis of all religious traditions, scriptures, and prayers. According to Pandit Vamadeva Shastri (Dr. David Frawley), when carefully chosen and used silently, mantras are said to have the ability to help alter your subconscious impulses, habits, and afflictions." They are considered sacred verses or phrases, and many use them in a repeated manner for meditation and for prayer. Mantras have a healing and soothing sound; to repeat the mantra is to speak to divinity and to calm the soul.

It just so happens that this busy girl needs to speak with divinity and calm her soul most while in rush hour traffic. While in the car I often listen to musical recordings of chants. Some of my favorite artists are Deval Premal, and an album titled "Yoga Music Mantras and Chants" by the Yoga Mantra and Chant Music Project. I recognize this isn't the most traditional way of chanting mantras, but it keeps me calm, relaxed, and focused on spiritual intentions. One of the simplest mantras you can try is "Aum," or "OM." If this is something that interests you I also recommend you speak with teachers who have done these for years. I also know of a local Kundalini studio that offers chanting yoga classes with gongs, which I hope to check out.

Candle Lighting Meditation

One meditation activity you can try on Imbolc allows you to disconnect from the hectic world and find comfort in quiet and simplicity. At dusk, turn off all the lights in your home. Put your cell phone in a drawer and turn the ringer off. Turn off your computer, turn off music. Light candles around your home and feel what it would be like without modern electronic conveniences for just a little while. Curl up in a blanket and slowly gaze into the flames of a candle. Watch it flicker and move, allowing your vision to go blurry when it wants to. If your thoughts start to become too overwhelming, try and turn your attention to your breath and the feeling of it moving in and out of your body instead.

Meditation makes a major difference in my life, and I know now that it is something anyone can try. Meditation is not just a practice of sitting in the Lotus Position for hours on end: it is an activity that allows you to center yourself, clear your mind of unwanted thoughts, and feel mindful in the moment. As a result, I hear my inner voice clearly: I feel what is best for my body, I sense what is best for my heart. You can make any moment a meditative moment: even if it is moving crystals around on your desk, working with a Zen garden, or joyfully folding laundry.

The goal of meditation is to get you in the moment, to make you sense peace and wonderment, and to allow your mind the opportunity to heal and feel good. I hope that after reading this you will also give yourself the opportunity to meditate, as it will transform the way you feel about yourself and this fantastic universe we all share together. You can take a moment now. Go on: close your eyes and feel your breath move in your nose and fill your chest with life…

LOVE SPELL SUBSTITUTIONS: PRACTICAL SOLUTIONS FOR LOVE SPELLS ON VALENTINE'S DAY

Having worked in the metaphysical community as a healer, diviner, and teacher, I have been approached dozens of times about love spells. There have been numerous instances where I've had to work with customers who come into the metaphysical shop, looking for the right ingredients to concoct a magical spell. They want love, immediately, sometimes from a specific person. They want the perfect man to come just drop into their laps, without putting in the effort to meet people or to make ourselves available. What I mean to say is this: spell work is not an easy, quick solution to your problems. During the month of February I want you to consider different ways for drawing love in your life.

I am going to ask you to put your love magic in your pocket and consider different approaches to drawing more love, joy, and happiness into your life. The mundane way. These are simply candid nuggets of wisdom, suggestions, food for thought, and recounts from my own experiences with clients. Even if you consider yourself a seasoned witch, I believe the advice below could be wonderful things to consider before rushing off to the metaphysical shop to buy out their selection of red candles and rose incense. Sometimes, all you need is a little faith and confidence. Have some faith in yourself; believe that you can feel love for yourself and others, and that others will show their love in return. So, let's look at possible ways to draw love in without the assistance of love spells.

When Love Spells Go Creepy

Love spells have been a topic of many intense discussions amongst the magical and modern Pagan community. It seems clear that most considerate and sane people agree that performing magic to manipulate the feelings of another specific person is a big no-no. Yet, still, I have been asked how to create a love spell to win the courtship of one specific mortal. One person went as far to say to me, "I want him to be bound to me, body and soul."

Really? Not only is that so immoral, it is fairly creepy. If someone is uninterested in you, and is not willing on his or her own accord to be in the kind of relationship you desire, then perhaps you should keep your chin up and wait to find that person who is romantically interested in you. But behaving like the Evil Witch from *Snow White* in attempting to bind the body and soul of a person to your own is probably not the best first date for anyone. Not only that, if you are part of the Wiccan tradition, you believe the Rule of Three, and realize that what you put out there will return to you threefold. Who knows what could result from this kind of demented spell work - a nasty relationship? An obsessive relationship? A realization that he wasn't the right guy for you after all, and now you

71

are in a rut and can't get out? A missed opportunity to meet the true prince or princess of your dreams? You never know what will result from manipulating the free will of another individual, but with most certainty, it will not benefit you in the end.

Read *He's Just Not That Into You*

Here is some tough love: if he isn't showing you the love you want, then he's just not that into you. If he's not returning your phone calls or your text messages, he's just not that into you. If he's married, he's just not that into you. If he isn't giving you the two "Big A's": Attention and Affection, he's just not that into you. If he's just a lousy lover, a deadbeat, a downtrodden person, a troll or a bully, he's just not that into you (or himself) . If he is putting you down or making you feel less like a goddess and more like a nagging burden, he's just not that into you. If he makes you "crash on his couch, " he's just not that into you. If he's too busy raiding on *World of Warcraft* or fixing his car to take you to the movies, then he's just not that into you. Stop ignoring the signs! Stop saying "it's complicated" and head for the hills!

Relationships are meant to be a place of comfort, devotion, support, happiness, caring, and sensuality. Remember those words the next time that guy doesn't text you back for a week and you are feeling distress and sadness from it. Practice patience in waiting for the right mate who is willing to give your relationship the attention it deserves to grow and flourish. Honest, heart-felt communication, dedication, and unwavering support are the qualities of a strong relationship. Think of your partner as someone who nurtures and supports you and someone with whom you can explore the many facets of love. When they are wishy-washy, prone to disappearing for long amounts of time, and/or unavailable emotionally, the commitment to a fulfilling relationship isn't there. Save the drama for *Vampire Diaries.*

What is your attitude towards finding love?

If you think you are "going to be a lonely cat lady" for the rest of your life, then so mote it be. Attitude truly shifts and changes the way you feel about yourself and the prospect of romance. Have a little faith in yourself! When I see pictures on Facebook that say things like, "I am sarcastic as a defense against idiots, " then I can only imagine the pain and loneliness the person must be experiencing. Once, I read cards for a person who wanted to know why she couldn't find love in her life. The pin on her shirt boldly read, "Back off, I'm a goddess." I do indeed believe we all have Goddess in us, but the phrase "Back Off" is clearly not a phrase that says, "I'm approachable and friendly." What vibes are you putting out into the world about welcoming love and people into your life? If you judge someone before meeting them, have a long "sh*t list, " or automatically believe that everyone around you is an idiot, then you are most likely blocking out potential opportunities for all kinds of relationships, romantic and platonic alike. Become accepting. Become friendly. Ask yourself what makes a person approachable. Love yourself; let others love you; love others. Like attracts like.

Stop saying that you attract the wrong mate.

How many times have you heard the phrases "I just attract mean guys, " or "I just attract crazy girls"? We've all dated someone who turned out to be not-so-much "our type," but if there is a continuous pattern of lousy lovers in your life, perhaps it is time to get back to the drawing board to reassess what it is you actually want in a relationship. Who is your ideal mate? What are the qualities of said ideal mate? Take a moment to write down those qualities, staying thoughtful and positive. In other words, instead of saying, "He can't be a loser" say, "He is highly ambitious." This is also another situation where you can contemplate your own self-love, your own needs, and your own desires. You deserve the best from a romantic companion. Look in the mirror every morning repeat the following: "I deserve to be treated like a goddess (god) ." Even if you have to force a grin on your face when you say it, after a while it will sink in and you will know it to be. And, more than anything, it is essential to meditate on the peace and simplicity of being happy with yourself, and not having to rely on others for good vibrations.

The love you take is equal to the love you make.

Thank The Beatles for this incredible slice of esoteric knowledge. Meditate on this one. The love you take is equal to the love you make. What kind of love makin' is going on in your life? Now, this is not a personal or cheeky question I'm asking you. How much love are you giving to the world? How kind are you? How affectionate are you? How interested are you in other people? What is your attitude about those who come to you in your life? Are you gracious, giving, trusting, and accepting? Or are you sarcastic, judgmental, cynical, and non-accepting? Sometimes just complimenting someone can make a world of difference.

I remember the other day I was in a slightly (okay majorly) lousy mood. I was at the hospital for blood work (it's an iron deficiency, don't worry) . The girl who was drawing my blood was clearly in the same kind of mood as I was. She was closed off, a little cold, and not so thrilled I was there before her second cup of morning coffee. Then I noticed: this lady had the most beautiful eyelashes. So I told her. "Your eyelashes are gorgeous!" Something changed in her demeanor. Her face lit up and she smiled, "Really you think so?" Soon enough, we were both smiling, joking, and talking about makeup and her work. We both shifted into much better moods, and I know that the rest of my day was much brighter.

So consider: when can you show compassion and love to people? Maybe there is a friend you are thinking about right now. Send them a text message and let them know. Perhaps you miss your parents. Send them a card in the mail. Perhaps you are just going to help an elderly lady walk across the street, or introduce yourself to your neighbors and invite them over for a cookout. Acts of kindness make you feel good, and they are contagious. Assist in making the world enjoy a better day, please, and it will be returned in love that you can happily cherish for your own well-being.

Activities for a Special Valentine's Day to Attract Love and Give Love

With all the advice above in mind, there are some wonderful activities you can do to draw love into your life that don't involve wagging a wand or stirring a cauldron. Here is just a small list of ideas to consider:

- Try a random act of kindness. Buy a latte for the person in line behind you at the coffee shop; open the door for someone; tell someone to have a nice day (and mean it); while at the pub, ask a stranger what song he/she wants to hear when you're filling the juke box. Have fun with it!
- Try a prepared act of kindness. Sign up to volunteer for a cause that rings true to you.

- Craft Valentine cards and send them to friends and family. Include a compliment in each.
- Bake a batch of cookies for Valentine's Day and share them with your co-workers.
- Study the mythology of Freyja, Frigg, Inanna, Ishtar, Aphrodite, Bastet, and Venus-- Goddesses associated with love and/or sensuality.
- Scatter birdseed out to the birds in your backyard.
- Adopt a pet.
- If you are single for the evening, pamper yourself with activities that bring you the most pleasure. Read a book on the Law of Attraction, write the qualities you love about yourself in a journal, paint a picture, go to a yoga class, go shopping for a new perfume or cologne, build a blanket fort with your kids, take a warm bath, walk your dog, cook an incredible meal, watch a favorite movie, or call your mother.
- If you are spending the evening with someone special, spend a moment to write a list of intentions for the two of you to share over the next year. What do you want to accomplish together? What do you want to explore together? Where do the two of you see your relationship going? Perhaps it is a great opportunity to try a new restaurant or activity, or revisit a favorite restaurant to reminisce about the wonderful times you've shared together.
- If you are crushing on someone, what's the harm in asking him or her out? You don't necessarily need to go the *Say Anything* route of blasting Peter Gabriel for him/her to show you care. How about a comfortable, laid back invitation to an afternoon cup of coffee? Or, invite him or her to join you to a concert, or to come along with a group of friends who are throwing darts at the bar on Friday night. And for goodness sake: compliment, compliment, compliment. They always win and show sweet affection.
- Embrace Valentine's Day as an opportunity to love love, and not an opportunity to make snarky comments about the greeting card industry. Hug the person who calls Valentine's Day a "commercial holiday."

Happy Valentine's Day. You are love and you are loved.

As a guiding force for our comfort, healing, inspiration, and joy, love is revered at Valentine's Day. Whether it is love for a romantic partner, platonic friends, or family, Valentine's Day can be looked at as one of multiple opportunities to express your feelings and appreciation for those you care about in your life. My hope is that you find this time of year as an opportunity to focus your thoughts and dreams on compassionate intentions, heart-felt communication, romantic excitement, blissful compliments, and self-love.

DIVINATION HIGHLIGHT: PYROMANCY

Growing up in New England, I knew that February was going to be a long, cold, and snowy month. But even in the cold of February, there was the hope of light around the corner, even if that meant that we still had piles of plowed snow melting in April! Regardless, fire is a powerful symbol of Imbolc: it is the spark of divine creation, warmth for comfort and healing, and the light of hopeful weather in the coming spring season. It is also a symbol associated with Brigid. The element of fire is one often turned to at Imbolc, so let's take a look at how we can divine with fire during this chilly season.

Divining Fire

One simple method of divination by fire is scrying. Scrying is divination by gazing, commonly associated with (but not limited to) crystal balls or dark reflective mirrors. Scryers will often gaze into a reflective surface with the intention of seeing divinatory messages. Fire scrying can be a relaxing exercise. Before your scrying session consider what questions you'd like to gain insight into. Rest comfortably by the fire and gaze into its gently glowing embers, allowing your focus to soften, your vision maybe even going a little blurry. If your thoughts wander try and return your attention to your breath and the motion of the fire. You may feel an intuitive answer to your question or see shapes in the embers that contain symbolic messages.

There are different ways to interpret the condition of the flames to divine future events as well. Have a question in mind prior to lighting the fire, and then interpret the way the fire lights and flames move. It is difficult to find any standard list of flame interpretation, and many sources just contain brief passages on the topic. Scott Cunningham suggests many flame interpretations in *Earth Power*:

- It is a good sign if the wood catches on fire and burns quickly.
- If it is difficult to get a fire going the answer is not as optimistic for the moment and needs to be returned to at a later time.
- Love and romance are omens if the fire moves to one side of the fire pit.
- Difficulties and challenges will follow if the fire crackles frequently.
- There is important news ahead if sparks fly into the air.

Divining Smoke

If gazing into a flame is not something of interest, there are two methods of interpreting the smoke of a fire as well. Capnomancy is the divination of the smoke from a fire. The direction of the smoke is said to determine the outcome of future events. In general it is believed that if the smoke rises straight up and high before dissipating it is a good sign. On the other hand, if the smoke lingers low and near the fire it is not as fortunate an omen.

If you are interested in trying something a little more small scale, you can do as the Babylonians did and divine with incense smoke. Libanomancy is the divination of smoke from incense. A collection of ancient Babylonian texts called *Three Collated Libanomancy Texts* reveals that incense smoke predicted the outcomes of battles and confrontations. The interpretations are challenging to modernize for today's diviners, especially with passages like "If the top of the incense gathers like a date palm and is thin at its base hardship will seize the man." Here are some suggestions for libanomancy interpretations to try:

- If the smoke comes towards you the answer is yes.
- If the smoke moves away from you the answer is no.
- If there is a lot of smoke you will have abundance and success.
- If the incense goes out you will have to wait longer to see results.

Objects in the Fire

An ancient method for conjuring messages from fire divination includes throwing objects onto the fire. Alomancy, sometimes known as halomancy, is divination using salt. Salt would be thrown onto the fire. The sounds of the fire as well as the color of the flame would then be interpreted. Daphnomancy is the divination of throwing laurel leaves onto the fire. Hold a bay leaf with a question in mind, and then throw the leaf into the fire. The louder the crackling is from the bay leaf burning, the more optimistic the outcome of your question.

Nuts have been thrown into fires as well to give answers. In Wales, there was a New Year's bonfire tradition associated with nuts. Throw a nut into the flames of a bonfire. If the flames dance when the nut is thrown in, it would be an exciting and fun year. If the flames do not change when the nut is thrown in, it will be a dull year.

Candle Divination

Pyromancy can be performed with candles as well, and there are different methods that can be used with a simple spell candle to look for future omens. Candle divination examines the condition of the flame and the shape of the wax for prophetic interpretations. In addition to scrying with a candle flame, you can also use the following list as guidance to messages:

- The higher and brighter a flame burns, the better the outcome.
- If the wick leans towards you, the outcome is yes.
- If the wick leans away from you, the outcome is no.
- A flickering flame indicates change is on the way.
- A sparking flame indicates possible challenges.
- If wax drips to the left side the answer is no.
- If wax drips to the right side the answer is yes.
- If wax drips equally on both sides there is no response.
- If there is no wax drip down the sides of the candle, ask again later.

Ceromancy is the divination of wax shapes. Light a candle and let it burn until there is melted wax collecting. Carefully pour the wax into a bowl of cold water. Take the wax out and interpret its shape. Interpreting wax shapes can feel similar to interpreting tea leaves: it is really up to the observations of the reader to see what shapes are in the wax and to determine a meaning. It may be worthwhile to note what shapes you see and follow up to see what outcomes followed after the reading. It may also be worthwhile to cross reference glossaries that the meanings of shapes in tea leaf readings. Perhaps if you see a heart it would represent love, or a coin would represent prosperity. If you see a baby, it could mean new beginnings. Or, if you see an animal it may be worth exploring the meanings of its spirit.

Spodomancy

One curious and neat divination brought up by Courtney Weber in her book *Brigid: History, Mystery, and Magick of the Celtic Goddess* is spodomancy, or divination with ashes. She suggests that you smooth out the ashes and soot in your fireplace before bed on Imbolc. Check on the ashes the following morning. If they look as if they have been disturbed or have footprints in the ashes, then Brigid came to visit and bless your home during the night. Another way to read ashes can be done as follows. Spread out ashes in an area that is exposed to a breeze: perhaps you have a stone you can spread them across that you can put in your garden, or on a tray that you can put near an outdoor altar, or on a porch that you don't mind sweeping. Write a question you have in the ash and allow it to sit overnight. Whatever letters are legible the following morning can be deciphered and interpreted to show the answer to your question.

You can also try out pyromancy, the divination method described above. Although there are no standardized interpretations for pyromancy, Imbolc is a wonderful opportunity to cozy up with the element of fire. It may take time to understand the messages or come up with your own interpretations, but it is worth the effort of working with such a relaxing and ancient form of divination.

IMBOLC CHAPTER NOTES

[1] Weber, Courtney. *Brigid: History, Mystery, and Magick of the Celtic Goddess.* San Francisco, CA: Weiser Books, 2015.

CHAPTER FOUR:
OSTARA

OVERVIEW, MAGIC, ACTIVITIES, AND CORRESPONDENCES

The Spring Equinox celebrates rebirth, growth, balance, and warmth. At the Spring Equinox we celebrate the growth of life around us: green is reappearing in nature, birds are singing in the morning again, flowers are returning, and gardens are being prepared for a season of growth. The Spring Equinox was an exciting time in ancient civilizations: at this point in the year, the cold spell of winter was broken. The soil was tilled and prepared for planting crops for the year's growing season. The warmth promised at the Winter Solstice finally arrived.

Today we may not be so connected with the land or the cycles of growing seasons. Strawberries are available all winter at the local grocery store and heat is not a scarcity as long as you keep up on the electric or gas bill. A wonderful opportunity with the arrival of spring is that it invites you to reconnect with nature. On sunny and warm days there is an invitation to see wildflowers on nature hikes or plant a garden in your yard. During severe thunderstorms and spring showers there is an invitation to deepen your appreciation for the power of nature. There needs to be a balance between sunshine and rain to create an abundant garden. The metaphor in this is useful, even for modern Pagans, who may not rely solar calendars for their livelihood as their ancestors did.

Maple Syrup and Honey Magic

In *Ostara: Rituals, Recipes, and Lore for the Spring Equinox*, author Kerri Connor makes an intriguing argument that links maple syrup and honey to the rituals of the Spring Equinox.[1] Maple trees are tapped for syrup between February and March. Bees begin to stir in spring after huddling in their hives during the winter, so at this time honey can be produced again. Both of these invigorating and sweet syrups have magical properties that can be celebrated during the springtime. Honey can be used for attracting love, good health, and happiness. Maple syrup can be used for attracting money and love. Both can be used to "sweeten" or enhance spells, and combined together they make a perfect offering to spring deities.

A common form of magic in Hoodoo is a honey jar, a jar full of honey said to draw sweet and positive magic to the creator. A honey jar for prosperity is a magical way to draw money and success into your life. The following list includes suggested items to add to a money jar that will draw prosperity to your home and family.

- Basil for money and family happiness
- Cinnamon sticks for love and money
- Patchouli for money and growth
- Lodestone, jade, or pyrite
- Petition paper (paper with your written intentions on it)
- Business card
- Dollar bills or coins

Add all the items that represent money and success to you to a clear jar and then fill it with honey. Seal it shut with a lid, and then light a green candle on top of the jar.

Seed Magic

Alfalfa seeds have the magical properties of prosperity, abundance, growth, and business success. At Ostara, collect alfalfa seeds and contemplate a major money project you would like to see

grow over the course of the spring. Whether it is a promotion, a new job, selling a house, or getting a record deal, hold your hands over the seeds and visualize the successful outcome of your money project. Say the following incantation over the alfalfa seeds: "Seeds of money, seeds of success, grow for me riches and abundance well blessed." Plant the seeds and keep them in your windowsill. As the seeds grow so will your success. You can also carry the alfalfa seeds in a small pouch with you or a small pinch in a coin purse.

Edible Flowers

Throw away the weed-wacker and lawn chemicals! Did you know that many so-called weeds are actually edible? Take dandelions for example. The leaves and flowers are edible, and the leaves have so many nutrients in them that they are a wonderful green to add to salads. The roots of dandelions can be dried and used as a tea substitute for coffee. If you are looking for an Ostara-themed dish to bring to ritual, look no further than your garden and yard (as long as you are positively sure how to identify wildflowers and herbs and know that they are not covered in chemicals). Some spring garden and wildflowers you may want to blend into a salad include: arugula leaves and flowers, chickweed, chives, cilantro, dandelion leaves, nasturtiums, and violas.

Another popular activity for edible flowers is candying violets. These can be used for garnishes and decorations. As directed by

Rosalind Creasy in *The Edible Flower Garden*, begin by selecting newly-opened violets in the morning. Cut the violets, leaving enough stem so you can hold them comfortably. Wash the flowers and allow them to dry completely. Slightly beat an egg white in a bowl. Holding the flower by the stem, gently paint the flower with a light coating of egg white. Then, sprinkle sugar onto the flower. All the flowers to dry on a cake rack or parchment covered cookie sheet. Make sure you gently put the flowers into their original shape with the petals opened. They can be dried in the oven, with the light on, though no extra heat is needed. In a few days they should be completely dried and stored in a sealed container.

Spring Cleaning

As the frost of winter melts into springtime, we begin to feel a little more energy and excitement. Clearing clutter and opening windows to let fresh air in can shift the energy of your home from feeling stuffy to vibrant. A clean space allows for clear thinking, productivity, and relaxation. There are ways to add a little magic to your cleaning as well.

- Mopping Rinse: If you want to wipe down your floors, consider using a magically charged rinse to bring a little extra magic into your home. For the rinse, fill an entire gallon bucket with water, unscented soap, and a couple drops of each of the following essential oils: lemongrass, pine or fir, cedarwood, and rose (or rose water). For a little extra magic, charge the water you use under the sun.
- Ostara Simmering Potpourri for Purification and Rejuvenation: Pour three cups of water into a small pot on the stove. Turn the burner to medium, and once the water has started to boil, turn it down to the lowest setting. Add sliced lemon, lavender, rosemary, sage, and a sprig of spring flowers. Allow the herbs to simmer; watching closely that the water doesn't boil down too low. Save the water to sprinkle in the garden for growth and recycle the discarded herbs in compost.

Ostara Comfort Basket

Self-care is always in season. In the Easter tradition, many people exchange gifts in baskets. These gifts often include candy, flowers, or even rabbit figurines. This Ostara, consider creating a comfort basket for yourself. This is a basket you can go to when you are having a tough day: the idea is that it will make you feel better by going through its contents. Think about what it is that brings you comfort: is it writing? Put some neat stationary, bullet point pages for motivation, and nice pens in the basket. Do you like to take baths? Put a sea salt bath soak in the basket. Are you fond of campfires? Put the ingredients for s'mores in there. Are there crystals that you really love? What about feathers, incense, or teas? The comfort basket is meant to give you a time to rest and return to nurturing yourself back to a vibrant and energized place. This can also be a wonderful present to share with a special someone. There is even something creative in the process of collecting different items that you believe will help you feel better, or brighten someone else's day. Peanut Butter or Cadbury Creme Eggs are always a winning treat if you need a good idea to start with!

Ostara Oil Blends

The fragrances for Ostara are bright, floral, purifying, and full of love magic. A simple blend for bringing love, fresh starts, and happiness into your home would be equal parts sweet orange and lavender. I tend to use this blend in an oil diffuser when I am cleaning. If lavender is a little too sleepy for you, switch out lavender for rosemary.

An oil blend I am very fond of is adapted from a recipe in *Llewellyn's Complete Formulary of Magical Oils* by Celeste Rayne Heldstab.[2] I enjoy this recipe because it combines earthy scents with floral ones, reminding me of the fresh fragrance of the forest in spring. Blend 3 parts vetivert, 1 part rosewood, 1 part geranium, and 1 part honeysuckle or ylang-ylang.

Ostara Journaling

This is the time of year when the sun starts to warm up, nature begins to grow, and we prepare for a season of gardening. At this time of the year, contemplate what you would like to see grow in your garden. Here are some questions to write about, journal on, or meditate on this Ostara:

• What goals would you like to see completed this growing season?

- What is the most valuable thing you think needs attention in your life right now?
- What does balance mean to you? What does wellness mean to you?
- How do you find energy and balance in your life?
- What are you looking forward to doing outdoors when the weather gets better?
- Create a daily schedule.
- Create a budget.
- Create a list of things you would love to manifest in the next week, month, or year.

Correspondences:
- Names: Ostara, Spring Equinox, Vernal Equinox
- Date of Celebration: Celebrated on the Spring Equinox (which usually falls between March 20th and March 23rd).
- Deities Honored: Bloduwedd, Cernunnos, Dagda, Eostre, Freya, Mithris, Persephone, Sita
- Magical Focus: balance, communication, fertility, growth, love, new beginnings, rebirth
- Activities: decorating eggs, egg hunts, gardening, hiking, spring cleaning
- Altar Decorations: animal figurines (robins and rabbits), decorated or painted eggs, spring and wild flowers
- Food and Beverages: apricot, artichoke, asparagus, avocado, bean sprouts, broccoli, carrot, cabbage, chicken, eggs, fish, green

onions, ham, honey cakes, hot cross buns, lamb, leafy greens, lemon, mushrooms, orange, potatoes, radishes, seeds, sweets
- Plants, Herbs, Incense: broom, cinquefoil, dandelion, dill, gardenia, honeysuckle, lemon balm, lemongrass, lilac, lily of the valley, mint, narcissus, parsley, thyme, tulip, vervain, violet
- Crystals: aquamarine, amethyst, fluorite, jasper, moonstone, rose quartz
- Colors: light green, pastels, pink, yellow

GODDESSES AND MAIDEN WITCHES OF SPRING

When we think of Ostara we think of Eostre, an Anglo-Saxon Goddess of spring.Unfortunately, there is very little information on Eostre, though the Venerable Bede makes mention of her in the 8th century, saying Easter was named after her. Furthermore, it is important to keep in mind that the name Ostara is a modern Pagan creation, one which Aiden Kelly adopted for the Spring Equinox in the 1970s. As blogger Jason Mankey explains, "There aren't any tales of Eostre throwing eggs to all of the good little Germanic pagans, or her riding a giant rabbit, so it's hard to say with certainty that she existed and is the source for the word 'Easter.'"[3]

Spring Goddesses like Eostre still deserve attention and tribute at the Spring Equinox, even if their connection to the Spring Equinox is based on symbolism and mythology. Spring Goddesses bring life and beauty back to nature. They stir love in us and their engagement in the wellness of the land gives us hope that growth can happen in the spring season.

Eostre and the Hare

In *Ostara: Customs, Spells and Rituals for the Rites of Spring*, Edain McCoy shares a wonderful story about Eostre meeting with a rabbit in spring.[4] Even if this is not one from mythological volumes of the days old, it is a sweet story that would be a fine one to share with children.

One of Eostre's finest devotees was a small hare who wished to give a gift to the goddess, but wasn't sure what he could offer the goddess of spring. One day, while looking for food, he came across a fresh egg. Although he craved the delightful egg for a snack for himself, he decided it would be a wonderful present for Eostre. He painted the egg bright colors and drew symbols and designs on it.

When the egg was complete, he offered it to Eostre. Eostre was so delighted by the hare's egg, that she decided that it would be a tradition that all children would receive eggs at the Spring Equinox.

Freyja

Freyja is said to be a goddess associated with the return of spring. From the divine Vanir family, Freyja is sister to Freyr. As one of the most revered goddesses in Northern mythology, Freyja is a goddess of love, fertility, and magic. In the *Edda*, composed by Snorri Sturluson, Freyja is described as a glorious goddess who "is the most approachable one for people to pray to... She was fond of love songs. It is good to pray to her concerning love affairs."[5] She is said to ride a chariot led by two cats. She is married to Odin, and while he is off on long travels, she cries tears of "red gold,"[6] which considering the region, is perhaps amber. Freyja isn't just a goddess of love and fertility. It is also believed that she was as adept in magic as Odin. Freyja was said to teach the Aesir a form of magic known as seidr, which involves trances and shamanistic rituals to divine and weave the future. Those who practiced seidr were said to have a powerful ability to access secret knowledge and share wisdom about future events. Not only was Freyja said to be a master at seidr, she taught the form of magic to Odin.

Blodeuwedd

Blodeuwedd is a Welsh goddess of flowers and fertility, often connected to the holidays of Ostara and Beltane. Blodeuwedd's story appears in the tale of "Math, the Son of Mathonwy," a story in the medieval Welsh book *The Mabinogion*. The story begins with the goddess Arianrhod shaming her son, Lleu Llaw Gyffes, saying that he could not be king unless she permitted it. Through her rule, she made it so he could not marry a mortal woman, thus stopping him from gaining the throne. However, Lleu has magical abilities that allow him to be safe from being killed, unless in the most complex of circumstances. As we learn: Lleu cannot be killed in a house or outside; on a horse or standing on the ground. This at least allows Lleu the time to search out a wife who is not human. Lleu's magical cousins Math and Gwydion are able to help him with this task. They create an otherworldly woman by using the flowers of oak, broom, and meadowsweet. By doing this magic, they created a beautiful maiden of the land they named Blodeuwedd, meaning "Flower-faces." Lleu and Blodeuwedd are married, and Lleu is finally able to take the throne, through marrying a woman of the land and not a human.

While Lleu is away hunting, a hunter named Gronw comes to the castle. When seeing Blodeuwedd, the two instantly fall in love. To be together, they plot a way to kill Lleu. When Lleu returns, Blodeuwedd tells him that she is afraid he could get killed. This, of course, is feigned and part of the plot to set up Lleu's death. Though Lleu tries to coax Blodeuwedd, she insists that he set up the circumstances in which he could be killed. So, they set up a bath on a river bank with a thatched roof. They bring one goat to the bank of the water. Lleu puts one foot on the goat and the other foot on the side of the bathtub. In this instant, Gronw throws a spear and hits Lleu in his side. Lleu turns into an eagle and flies away.
Gwydion finds Lleu as a wounded eagle high in a tree, and by chanting, gets him to fly down. With the help of a magical wand, Gwydion turns Lleu back into his human form. Gwydion then sets out to find Blodeuwedd and turns her into an owl, banishing her from seeing the light ever again. When Lleu is completely healed, he slays Gronw.

For me, the story of Blodeuwedd is tragic and beautiful: she has an otherworldly creation, made with magic from flowers, with the intention of wedding a human hero. Unfortunately, her curiosity for feeling love and her passionate desires condemn her back to nature. As Winter Cymraes reflects in her article about Blodeuwedd, "She is never asked whether she loves him or desires to marry him. She was created for his purposes, solely to assure his right to rule the land. Her own desires are impossible to achieve while Lleu lives and she is often seen as the epitome of non-assertive femininity, fickleness, and the faithless wife, using the passion of two men for her to seal the doom of both."[7]

I see this as an allegory of what many women encounter when trying to find themselves, their positions in society, and their roles in relationships. Sometimes it feels as though it is hard to be heard, that her words are lost through an otherworldly barrier, her needs met only with sacrifice. Honor Blodeuwedd at Ostara by lighting nine candles decorated with the flowers that created her, or by decorating your altar with an image of an owl.

Persephone's Return to the World of the Living

Persephone is the gentle and beautiful Greek goddess of the dead and afterlife. Daughter of Demeter and Zeus, she was abducted by Hades, Lord of the Underworld. Demeter mournfully searched for Persephone, and as she continued to search, the earth began to decay and die. The world continued to grow cold and icy, the land barren as Demeter was in deep grief over the loss of her daughter. Seeing this, Zeus sent Hermes to the underworld to fetch Persephone, on the one condition that Persephone does not eat anything while in the underworld. Hades then pressed one single pomegranate seed into Persephone's mouth, condemning her to the underworld for half the year. Thus, Persephone spends part of the year in the underworld with Hades, and during this time Demeter mourns and the earth is bare and cold. But when Persephone returns, so does the warmth and growth of nature.

Easter Witches of Sweden

In Sweden there is an ancient tradition of children dressing up as witches at Easter. They dress in long skirts, bright shawls, and carry brooms or kettles, wear face paint, and go from door to door asking for gifts, just as American children commonly do at Halloween.

Apparently, there was an old belief that witches were up to no good the week of Easter, leaving their homes and causing havoc and mischief on their flights to a place called Blakulla, where they danced with the devil. People would light bonfires to keep their evil influences away, while children get to mock them in costume and get treats as a prize. What is most fascinating about this practice at the Spring Equinox is that we see young girls dressing up in magical forms of witches. It is as though they transform themselves into otherworldly maidens, who, like the goddesses of spring, welcome in the changing of seasons and the growth of the land.

MYTHOLOGY AND MAGIC OF THE EGG

The most prominent symbol of Ostara and the Spring Equinox is the egg. As the source of life for all living creatures, eggs represent birth, rebirth, the soul, and fertility. The egg has played its role in many myths and in magic, spanning many cultures. It is seen as an enchanting vessel of life, abundance, and infinite possibilities. Here, we will examine the mystifying and magical qualities contained in the egg as interpreted through mythology, as well as explore ways to enjoy this magic at Ostara, or year round if so pleased to.

The Cosmic Egg

The notion of infinite potential is contemplated in the idea of the "Cosmic Egg." The cosmic egg represents the place from where the universe is created. Myths which span many ancient cultures

describe the very beginnings of the universe coming forth from an egg. It is as though the universe bursts out of the egg, dividing into different aspects that make the universe, comparable perhaps even to the Big Bang Theory.

The ancient Babylonian goddess Astarte was said to emerge from an egg. The story goes that the egg was in the Euphrates river, where it was pushed to shore by fish. Once on the shores doves rested on it, incubating the egg until Astarte was born from within it.

In Hindu myth, a seed appears in the primordial waters. This seed transforms into a brilliant, golden egg. The god Braham meditates for one year within the egg, then breaks forth from the egg to create the sky and the earth. In addition to the creation myth, the Lingam Stone from the Narmada River in India is a valuable stone which is shaped like the Cosmic Egg.

In a Chinese creation myth from the 3rd century C.E., Pan-Ku slept within an egg for 18,000 years. He grew into a giant, and when he hatched from the shell the white of the egg (Yin) rose upwards to become the sky and the yolk of the egg (Yang) descended downwards to become the earth. Pan-Ku spent the next 18,000 years pushing the two elements apart from each other to keep them from blending. When the sky and earth were finally separate, Pan-Ku laid down and died. The world grew from his corpse.

In the Egyptian city of Khemnu (Greek word is Hermopolis), the Ogdoad were a group of four couples, eight deities in total, who were worshipped. The Ogdoad, who were often depicted as frogs or serpents, represented primordial waters, eternity, darkness, and air. One myth says that the Ogdoad created a giant Cosmic Egg which birthed the sun god Ra. Other versions say the egg was laid by an ibis, a bird sacred to Thoth. There is also legend that the very shell of this Cosmic Egg is buried within a temple at Hermopolis.

The Pelasgians, settlers in Greece who predated the Hellenistic Greeks, also had a creation myth involving the Cosmic Egg. They believed that in the beginning there was only chaos. From the chaos the Goddess Eurynome rose. She created the sky and sea, and from the sea she danced. She spun around, creating a whirlwind. She rubbed the wind between her hands and created the serpent Ophion, with whom she mated. Eurynome turned herself into a dove and laid the Cosmic Egg. The three beings created a sacred trinity: Eurynome representing femininity, Ophion representing masculinity, and the egg representing the love child. Ophion wrapped himself around the egg seven times to incubate it. When the egg hatched the universe was birthed.

Also valuable to the Greeks was the Omphalos, a conical stone that was worshipped as sacred. Omphalos means "navel," and these stones are often called "Earth Navels." In Delphi it was believed the Omphalos was the stone accidentally swallowed by Chronos. In Delos, there is an omphalos which has a serpent wrapped around it, clearly linking the stone's shape and the Cosmic Egg (the serpent representing Ophion). These stones are not only found in Greece, but in other areas of the world, as well. One such stone is the Lia Fail, which is found on the Irish Hill of Tara, considered to be the birthplace of Samhain. Some theorize that the egg-like stones connect across the world to create a sacred grid system.

Eggs as Talismans

Roman philosopher, naturalist, author and explorer Pliny the Elder spent time observing the traditions of Druids in Gaul. In his works he described seeing a Druid's amulet which was called an anguium. It was described as being egg-shaped, having been created by the form of serpents wound tightly together. The Druid's Egg was said to have magical powers: it aided people in legal matters, helped draw attention from royalty, and had healing powers. Egg-shaped shaped crystals and glass have been discovered, leading some to believe these were the Druid's egg amulets. Interestingly enough, the serpent and the egg come together in the Gaulic Goddess Sirona, a fertility goddess of healing and rebirth. Sirona was depicted carrying a bowl of three eggs. She had serpents coiled around her arms, reaching towards the bowl of eggs.

Pysanky are the ornately decorated eggs with a long, even ancient, tradition in the Ukraine. They are raw eggs, not to be eaten, but to be gifted and used as talismans. They are given to friends and family for good health and prosperity. They are fed to animals to give them good luck in producing many healthy babies. They are saved in homes or buried under homes for protection against fire and storms. They are buried in fields to bring good fortune to the year's crop. The fascinating aspect to the pysanky are that their decorations are full of magickal and ancient symbols: trees, flowers, spirals, and birds depict images steeped in mythology and magic commonly associated with springtime.

Egg Magic

Working with eggs in magical work can be quite fulfilling. They can be used in spells for good fortune, fertility, love, creativity, alchemy, transformation, and protection.

- *Egg painting magic in the home.* Consider making the practice of egg decorating a magical one. Consider a goal you wish to achieve within the coming season of growth. Ask yourself where you wish to see abundance in your life. Magically decorate the eggs in a manner to reflect your wishes for abundance by using magical symbols and colors. For example, paint an egg red or pink and decorate with hearts to reflect wishes for love. Paint an egg green and adorn with gold glitter to reflect wishes for money. Paint an egg purple and glue violets on it for intuition and spiritual growth.
- *Cascarones.* Cascarones are hollowed out eggs that have been filled with items like glitter, flour, or perfumed herbs. Traditionally, they would be playfully broken on a person's head. If you are talented and patient, empty an egg and refill it with herbs and oils that correspond with something you wish to grow in your life. Break it at the time you really want to see that wish manifest itself.
- *Powdered Egg Shells.* Powdered egg shells, also known as cascarilla, are used in Santeria, folk, and hoodoo magic. Cascarilla can be sprinkled around the borders of rooms for protection and peace. Because it creates a chalk-like substance, it has also been used to draw sigils and magical symbols. It can be added to floor rinses for protection in the home. To make cascarilla, clean and rinse egg shells thoroughly. Bake the shells at a low temperature in the oven (I recommend starting at 250 degrees F) for about 15 minutes. Grind them to a very fine powder with a mortar and pestle.
- *Egg magic in the garden.* If you are talented and patient, hollow out eggs and make ornaments out of them with ribbon. Or, use plastic eggs as an easier substitute. Hang the eggs from tree and shrub branches in your yard or garden for abundance

and good luck. To bring growth to your garden, paint an egg brown and green and mark it with symbols of growth and fertility. Plant it in your garden, and walk clockwise around the garden, saying "Egg of the Goddess, giver of all things, grow my garden abundant this spring. Strong and sacred this place must be, springing forth its bounty, so blessed be."

- *Magickal Egg Hunt.* Here's an opportunity for children of all ages to enjoy Ostara egg hunts. Fill plastic gift eggs with small magical amulets, charms, crystals, bags of seeds, herbs, small vials of oil, jewelry, or incense. With it, include a small fortune or inspirational quote. The people involved in the egg hunt will find the egg that offers the most valuable fortune and gift they need for springtime.

- *White Light Bubble as a Protective Eggshell.* For many people in the metaphysical world, the idea of the "White Light Bubble" describes a visualization exercise of seeing white light surrounding the body for protective energy. For the purposes of Ostara, consider morphing the white light bubble into an egg shell. Take a moment to quietly pause. Close your eyes and take long, deep breaths. Visualize yourself surrounded by a warm, comforting, and protective eggshell. See the infinite oval shape of the shell surrounding you, knowing that nothing negative or harmful can penetrate your personal space. Consider yourself at the very center of the Cosmic Egg. What are the properties necessary in this centered place to create life and the universe? When it is time to emerge from the egg, take a moment to see how it feels to be "born." What sensations do you feel? What do you see? What are the immediate priorities you want to tackle? Contemplate how this exercise feels similar or different to the white light bubble.

- *Eggs on Ostara Altars.* The altar is a perfect place to display the egg. Whether embellished with magical symbols or left natural, their presence on an Ostara altar reflect the rebirthing of nature in the spring. In addition to actual eggs, put on display objects such as lingam stones, faberge eggs, egg-shaped crystals, or egg-shaped chocolate. Take time to gaze at the egg and consider what the egg symbolizes for you.

Natural Egg Dyes

Making natural egg dyes is a fun way to create beautiful, natural looking colors from plants. Simply boil two cups of water with each of the ingredients below. Allow the ingredient to cook for thirty minutes. If you want a bolder color, add more of the ingredient. Pour the liquid through a strainer into a bowl. Then stir in one tablespoon of vinegar. Dip the hardboiled eggs into the dyed water for about 10 minutes, longer for a brighter color.

- For Yellow Dye: Use 2 tablespoons of turmeric.
- For Orange Dye: Use ½ cup of yellow onion skins or 2 tablespoons paprika.
- For Deep Blue Dye: Use ½ cup of chopped up purple cabbage.
- For Blue Dye: Use ½ cup of blueberries.
- For Pink Dye: Use ½ cup of chopped up beets.
- For Brown Dye: Use one teabag of black tea.

Eggshell Seedlings

If you are more interested in a gift that you can share with your green-thumbed friends, consider creating eggshell seedlings. Take an eggshell that has been broken closer to one end (approximately one third down from the top) and gently rinse it out. Return it to an egg carton and allow it to dry. Poke a hole into the bottom of the shell. Add a scoopful of potting soil into the eggshell. Place seeds into the soil as directed on the seed packages. When the seeds have sprouted simply transplant the egg directly into the soil outdoors.

Divining with Eggs

Egg divination has long been practiced, and at times in history it was a popular form of divination. While some methods are easier than others, and some are neater than others, they are all fun to experiment with during the season of Ostara.

- *Oomancy*: Oomancy is divining with the egg white. Bring a pot of water to boil, and then lower the heat slightly. Break an egg and separate the white from the yolk. Pour the egg white into the boiling water and interpret the shapes made from the egg whites. When divining the shapes, consider your immediate reaction to what you see.

- *Oomantia*: Oomantia is the divining of the egg shell. An excellent egg divination described by Nancy Vedder-Shults in her article "Egg Divination" suggests to hard boil an egg.[8] Draw different symbols on the egg, giving meaning and interpretation to each of the symbols. Hold the egg and think of your question, and then gently roll the egg. When it stops rolling, your answer is in the symbol facing upwards. Another method for reading eggshells include cracking a hardboiled egg and interpreting the shapes and lines made with the cracks in the shell.
- Ooscopy: Ooscopy is the divination of reading the egg itself. A fun, yet messy form of egg divination that involves reading the shell, white, and yolk. Hold an egg for a moment and concentrate on a question you have. Throw the egg onto the ground, or perhaps in a dish. Interpret the shapes of the shells and egg to come to a divine answer.
- Egg Superstitions and Old Traditions: There is an old tradition that says you will have a lousy day if you crack an egg at breakfast and break the yolk. Cracking an egg with a double yolk is usually a good sign, often signifying a pregnancy or happy union, unless you are British, in which case a double yolk is a sign of death or ill fortune. An old Scottish divination said to fill your mouth with the white of an egg, not swallowing a drop. You are then to go out and about in the world until you hear the name of a man or woman. This is the name of the person you will marry.

Reverence for the Egg

Humanity has long revered the egg as a symbol of birth and creation, but also as a magical object that could be used for fortune and protection. Ostara is an excellent time to contemplate how such a fragile object could contain all the makings of our universe. Perhaps it is worth considering how vulnerable the egg is: with love, care, and devotion, life can spring forth from it. The mystical and soulful egg reveals the very same needs and nature of humanity.

SPRINGTIME WILDFLOWER MAGIC AND FOLKLORE

Above all, the Spring Equinox is the celebration of light and hope; it is the rebirth of nature and the return of growth and manifestation. A simple walk in nature reveals the beautiful palette of spring in the array of wildflowers. Their fragrance carries through the woods, just as their magical energy can for witches and healers. This is a collection of some of my favorite springtime flowers, their lore, and their magical properties. Although it is not a complete list, it compiles some commonly found wildflowers in northeast America (and beyond). Please keep in mind the arrival of these flower may vary depending on where you live. In Tennessee I begin to see wildflowers at about the time of the Spring Equinox.

- **Anemone**: Rue anemones and wood anemones are sweet little flowers dotting the landscape in the first part of spring. There are many species of anemones, with over 25 in North America. The name from the flower was inspired by Anemoi, the Greek god of winds. Some say that anemone got its name because it seems to bloom when the wind blows, and consequently, it is one of the first flowers seen in the spring. Because of its connection to wind, anemone can be used for spells concerning the element of air. These flowers of the wind were also said to grow from Venus' fallen tears, who was grief-stricken over the death of Adonis. Anemone thus can be used to help mend a broken heart, and to hold them is to receive comfort during the grief of losing someone you love. It gives you power to stand strong, even in the face of adversity.
- **Bloodroot**: The name bloodroot was inspired by the red juice that comes from its stems and roots. Native American Indians used the juice as a face paint and dye. Bloodroot is carried to attract love and protect from negativity. Do not ingest bloodroot, it is poisonous.
- **Bluebells**: Brian Froud said, "The Bluebell is one of the most potent of all faerie flowers, and a bluebell wood is an extremely hazardous place to be – a place of faerie-woven spells and enchantments."[9] Bluebells are used for truth and luck spells.
- **Chickweed**: Chickweed is also known as bird seed or starweed. Young chickweed is an edible plant and the greens have vitamin A and C in them. Chickweed is also said to predict the weather. If the blossoms are shut there will be rain, but if they remain open it will be sunny and dry. Chickweed can be used in love magic, as it attracts love and keeps relationships healthy.

- **Coltsfoot**: Coltsfoot is a bright yellow flower that was once used in cough syrups and candies. Coltsfoot is used in love spells and can aid in returning to a place of peace and tranquility. Its leaves are smoked and can cause visions. These bright yellow and orange blossoms are a celebration of the return of the sun and spring equinox.
- **Columbine (wild)**: Not only does columbine attract hummingbirds, it is said to attract faeries. Native American Meskwaski Indians used to mix seeds into their smoking tobacco to create a divine scent that they also thought would attract love. The seeds are used in love potions and it is believed that carrying wild columbine can spark courage.
- **Daffodil**: Daffodils can be placed on altars for love spells, as well as to welcome the Spring Equinox. They will bring brightness, joy, and hope to a home. Fresh daffodils in the bedroom are said to increase fertility.
- **Daisy**: Sweet daisies relieve tension and stress, removing complexity from situations to reveal simple joy and truth. They can be used for purification. Add a vase of daisies to a recently cleaned, cleared, and decluttered space to enhance clarity and simplicity. Daisies are associated with Freya and Artemis. According to Scott Cunningham, you can sleep with daisy under your pillow and an absent lover will return to you. Paul Beryl says, "Dryads are attracted to those places where daisies grow, and sitting among them is a means of learning to communicate with the Devas of herbs."[10] It was also believed that daisies were connected to St. John and could protect a home or person from lightning.
- **Dandelion**: Dandelions are not just a weed! The name comes from French, meaning, "the tooth of the lion." They are versatile, practical, and magical flowers. Dandelions are said to enhance intuition. They can be used in divination incense, and dandelion root tea can be drunk to assist in psychic work. There is a belief that if you whisper the name of a loved one and then blow away dandelion seeds that person will receive your amorous message.
- **Geranium (wild)**: Also known as cranesbill, crowfoot, alum root, and old maid's nightcap, wild geranium is carried to attract prosperity and enhance happiness. It is linked to Venus and the five-pointed star, thus having powerful feminine and goddess

energy. Geranium has a nurturing spirit and can be used to help heal a broken heart and open yourself up to loving experiences.

- **Honeysuckle**: Honeysuckle has one of the most notable fragrances: sweet and inviting, it is a welcoming fragrance for the spring. Honeysuckle is used for prosperity and good luck. The flowers can be used in money charm bags. Although oil-infused honeysuckle does not smell as sweet, it is a powerful addition to prosperity and wealth oils. Honeysuckle is also used to release unwanted emotions: breathing in the scent releases shame, fear, and ego. It is also helpful during transitory times of change. Honeysuckle can be used for rituals and magic with Cerridwen.
- **Iris**: The beautiful Iris helps with creativity, activating psychic abilities, and recognizing divine messages. The three points are said to represent faith, wisdom, and valor. Iris is also the name of the Goddess of the rainbow. The root of iris is often called "orris root," and is used in attraction and spiritual protection spells.
- **Jack-in-the-Pulpit**: The Jack-in-the-Pulpit took its folk name  from its shape, a conical shape with a hood covering it. Native Americans had many purposes for it, and although the root is incredibly acidic and poisonous, they would dry or roast the root and use it for treating coughs and sore throats. The shape of the Jack-in-the-Pulpit represents shelter and protection, like the safety a loved one can give you. It is a flower connected to the spirit of the Green Man.
- **Lilac**: Blossoms from the lilac tree are otherworldly, and according to author Tess Whitehurst, "Lilacs in bloom create doorways of light between this world and the next."[11] Lilacs can aid in revealing psychic abilities and communication with the spirit world. They are also used in love potions and are said to have protective qualities.
- **Lupine (wild)**: Lupine comes from the Latin word lupinus, meaning "wolf." Because of this, lupine can be used for healing dogs. It is an otherworldly herb that can be used for spirit

communication and mediumship. It is a flower closely connected to faeries, imagination, and daydreaming.

- **Mayapple**: Mayapple is also known as American Mandrake, and is often used as a substitute for European Mandrake, even though the two are not related. Mayapple can be used for prosperity and money magic and to also bring protection to the home. Please note that the roots and leaves are incredibly poisonous, and it is important to mention that the berry alone is edible but has a well-known laxative effect.
- **Peony**: Peony removes blockages and old patterns. It is also said to be protective against harm – its roots and seeds would be hung around children's necks to protect them from mischievous spirits. Roots would be collected and carved into amulets, similar to customs with mandrakes. In China it is a flower of wealth. Place a bouquet by your bed for healing and to aid in relaxation.
- **Periwinkle**: Also known as blue buttons, sorcerer's violet, and devil's eye. Place over the door to protect your home and make it a peaceful homestead. Use in love spells and place by the bed to increase passion. It is believed that if a husband and wife eat periwinkle leaves they will always love each other. The shape is linked to a pentacle and the color is said to reduce anxiety.
- **Phlox**: The word "phlox" comes from the Greek word meaning "flame." Phlox helps with courage, meditation, and expressing love. The Pink Moon of April was given its name after the blooming phlox flowers.
- **Shooting Star**: Also known as American Cowslip. The flower has been used in wealth charms and love spells. It is said to help people reconnect with their cosmic origins.
- **Solomon's Seal**: It is believed that Solomon Seal was given its name because the shape and stars on its rootstock looks like a royal seal. Place Solomon's Seal in the four corners of your house for protection. Solomon's Seal is used in sacred and ceremonial magic, especially when truth and sacred oaths are made. It is also used to consecrate magical tools and places.
- **Spring Beauty**: Spring Beauties often are the first flowers to appear in the springtime. As a bright white or pale pink flower with five petals, it is often connected to the powers of Venus. Spring Beauties have many talents for surviving the harshness of early spring. The pink lines on its petals help guide bees. They

also have very strong and flexible stems that do not break in the wind. Because of this, Spring Beauties can be used for feminine empowerment, self-love, and to strengthen self esteem.

- **Trillium**: Trillium is a wildflower revered by Native Americans as sacred and feminine; thus, it was used as an aphrodisiac. The root would be boiled and a drop of the concoction would be dropped into the food of one's love. Its three petals celebrate the phases of the Goddess, and carrying trillium is said to bring luck and attract money.
- **Violet**: Ancient Greeks decorated Athens with violets, which were a symbol of the city. Ancient Romans made wine from violet blossoms. Violets create a feeling of calmness, clarity, and serenity. Keep violets on your altar when you are in a phase of self-exploration. They help to rid negative self-talk and invoke self-love. Violets are also used in love spells and said to aid in renewal of romantic love. Violets are excellent for creative minds as they are said to help inspire brilliant and beautiful ideas. According to Scott Cunningham, if you gather the first violet in the spring you will have a wish granted.[12]
- **Wood Betony**: Wood betony is used for protection and purification, making it a nice incense in Midsummer bonfires. It used to be used in charms to protect against anything that could bring you harm or illness. You can grow it in your garden to bring protection to your home and to add into spells for love and healing.
- **Yarrow**: Yarrow serves many magical purposes. It is a common herb in love spells. Large patches of yarrow growing in a field indicate a very powerful energy point: sit there, relax, re-center and feel grounded again. It is said to help bring harmony and flow to energy, thus a good herb to have in a house that needs balance and love. Yarrow can be used to attract friends, and when carried, can enhance courage. If placed under a bed or inside a pillowcase, you will dream about love and romance.

When harvesting wildflowers please be mindful to do so in a responsible manner. Wildflowers in public parks and forests are not to be picked, nor should any be picked without the appropriate requests. Harvesting rare and hard-to-find wildflowers is not recommended: only harvest what you need, and in small quantity.

Know about what you are working with: if you are prone to allergies, perhaps you do not want to handle the flowers. Read up on which flowers can be poisonous, avoid them, and proceed with caution. It isn't necessary to pluck and press every single flower you see on your path to feel the full potential of flower magic. Stopping to admire flowers and meditate with them can also give you a spiritual connection to their energy as well as add to your own understanding of how they function magically. Make the old phrase "stop and smell the flowers" one where you breathe in the power of nature, letting it evoke memories, joy, healing, and growth.

DIVINATION HIGHLIGHT: RUNES

In honor of Germanic Goddesses Eostre and Freya, this chapter will conclude by looking at the divination of runes. Runes have a fascinating history: they are connected to magic, myth, and the adventures of Vikings. They have been used to dedicate stones to historic families, evoke the strength of gods in weapons, and lead modern day archaeologists on a trail of where the Vikings once explored. Studying runes takes time and dedication, as well as an interest in history, archaeology, and ancient magic. Working with runes takes respect of the Germanic mythology and religions, thus making it an enlightening and empowering experience. They are truly a powerful alphabet that conjures images and interpretations as deep as Mimir's well of knowledge.

Even though rune shapes are fairly simple in their linear appearances, they have far from simple interpretations. In *Rudiments of Runelore*, author Stephen Pollington defines runes as "a Northern European writing system developed primarily for carving on wood, horn, or other organic material, and consisting of simple straight lines in a limited set of formal combinations."[13] Runes function as letters and symbols, and runes can spell out a word or stand for words. Although their origin and historical use are often debated in the academic world, many believe runes are based on the alphabets of Mediterranean languages and older Germanic symbols.

The names of each of the runes are culturally significant: each rune letter has a name which means something significant to the Germanic cultures who carved them. Some runes speak of gods, while others represent important animals on Germanic farms. Although it is still debated by some runologists, there is some evidence that hints at runes holding magical significance and being used for divination. An example is the Lindholm Amulet, a crescent shaped piece of wood with a mysterious "alu" inscription on one side of it. The inscription of "alu" has been found on a number of archaeological objects, leading many runologists to consider it as a magical amulet. The basic meaning of "alu" may be "ectasy" or "magic." Stephen Pollington believes that when alu is engraved, it inspires confidence and is "associated with things which are removed from the world of everyday experience. It makes them special, gives them religious or magical power."[14] Runes may have also been used in divination by Germanic tribes through the practice of casting lots. Tacitus, a Roman writer during the first century AD, wrote about the Germanic practice of consulting omens by scratching signs into twigs.

Runes are also commonly found in Germanic mythology, the most popular being in the *Poetic Edda's* story "The Sayings of the High One." In this passage, Odin narrates his self-sacrifice to discover the runes. After hanging from the tree of knowledge (Yggdrasil) for nine days he discovers the runes and then shares them with the world, describing the spells he has discovered for the runes. In "Skirnir's Journey," Skirnir threatens to curse Gerd by carving three runes on her head. In the "Lay of Sigridrifa" the valkyrie
Sigridrifa gives runic wisdom to the hero warrior Sigurd. She speaks of the ale-rune, which may be a reference to the magical "alu" inscription.

Today many modern Pagans and witches have rediscovered the power and magic of runes, utilizing them for divination and magic. Many people read runes as a way to divine the future. Try pulling one rune a day and contemplating its meaning. Perhaps you want to consider theme words to associate with the rune or meditate on the rune. Or, try pulling three runes: the first representing the past, the second representing the present, and the third representing the future. As a tarot card reader, I enjoy using runes during tarot readings. After the cards have been read, I ask the querent to take the runes and throw them over the tarot spread. Whichever runes are face down get taken away, while the runes which remain face up get read in relation to where they have fallen in the spread. Another interesting exercise is to see if you notice any runic symbols in nature. It's surprising to see how many runes can appear in trees, shadows, and even architecture. Runes have been used as amulets to attract specific energies as well as enhance magic. Consider carving specific runes into candles, drawing runes on sachets or in grimoires, or wearing a rune on a piece of jewelry. Carry a rune which has energies you wish to attract into your life and see how it assists you.

You will find that studying runes is an endless evolution of spirituality and reverence for history and the ancient culture of those who first carved these deeply mystical and historical symbols. Enjoy the journey, as it will guide you towards ancient wisdom.

Runic Alphabet and Interpretations

There are many variations on runic alphabet, as different regions had varied letters depending on the local language. The most common, standardized set of runes has 24 letters and is known as the Common Germanic Futhark, named after the first six runic letters. Here are very simple overview translations listed of each of the Futhark runes, however it is recommended that you follow up with books from the bibliography and recommended reading list at the end of this book. The name of the rune is listed, along with its corresponding letter and meaning. The divinatory meaning represents its interpretation in divination readings and the amulet meaning represents how it can be used in magic, spells, and amulets.

FEHU - f - word for "cattle, moveable wealth." *Divination:* The rune of wealth. Abundance and prosperity have been won or earned. Success and energy. *Amulet:* This rune can help draw prosperity and wealth into your life.

URUZ - u - word for "aurochs," which were a type of primitive cattle that youths had to battle against to test their courage and skills. *Divination:* The rune of strength, energy and good health. Through focus, confidence, and dedication success can be achieved. *Amulet:* This rune is used for abundance, energy, and action.

THURISAZ - th - word which may be translated to "giant," but also known as Thor's rune, as the shape is said to resemble Mjollnir (Thor's hammer). *Divination:* The rune of chaos and temptation. Force, catalysts, and purging. Always know what your purpose is and do what you can to feel powerful, strong, and closer to divinity.

ANSUZ - a - word for a member of the Aesir, the family of Norse gods. The Old English rune poem translates this word to "mouth." *Divination:* The rune of messages and communication. Insight, clarity, and answers are available. *Amulet:* This is a rune useful for communication, teaching, studying, writing, and speaking.

RAIDO - r - translates to "act of riding." *Divination:* The rune of travel. Activity, movement, and a time to be proactive in your life. You are the one in control and the one who leads your own existence. *Amulet:* Use this rune to bring movement, physical or metaphysical, into your life or use as a journey charm.

KENAZ - k - word for either "ulcer" or "torch," but often connected to the spark of inspiration. *Divination:* The rune of inspiration and visions. A time of creativity and transformation. Always do what inspires you and do not be complacent. *Amulet:* This rune can be used for those who are creative and need divine inspiration.

GEBO - g - translates to "act of giving." *Divination:* The rune of love. Harmony, friendship, and joy. Have trust in love, work on self-love, and love for others will come naturally. Find balance between giving and receiving. *Amulet:* Used in love charms and bringing loving energies into your life.

WUNJO - w - word for "joy" or "pleasure." *Divination:* The rune of joy. Pleasure. bright times, and feeling close to divinity. Consider what brings you happiness. Look for solutions as opposed to focusing on problems. *Amulet:* Use to bring happiness, serenity, and joy into your well-being.

HAGALAZ - h - word for "hail." *Divination:* The rune of disruption. Time of confusion and miscommunication.

Challenges are occurring and it is time to face them. Listen to yourself and pay attention to what your body needs.

NAUDIZ - n - translates to "need" or "distress." *Divination:* The rune of necessity. This is a rune of distress and arrives during times of anxiety, delays, confusion, restrictions, and self-initiated change. It is also a time to reconnect with divinity.

ISAZ - i - word for "ice." *Divination:* The rune of ice. Blockages, frustration, and a time to turn inwards. It is drawn when time feels frozen and there is a feeling of oppression. Take this time to step back and realize the world is in constant motion around you. Return to a natural flow and turn inwards.

JERA - j - word for "year" and the measurement of time and harvest. *Divination:* The rune of harvest. Efforts and hard word realized with abundance, hope, peace, and patience. *Amulet:* A rune for fertility, gardening, health, and abundance.

EIHWAZ - ae or I - there is no agreement on the meaning of this rune, though it may be "yew tree." Yew was connected with protection and magic. *Divination:* The rune of stance. A time for honesty and diplomacy. Stay focused to achieve the best end results. *Amulet:* Use for strength, endurance, and enlightenment.

PERTHO - p - a mystical rune whose meaning, according to the Old English rune poem, may be "dice box" or "chessman." *Divination:* The rune of mystery and chance. A time of spiritual evolution. Take chances and embrace the supernatural. *Amulet:* This tends to be a rune for those who take interest in magic and the supernatural.

ALGIZ - z - the original meaning may have been "protection" or "guard," but it is also associated with elk.

Divination: The rune of protection. Follow your instincts and feel the presence of the gods. There is safety as long as you are not reckless. *Amulet:* This is a rune used for protection and shielding.

SOWULO - s - word for "sun." *Divination:* The rune of vitality. Good fortune and energy. A time to have a positive attitude to achieve positive results. *Amulet:* This rune is used for success, growth, victory, and healing.

TEIWAZ - t - the rune is named after Tyr, a god of war before Odin. *Divination:* The rune of the warrior. Victory, success, and willingness for self-sacrifice. Have courage in your own abilities. Be diplomatic in all matters, including those matters that battle in your mind. *Amulet:* This rune may have been used as a victory charm and was found on many weapons. Use for courage, justice, strength, and feeling like a warrior.

BERKANA - b - the word for "birch tree," but it is associated with fertility and springtime. *Divination:* The rune of growth and fertility. Regeneration and the promise of new beginnings. Through nurturing yourself and others, the gift of giving will spread. *Amulet:* A rune commonly used for expecting mothers or those who wish to be mothers.

EHWAZ - e - the horse rune, as the shape of the rune may represent its legs. Horses were sacred to the Germanic people. *Divination:* The rune of momentum. Steady progress, harmony, trust, and ideal partnerships. Always be willing to forgive and not to take offense. *Amulet:* This rune is an amulet of motion, evolution, and progression.

MANNAZ - m - the word for "man" or "mankind." *Divination:* The rune of humanity. A time of cooperation or assistance. Innocence and returning to a simple place. Contemplate your place in the world and your attitude towards others. *Amulet:* This rune is used for teamwork, development of skills, and increased intelligence.

LAGUZ - l - word for "water" or a body of water such as a lake and can be connected to rituals in water. *Divination:* The rune of water. It could indicate confusion and a need for quietness to hear intuitive guidance. Follow your intuition and go with the flow. *Amulet:* This rune is used for developing psychic abilities and connecting with the Otherworld.

INGUZ - ng - reference to a fertility god who was a green man, counterpart to the mother goddess, and a divine hero. *Divination:* The rune of peace. A time when all tasks are completed and there is a stage of rest. Grow closer to nature to feel a oneness with divinity. *Amulet:* This rune is used to alleviate anxiety and bring forth a warm peace.

DAGAZ - d - word for "day" or "daylight." *Divination:* The rune of transformation. A rune of hope, release, happiness, and certainty. Believe in yourself and that you can have the best for yourself. Life will give you what you ask for. *Amulet:* This rune is used for balance, finding direction, and having brilliant breakthroughs.

OTHILA - o - translates to "inherited wealth," "homeland," and "family estate." *Divination:* The rune of family. Safety, increase, and abundance. A time to reconnect with loved ones and spirituality. Share without boundaries: share wealth, knowledge, and love, and you will be rewarded. *Amulet:* This rune is used to connect with heritage and ancestry. It can also be an aid on spiritual quests.

OSTARA CHAPTER NOTES

[1] Connor, Kerri. Ostara: *Rituals, Recipes, and Lore for the Spring Equinox*. Llewellyn Publications: Woodbury, MN, 2015. P. 55.

[2] Heldstab, Celeste Rayne. *Llewellyn's Complete Formulary of Magical Oils*. Llewellyn Publications: Woodbury, Minnesota, 2012.

[3] Mankey, Jason. "Eostre, Easter, Ostara, Eggs, and Bunnies." *Raise the Horns*. 12 Mar. 2013. www.patheos.com.

[4] McCoy, Edain. *Ostara: Customs, Spells and Rituals for the Rites of Spring*. Llewellyn Publications: St. Paul, MN, 2002. P. 4.

[5] Sturluson, Snorri. *Edda*. Trans. Anthony Faulkes. London: Everyman Library, 1995. P. 24.

[6] Sturluson, Snorri. *Edda*. Trans. Anthony Faulkes. London: Everyman Library, 1995. P. 24.

[7] Cymraes, Winter. "Blodeuwedd." *Druidry*. www.druidry.org.

[8] Vedder-Shults, Nancy. "Egg Divinations." *MatriFocus: Cross Quarterly for the Goddess Women*, Vol. 6-3. May 2007. Web. 5 Mar. 15.

[9] Froud, Brian and Alan Lee. *Faeries*. New York: Harry N. Abrams, Inc., 1978.

[10] Beryl, Paul. *The Master Book of Herbalism*. Blaine, WA: Phoenix Publishing, Inc., 1984.

[11] Whitehurst, Tess. *The Magic of Flowers: A Guide to Their Metaphysical Uses and Properties*. Woodbury, MN: Llewellyn Publications, 2015.

[12] Cunningham, Scott. *Cunningham's Encyclopedia of Magical Herbs*. St. Paul, MN: Llewellyn Publications, 1987.

[13] Pollington, Stephen. *Rudiments of Runelore*. Anglo Saxon Books, 2008. P. 10.

[14] Pollington, Stephen. *Rudiments of Runelore*. Anglo Saxon Books, 2008. P. 37.

CHAPTER FIVE:

BELTANE

OVERVIEW, MAGIC, ACTIVITIES, AND CORRESPONDENCES

At Beltane we finally arrive into the warm, vibrant, and fertile season of the year. Wildflowers are blooming, there are thunderstorms, and the days are brighter and longer. Beltane is a time of growth and traditionally celebrated as a fire festival. Beltane comes at the opposite point in the calendar to Samhain, and marks the passage into the light side of the year. This is a time of growth, vitality, passion, and fertility. Both Beltane and Litha are often associated with faery folklore; however, I tend to think of Beltane as a passionate and abundant celebration of life and growth, whereas Litha is a time of dreams, love, happiness, and faery magic. Even though I personally make this distinction for keeping order in this book, feel free to use the summer season as an optimal time for work with the Fae.

Festival of Floralia

The Romans celebrated the Festival of Floralia at the end of April and the beginning of May in honor of the goddess Flora. Flora was a goddess of flowers, spring, and fertility. Myth tells of Flora, who was originally a nymph, having gone for walk outdoors on a spring day in her original homeland of Elysium. Zephyrus, god of the

West Wind noticed how beautiful she was, chased her, and then named her his bride, making her a goddess. Flowers were the main decoration for Floralia.

Even during the Roman festival, the awakening of nature heralded in a sensual, evocative, and celebratory event. As nature was seen as untamable and wild, so were the celebrations. Melanie Marquis in *Beltane: Springtime Rituals, Lore, and Celebration* describes the celebrations of Floralia: "Though ultimately a serious event expressing great reverence for Flora, the festival had a strong element of fun that predominated it. Lots of wine and lots of boisterous singing and dancing created an atmosphere of raucousness, the noise of which may have been believed to help Nature fully wake up and get energized after a long winter's slumber."[1]

Celtic Fire Festival

In the Celtic regions, May 1st was considered the beginning of the summer season. This was a major fire festival celebrating the season of fertility and growth. The word "Bealtaine" comes from the Celtic word meaning "Bright Fire." The name is also in honor of the Celtic deity Bel, a god of the sun, much like Apollo. Bel is a god of healing, crops, and springs. In *The Provenance Press Guide to the Wiccan Year*, Judy Ann Nock explains the reason why a sun god can also be connected to water: "The Celts believed that by night, the sun traveled underneath the world to heat the waters in the thermal springs, uniting the energy of the sun with the healing properties of water."[2]

Beltane was a time for fertility, health, and good luck rituals, many of which involved the bonfires lit at this holiday. According to

Melanie Marquis, the fires were sacred and magical: "Their flames, their smoke were all believed capable of granting health and protection."[3] Men and women would leap the fire for good luck in the coming year. Animals were herded through the smoking embers for purification and protection. The ashes from the Beltane bonfires would be scattered on the fields to ensure a bountiful crop. Hearth fires would be extinguished, and would be relit with embers from festival bonfires.

Today in Scotland there is still a very popular celebration in Edinburgh called the Beltane Fire Festival. According to their website, the event is meant to reconnect participants to nature: "It is important to note that the purpose of our festival is not to recreate ancient practices but to continue in the spirit of our ancient forebears and create our own connection to the cycles of nature." The festival is held at Calton Hill where there are performances and drumming, many in extravagant costume and makeup. Thousands attend the event each year, inviting people to experience the sacred and theatrical aspects of the ancient Beltane fire festival.

Season of the Faeries

Beltane marks what I consider the beginning of the season of Faeries. When nature grows, so does the influence and presence of the Fae in nature. It is believed that the ancient faerie race of Ireland, the Tuatha De Danann, arrived in Ireland on Beltane. There are other legends that say trooping faeries moved from their winter homes to their summer homes on Beltane Eve. Bells were carried to keep away mischievous faeries, who were thought to be extra

curious about humans at this time of year.

Maypoles

The origin of the maypole was most likely a fertility ritual in parts of Europe. The pole has been described as a phallic symbol, representing the fertility and growth of nature and the land. In the book *In Nature's Honor*, Patricia Montley explores the idea that the maypole could be connected to ancient Roman pillars called *herms*, which were statues of the god Hermes with an erection.[4] This statues were often decorations in gardens and meant to be an amulet to bring growth and abundance to the garden. However, through the research of author Ronald Hutton, Montley concludes that there is no solid evidence that could indicate a link between the maypole and the herms. There are however, theories that the maypole could have been a way to worship the blooming tree of awakening summer. It is possible that societies such as the Druids, who worshipped oak trees, created a display of a world tree. Perhaps even the dance around the tree was a way to show nature coming back to life, or a ritual to help it grow.

Maypoles would be erected (no pun intended) in villages and decorated as part of the May Day celebrations. Villages selected a May King and a May Queen to lead the processions. Maypoles were crowned with a flower wreath and then decorated with ribbons, which were woven on the pole by dancers weaving around each other with the ribbons. This practice of dancing around the maypole has continued up to this modern day, even with many schools having special May Day celebrations that include dancing around a maypole.

May Bush

May bushes were usually small bushes that would be decorated with fresh flowers and bright ribbons. Some would be near the doors of private homes, while some would be in neighborhood areas. Consider decorating a bush by your door at Beltane to bring luck and joy into your house for the summer. Decorate it with flowers and ribbons and tie petitions or wishes to the bush as well.

Create a Miniature Maypole

A miniature Maypole can be made by a single practitioner. Miniature Maypoles are a beautiful decoration on altars, in potted plants, or in gardens. Find a twig or branch and wrap it in ribbons. If you would like to use the powerful prosperous energy of this year, write a wish on each of the ribbons or a goal you would like to see manifest, using a corresponding colored ribbon to match the wish's intent. For example: if you have a wish about romance, use a pink or red ribbon. If you have a wish about money, use a green ribbon. If you have a wish about good health, use a blue ribbon.

Collecting Dew

There has been a belief that dew collected on Beltane had powers of restoring beauty and youth. The dew was said to enhance health, beauty, and happiness. One way to collect dew is to use a clean towel or piece of cloth and wipe the dew off of leaves and grass early in the morning, then wring the dew out into a container. You can also gently shake dew covered leaves in a jar. Use the dew for washing your face, or save it for spells for love or abundance.

Berry Love Spell

This spell can be used for enhancing fertility and attractiveness. You will need a bowl of berries, strawberry leaves, raspberry leaves, and a berry-scented candle. Light the candle and repeat the following three times: "Berries ripe with love, berries strong with life: as I eat these, my happiness will shine. Strength and romance, abundance and prosperity: as I eat these, my life attracts fertility."

Spirit Animal Meditation

A Spirit Animal is said to be a personal spirit guide which takes the shape of an animal. Each animal is said to have values, lessons, and gifts to share with you. Some of the traits of the Spirit Animal are even said to reflect your own. Spirit Animals have also been called Animal Totems, Power Animals, Nature Totems, and animal guides. All cultures, modern and ancient, have myths and beliefs about animals. Cultures from Native Americans to Pacific Islanders, from Ancient Romans to Ancient Celts share stories of animals interacting with humans. Many tales speak of shamans and magical people being able to transform into animals, or shapeshift. By shapeshifting into an animal, the shaman is able to take on the qualities and powers of that animal. Native Americans have tales of humans shapeshifting into wolves. In Norse mythology, Odin transforms into an eagle, and in Celtic myth the goddess Morrighan transforms into a raven at battle.

There has been a great deal of research and literature written on how the myths and stories of animals can correspond into lessons for our lives. Carl Jung wrote about how animals play roles in our daily lives. Modern day authors and metaphysical practitioners have written on the natural qualities of animals and how their mythology can be interpreted into spiritual growth.

There are many ways to connect with your Spirit Animal. You may have even found that certain animals have reached out to you. Do you ever dream about specific animals? Do you ever have peculiar interactions with specific animals? Or are there animals that you are fascinated by? Other methods for connecting with Spirit Animals include meditation, shamanic journeys, and even oracle decks. This visual meditation can help you connect with a Spirit Animal trying to share a lesson in your life. To begin, as you would with any meditation, create a safe location where you would like to begin your journey. Use whichever techniques are best for you to get yourself into a deep and relaxed state of meditation. When you are ready, follow the guidelines below:

You are at the entrance of a cave. Know that it is a safe place for you to explore yourself and connect with your Spirit Animal. You will find that as you move along into the cave you descend deeper and deeper down. Keep moving forwards: you will soon see a light growing ahead of you. The light gets brighter until you see an exit ahead.

When you exit you will be in the natural environment where you will connect with your Spirit Animal. Where are you? Are you in the jungle? A forest? The desert? The ocean? The mountains? Is it night or day? Hot or cold? Perhaps it looks like your favorite nature path in the wilderness. Take a good look at your surroundings. What do you see and hear?

Look around until you find a path that will lead you to your Spirit Animal. This path could be defined or simply a direction that feels right to walk in. Either way, as you walk along it will become clear that you are meeting with your Spirit Animal. Walk along, taking in your surroundings and listening to the sounds around you. Have you connected with your Spirit Animal yet? If not, ask for your Spirit Animal to come forward if you wish.

When you are in the presence of your Spirit Animal consider how you are feeling. Do you see one animal or are there others? Feel free to introduce yourself. Do you have any questions you wish to ask? Does your Spirit Animal lead you anywhere else? Take a moment to connect with your Spirit Animal, asking if there is any information you need to take with you from your interaction. Know that you will remember the most valuable lessons and interaction.

When you are ready to end your conversation or connection with your Spirit Animal, say thank you for allowing you to have this experience. Recognize that you can connect with your Spirit Animal any time through meditations and dreams, or possibly via a sign in waking life as well.

Head back towards the cave. Take in your surroundings one last time before entering the cave and climbing upwards to where you began. Climb upwards, towards the entrance of the cave. Finally, you return to the safe location where you began.

Journaling at Beltane
- If you could have three wishes right now, what would they be?
- Have you ever had an encounter with faeries? If so, what happened?
- Who is someone you've loved romantically? How has that shaped your life?
- What opportunities are happening right now that you think will be a benefit to you?
- What are you excited about doing over the summer?
- What projects or activities outdoors are you eager to catch up with and make some progress on?

Correspondences
- Names: Beltane, May Day
- Date of Celebration: May 1st , or the sun is positioned 15 degrees relative to Taurus, or the cross point between the Spring Equinox and Summer Solstice.
- Deities Honored: Aphrodite, Bel, Cernunnos, Dionysus, Flora, Freya, Green Man, Maia, Pan, Venus
- Magical focus: Abundance, Divination, Faerie Magic, Fertility, Growth, Love, Passion, Prosperity, Purification
- Activities: bonfires, camping, cleaning, collecting dew, dancing around a maypole, divination, gardening, having a bonfire, hiking, hosting an outdoor feast, making daisy chains and flower wreaths, planting seeds, sacred sex, swimming
- Altar Decorations: Chalice, May Gad, Wildflowers

- Food and Beverages: almonds, berries, cream, greens, honey, mead, oatmeal cakes, salad, white wine
- Plants, Herbs, Incense: bluebells, cinquefoil, daisies, fern, foxglove, hawthorn, hibiscus, honeysuckle, ivy, jasmine, marigold, mint, musk, peach, primrose, rose, rowan, sweet woodruff, thyme, vanilla, ylang ylang
- Crystals: carnelian, emerald, fluorite, rose quartz, sapphire
- Colors: blue, burgundy, hunter green, plum, white

THE MYTHOLOGY OF THE GREEN MAN

The Green Man is a personification of the forest: he is the essence of the wild landscape, a reminder that we are interconnected with our environment. He transforms with the seasons: at Beltane and Litha he is lush, green, powerful, and virile. The most familiar form the Green Man takes on appears in art and sculpture frequently: this is in the guise of the *foliate head*, which shows his face surrounded by lush and green vegetation. Gary R. Varner, in *The Mythic Forest, The Green Man, and the Spirit of Nature*, reflects on the importance of the Green Man in culture and myth: "The Green Man is an embodiment of the heart and soul of the mystery of nature, the cyclical character of life and death, and where we as individuals fit within this cycle."[5]

Green is associated with nature: it is symbolic of growth, fertility, and abundance. For the Green Man to have been assigned the color of vegetation, he not only aligns himself with the natural world, but also the supernatural world. Varner points out the color green's magical connection: "Green was a color shunned by many as being associated with the forest and fairy-folk. But why green? Green is associated with nature, with ripening life and with fertility, paganism and the supernatural – things that the church could not control. Perhaps more importantly, green symbolized not only enchantment but also divine beings."[6] It is the color of the untamed world outside the church and castle, the wooded area where the faeries roam and humans do not have control. Here, we will briefly review some of the enchanting and divine characters in mythology and culture associated with the Green Man at the time of Beltane.

Pan

Pan is a recognizable god of the forest. David Adams Leeming in *The World of Myth* notes that Pan "personifies humanity's animal nature."[7] With goat horns and hooves, he is said to wander through the forest, playing his flute and falling in love with nymphs. Said to be the son of Hermes, he was honored by herders in Ancient Greece, but he also has a sexual and vivacious side as well. Sometimes associated with Dionysus, his sensuality and ability to be playful show his departure from the civilized world. He is free to be as wild as he pleases.

Enkidu and Osiris

There are gods from the Ancient Egypt and Sumeria that have been tied in with the Green Man theme as well. In the epic tale of Gilgamesh, Enkidu is described as being both an animal and a man. Like the Green Man, his sacred space is the forest, where he is a protector of animals. He transformed from being a wild man of the forest after he slept with a woman. It was as if the sacred act of sex helped him shift into a different, wiser, more civilized human. Some have also made connections between the popular Egyptian god Osiris and the Green Man. Osiris is a resurrection god, one who taught the Egyptians how to cultivate grains. Like the Green Man, he is depicted as having a green colored skin.

Jack in the Green

In England there was a tradition of someone dressing as "Jack in the Green" on May Day. This person would be dressed in elaborate green costumes of foliage and would be a loud and wild addition to May Day celebrations. In *Craft of the Wild Witch*, Poppy Palin explores Jack in the Green as a trickster spirit with an unpredictable nature: "In truth he is both the hunter and the hunted, eternally dancing between light and darkness, crowned by glossy leaves of oak and bound to man's law."[8] Her description of Jack in the Green coincides with the Green Man, a powerful figure of the forest transforms with the seasons and reveals to us wisdom through the cycles of life and the mysterious nature of the wooded area he inhabits.

Cernunnos

One god that always makes himself apparent during the Beltane celebrations is Cernunnos, the horned god of the forest and hunt. He has been compared to the Celtic god Dagda and to the lord of the

Underworld Arawn. His image and story is of great value to many in the modern Pagan communities, though curiously, there is minimal historic information on him. We rely heavily on our understanding of him through historical images. The oldest image of him comes from a 4th century BCE rock carving in northern Italy, where he is has antlers and torcs on each arm. The most notable image of him comes from the Gundestrup Cauldron, where he is surrounded by forest animals. He sits with his legs crossed, holding a serpent. Miranda Green in *Symbol and Image in Celtic Religious Art* suggests that he was worshipped as a god of prosperity, animals, and crops. She suggests that he has shapeshifting abilities, able to move through the forest with grace to protect the animals and connect with the Otherworld.[9] Cernunnos is a favorite deity for many, and perhaps this is because he can be called on for abundance and the opportunity to explore the Otherworldly wild woods through shamanic journey.

The Green Man and the Cycle of Life

Ultimately, the Green Man is tied into the seasons and cycle of life. He is a remind that what is barren can again grow, and what is grown could be harvested. Seeds can be planted, and the cycle starts again. The Triple Goddess has often been said to represent cycles. For some: the cycle of maiden, mother, and crone represents the cycles of life or the moon cycles. In this same manner the Green Man could be said to represent the cycles of nature and growth. The Green Man reminds us that we are connected to the earth, dependent on its growth, harvest, and wellness. When you are feeling the desire to leave behind the stresses of modern life, take a break from the technology that surrounds us all, and playfully reconnect with nature, you are connecting with the spirit of the Green Man.

PROSPEROUS LIVING AND MONEY MAGIC

Let's start with the hard truth: there are most likely practical solutions that you can try out to conjure more money and prosperity in your life than magical ones. This shouldn't stop a witch from trying to enhance her situation by bringing a little money magic, it should just give her reason to take stock of what she has and create meaningful plans to reach the outcomes she desires the most. The hope of this section is not only to have you using magic for prosperity, but also to get you planning and motivated to create the changes in your life necessary to develop more success and financial stability.

Let's begin with contemplating the following questions before reading on:

- What is your relationship with money?
- How do you speak about money?
- Where is there resistance in your financial flow?
- When is prosperity not associated with money?
- How are you already prosperous in your life?
- What are you already grateful for in your life?
- What struggles have you already overcome?
- What do you believe you deserve?

Sometimes we think we have major blockages in our paths to financial success, and don't even realize how much we've already overcome in our lives. It is also interesting when you think about your relationship with money: some people feel bitter about those who are earning more, some people feel completely frozen and scared when thinking about tackling bills. These are difficult questions, but they can begin the process of looking at whether your relationship with money is healthy or not.

Difference between Prosperity and Money

There is a difference between prosperity and money. For me, prosperity is an all-encompassing word; one that defines where you are fulfilled and your wants are met. It is a feeling of abundance and represents an aspect of your life where you feel you satisfied and comfortable. You can have a prosperous home life or love life; you can feel prosperity in your social circle or with your work benefits. Prosperity does not need to be a dollar amount in your bank. Money can definitely be a part of your feeling of prosperity: it is what allows you to live in comfort, get the medical attention you need, buy food, and be responsible for your own well-being. You can have financial prosperity, but having a lot of money does not solve every issue, especially those tied to emotional relationships and personal peace of mind. This is important to keep in mind: money is not going to make you any happier: it will just make life a little bit easier.

Non-Magical Methods for Enhancing Financial Comfort

There are plenty of practical methods for bringing more financial comfort into your life, and though they sometimes are not fun, they will be worth working through. One credo I have always held close to my heart when thinking about prosperity is the value of time: your time and energy are precious commodities.

- Time Management: Take a moment to think about or write out how you spend time. How many hours are you working? How many hours are you taking care of yourself, or doing fun activities?
- Budgeting: For a month, write out everything that you spend money on to see where your money is going.
- Financial Empowerment: Along with seeing where your money is going, understanding your finances and debts will keep you aware of bills. I personally write down the bills I have due on my calendar. I have a clear picture of what is due and when. When the bill is paid, I check it off, which gives me a sense of accomplishment.
- Ask for Help: Asking for help is okay. There are services in your town that can help you; from social programs to financial programs, you may find that there are opportunities to get help as well as support with your money. We have a "financial empowerment center" in Nashville, which is free to use, and allows people to sit with experts to create budgets and get a handle on bills. My credit union has been a lifesaver for me as well; they have helped me with car loans and improving my credit score.
- Have healthy role models: Look for people in your field of work, or someone who has your dream job or your dream income and see what advice they'd give you. If it is someone you know personally, ask them if you can have a conversation about how they got to where they did. Here are some books to consider reading for extra motivation and advice:
    - *How to Win Friends and Influence People* by Dale Carnegie
    - *Think and Grow Rich* by Napoleon Hill
    - *The 9 Steps to Financial Freedom* by Suze Orman
    - *The 7 Habits of Highly Effective People* by Stephen Covey

Creating a Plan for Success

Prosperity and success require patience, planning and hard work. Take a moment to write out the most successful, most benevolent outcomes you would like to see in your life. There are no wrong answers on this list: explore your goals, both small and big. Next, look at the list and determine which are the top priorities for you. They may all be significant, but think about the one that stands out as the most important and valuable to you. What are some of the things you must accomplish to reach this outcome? Creating a plan may help you keep on target, both in obtaining short term goals and long term goals. This allows you to have a clear picture about what needs to be done and motivate you to take the actions necessary to complete the tasks at hand. Create a list of the things that need to happen, starting with what you can do today to get one step closer. Even if you don't know what to do, the first thing on your to-do list may be  "ask for help." This may then lead you to thinking about who you can ask for help. Perhaps one of your goals is buying a new car. You may want to speak to someone who recently bought a car and find out what their experience was with it. You may want to ask for help at your credit union with a loan officer. Write out lists and strategies to help you reach the answers and successes you want to see in your life.

Visualization Exercises and Inspiration

This section is meant to offer ideas for shifting your way thinking into a positive, hopeful, and inspired mindset. How is your attitude about money and your ability to gain it when you need it? Has there ever been a time when you thought you'd always be broke, always struggle, or never reach a goal you had? It probably did not help you move forward in any way to hold those attitudes in your mind because they are defeating.

Visualization exercises and magic are wonderful supplements to help you focus your mind on success and know you are deserving of comfort, prosperity, and success. It is important to reprogram your mind when thinking about money in your life. This may mean believing that you are deserving of money, that your product has value, or that you have the best skillset. Here are some activities to help you turn your attention to plans, and keep inspired and motivated:

- Create a vision board. This is a fun arts and crafts exercise where you simply collect images that speak to you and that reveal things you'd like to see in your life. You can do this by printing out pictures you find online, collecting images you find online, or drawing your own illustrations and piecing them together in a collage. I have an internet version of a vision board on Tumblr, where I collect pictures of homes and travel that resonate with me. It is a comfort to visit the page and remind myself why I work so hard.

- Practice acts of gratitude. Pay it forward. Get the door for someone. Give a compliment. Volunteer for a cause. Bake cookies for the folks in your office. Generate abundance for those around you and you'll see abundance return to you.

- Behave like your "most benevolent outcome." In other words: think about the end goals that you had in mind when you were creating your list of things you would love to see manifest in your life, and act as though those goals have been achieved.

Magical Spells and Amulets

- Lucky Green Rice or Lucky Green Salt. Green rice is often associated with Hoodoo magic and is used to attract money, prosperity, successful business ventures, and good luck into your life. Mix together 1 cup of plain white rice with seven drops of green food coloring. Blend it well so all the color gets onto the grains evenly. If you would like, add shredded money, small chips of pyrite, dried mint, dried basil, or flax seed. You can also add a couple drops of an essential oil if you would like, such as bergamot, bayberry, or patchouli.

After everything has been blended you can scatter the green rice outside your doorstep or keep a small amount in your wallet. I have a small decorative container I keep my rice in near the place where I keep my money.

- Kiki's Fast Money Oil. I have found this to be a very powerful blend. It's perhaps not the prettiest of scents, but it is a great oil to wear if you are trying to draw in business, enhance money making opportunities, and find fortunate methods for making money quickly. This recipe is for a 15ml bottle.

> Carrier Oil: I recommend sweet almond oil.
> 7 drops patchouli
> 6 drops cedarwood
> 4 drops bergamot
> 1 drop cinnamon
> 1 drop basil
> Optional items you can add: small pieces of aventurine or pyrite, honeysuckle petals, or a drop of water collected during a thunderstorm.

- Dollar Bill Spell. Take a dollar bill that you are willing to write on and not spend. Write a sigil on it or draw symbols on it. Write around the borders of the bill "This dollar will multiply: success and fortune are mine." Anoint the bill with a prosperity oil blend and keep it in your wallet.
- Money Mojo Bag. Get a small green pouch or sachet and fill it with the following: aventurine, jade, basil, dill, dried beans, almonds, and tonka beans. (Add the amount that is best suited for size of the bag and what you have on hand). While you hold the bag visualize holding a stack of money. Keep this with you when going on business or money-making ventures.

Correspondences: Working with Prosperous Materials

- Gods and Goddesses for Prosperity: Aphrodite, Dagda, Ganesha, Hecate, Jupiter, Lakshmi, Nerthus, Tyche, Zeus
- Plants and Herbs: Alfalfa, allspice, basil, chamomile, cinnamon, cinquefoil, cloves, dill, galangal, ginger, High John the Conqueror, honeysuckle, Irish moss, mint, nutmeg, pine, red clover, tonka beans.

- Foods: Almonds, dried pumpkin seeds, honey, orange, rice
- Oils: Bayberry, bergamot, cedarwood, orange, patchouli, peppermint
- Crystals: Aventurine, chrysoprase, citrine, green calcite, jade, lodestone, peridot, pyrite, tiger's eye
- Symbols: Feoh rune, frog, symbols for currency
- Best Timing for Money Magic:
  - New Moon for new beginnings: creating new goals, new plans, new strategies
  - Waxing Moon for manifestation: manifesting money, support, wealth
  - Full moon to get rid of what no longer helps you: removing obstacles, stress
  - Waning moon to banish something negative: banish debt

GREEN WITCHCRAFT AND MAGIC IN THE FOREST

The forest has always been a place of Otherworldly power, just outside of the civilized world, where all things wild, magical, and mysterious can wander. The benefits of visiting the woods are based in reality, however. Walking through the woods is not only a great way to get exercise, but studies show that the trees and flowers give off fragrances that enhance immune system function, reduce stress, and lower blood pressure. Being in the woods can be an opportunity to take a moment away from the hectic and technological world. Think about a time you walked in the woods: how did you feel when you arrived? And, in comparison, how did you feel when you left? I have arrived for hikes in a stressed out mood, and only after a couple of miles, I feel calm, centered, and grounded. At Beltane, give yourself the opportunity to immerse yourself in the benefits and the magic of the forest. It will revive and inspire you.

Green Witchcraft

Green witchcraft is an integral part of magic in the forest and nature. Green witches feel a great connection with nature, the elements, and faeries. They enjoy spells with items from nature, learning about the elements, and feel a connection to seasonal celebrations. They conjure magic with the flowers of spring. They

may enjoy doing rituals, spells, or meditations outdoors or creating a sacred space in a natural setting.

A green witch utilizes herbs and plants to tap into her diverse spiritual and magical energies. She will study trees, herbs, wildflowers, and wildlife. She may study botany, geology, or caretaking of animals. Her tools may be natural: found feathers, special stones, leaves, wooden wands, or a boline for collecting herbs. Green witches do not need to live in a cottage tucked away in the middle of a dense forest, either; they can live in urban areas and have small apartments. Do you consider yourself to be a green witch?

Welcoming Meditation for Entering the Forest

This is a short meditation I like to do when I arrive at the woods.

Take a minute to close your eyes and settle into where you are sitting. Take a deep breath in, feeling the breath move through your nose and fill your lungs. Breathe in deeply, paying attention to what you smell. Do you smell flowers? Does it smell earthy to you? Envision this welcoming fragrance as a bright green light, filling you with healing energy.

Pay attention only to the sounds of the forest. What do you hear? What sounds are soothing to you?

In your mind's eye move through the forest, finding a tree or location, real or fantastical, where you feel at ease. Rest there for a moment. What do you see? What are your goals for entering the forest?

In your mind, introduce yourself to the world around you. Repeat the mantra, in your mind, "Hello, we are all connected."

After you feel you've repeated the mantra enough take a moment to recenter. What are you drawn to in the forest on this trip?

Thank the woods, the trees, and the spirits of the woods for being present with you, protecting you, and guiding you on a trip that brings you peace, healing, joy, and inspiration. When you are ready open your eyes.

Deities of the Forest
- Abnoba: A Gaulish goddess of the forest and rivers, she protected waterways and wildlife. She was worshipped by the Black Forest. Avon may be a variation on her name.
- Aranyani: A Hindu goddess of the forest who was quiet and preferred the most remote of wild places.
- Arduinna: A goddess of the Ardennes forest, which is an area near Belgium and Luxembourg. The boar and spear are her sacred symbols. She was an untamed free spirit that healed those of her region.
- Artemis: Greek Goddess and huntress whose domain is in the wilderness. She is seen carrying a bow and arrow, accompanied by a deer. Her Roman equivalent is Diana.
- Flidais: Mother to mythological heroes, she is seen as an Earth goddess who protects wild animals and forests. She is a shape-shifting goddess of sexuality who is part of the Tuatha de Danaan.
- Medeina: A Lithuanian goddess of forests, trees, and animals. Her sacred animal is the hare. Unwilling to get married, she instead spends her life tending to the forest.
- Silvanus: A Roman forest god who watches over the grow of wild trees.

Forest Magic
- Acorns: Acorns are a symbol of abundance, fertility, luck, and longevity. They are sacred to Diana and Cernunnos. Gather them at the full moon to use as a faerie talisman.
- Hag Stone: A hag stone is a stone with a naturally formed hole in it. The stone is carried to protect its owner from harm. It is said the hag stone was by witches to cast spells. It is also believed that you can look through a hag stone to see faeries. You can usually find hag stones by rivers or streams.

- Maple Leaves: In her book *Traditional Witchcraft for the Woods and Forests*, Melusine Draco suggests that maple leaves can be used for good luck and abundance. She suggests you take two golden maple leaves and two golden coins and place them in a yellow sachet or bag. Keep this bag at the entrance of your business to draw in success and prosperity.[10]
- Birch and Oak Wood: According to Richard Webster in *Flower and Tree Magic*, birch and oak trees are a compatible pairing: "Folklore says that an oak tree will usually be found close to a birch tree, as they are considered husband and wife."[11] If you live with your loved one, take a walk in the woods together and find a stick of birch wood and a stick of oak wood. Tie them together with red and pink ribbon, add a rose to the bundle if you would like. Keep this in your home to symbolize your love and devotion to each other: it will keep you both connected and supportive of each other.
- Themed Gardens and/or Forest Altars. If you do not plan to make it deep into the woods any time soon, there are still ways to celebrate and honor the power of the woods at home. One way to do this is to create a themed garden. For example, you can make a moon-themed garden with blue and white flowers. Or, you can make a faery-attracting garden with yarrow, thyme, roses, rosemary, foxglove, and berries. Having an altar that honors the forest can be done in a respectful and honorable way. Be mindful of picking anything

you do not know, or taking anything from city/state/national forests. Along your travels, though, you may find fallen empty robin eggs, special stones, twigs of wood, or leaves that are precious to you. Make an area for the forest with a green backdrop, images of places in the wild you love, or a statue of Cernunnos or a nature deity. Perhaps even a potted plant of something that is native to your area. There are even people who grow edible mushrooms at homes, so if it is something safe and contained, a forest altar seems like a fitting place for mushrooms to do their thing!

Rules of the Woods

1. Do not litter. This seems like a very obvious and straightforward notion, but I have always been surprised at the amount of litter I have found in the woods. From beer cans to cigarette butts, energy bar wrappers to empty water bottles: people have found a way to leave their mark in places far from their homes. You are a visitor in the woods, be so kind to treat it well and clean up after yourself. If you are so inclined, bring a bag with you to clean up garbage left behind by others. Mother Nature will be thankful for your efforts in preservation.

2. Quiet, please. It is very odd to me that people would talk on their cell phones, at loud volumes, on a walking trail, blocking out the sounds of nature and just permitting those around them access to their private (and often irritating) conversations. The woods are a sacred space: for many, it is the only time of the day (or week) when they can get away from the noises of a busy neighborhood and life. Be respectful to those around you, even those you cannot see. Bring headphones for music, turn your cell phone ringer off, or just shut off your cell phone. If you are with others, enjoy conversation at a lower level, and be mindful that sound carries in the forest. I've heard all sorts of fascinating tales just by being in the proximity of gossipers at the wrong time.

3. Do not disturb the wildlife. Be mindful of picking up things that don't belong to you! Although many people like to forage in the forest, it is important to know that if you are not on your own property you are taking something that isn't yours. If you are visiting a local, state, or national park, ask what the rules of picking mushrooms and flowers are. You don't want to pick

something that is rare. There are Lady Slippers in the woods near my house, but no naturalist will share their locations out of fear someone will pick the precious flowers that only blossom every few years. If you see animals, let them do their own thing. You don't need to snapchat your black bear encounter, and you don't need to feed the squirrels. In the case of a black bear you should probably keep moving, but otherwise, harmless animals are pleasant to observe in the moment.

4. Learn the folklore and stories of the area you are visiting. Every area has a good story to tell. See if you can learn about the history and traditions of the area you are walking through. Knowing that many have taken the same path before you and discovered something that became sacred and legendary makes it an even more enriching and inspiring experience.

DIVINATION HIGHLIGHT: DIVINATION IN THE FOREST

The forest during this time of year is at its most lush: the warmth of the sun has helped nature to bloom. The woods are green and full of life. Perhaps one of the ways you can escape the heat is by hiding under the shade of the canopy on a wooded trail. The forest has always been considered a place where the wild and mysterious thrive, a place where the supernatural and magical can easily manifest away from the civilized eye of town life. There are many forms of divination that can be practiced in forest and, as you will discover in this section, many forms which require your own intuition and personal interpretations.

Orinthomancy

Divination using birds is known as orinthomancy or augury. The type of bird observed, their cries, and the direction in which they fly have been used as means of divining. To begin in orinthomancy, find an area where you would like to try to observe birds. You may find that in your town there are places or observatories that bird enthusiasts like to visit. Or, you may just wish to find a private place in nature and see what birds come visit you first. Does it seem to approach you, or does it observe you from a high branch? If you have a question in mind, it is believed that if a bird appears to your right the answer is positive. If the bird appears to your left the answer is negative. What type of bird is it? You may want to become acquainted with common birds in your area with a bird guide. For additional information on the spiritual interpretations of birds I recommend *Birds: A Spiritual Field Guide.* Crows tend to be harbingers of change and psychic abilities, and their closely related counterpart raven teaches of otherworldly connections and witchcraft. Hawks remind you to connect with divinity, enjoy nature, and focus on your health. My mother's favorite, the hummingbird, reminds you to be playful and mindful about how you budget time and energy. Owl asks you to be keenly observant of life around you, to dig into your knowledge, and to discover your own personal brand of wisdom through meditation and dreamwork. Some say the Fae and forest spirits will leave a feather in your path as a gift and message. With this in mind, consider what type of feather it is, and interpret it accordingly.

Animal Messages

When we go into the woods it is common to have encounters with wildlife. But have you ever gone into the woods and had unusual interactions with animals? Do you see the same kind of animal multiple times over a period of time? When deciding whether or not to move to England I asked the universe to show me a sign. After asking for a sign I had a very clear animal message while sitting on my parents' back deck in a rural part of Connecticut. I heard a flock of crows flying from the right of me, they were flying low, and incredibly loud. As they flew by I noticed a fox dash through the yard below the crows. It turns out foxes are linked to Merlin energy, and seeing the crows fly from the right was optimistic. The following fall I was registered in Arthurian Legend Studies at the University of Nottingham. Have you had special encounters with animals like this as well? Seeing a coyote offers lessons of enduring love, and asks you to contemplate trickster energy. Seeing deer asks you to reconnect with family and friends as well as practice forgiveness. Seeing a butterfly asks you to allow transformation in your life and develop your psychic abilities. Seeing a rabbit asks you to focus on your health, enjoy life, and practice herbal magic.

Seer in Nature

In Scotland people with "the sight" were called frithirs. According to Caitlin Matthews, frithirs when through a specific ritual to give prophecy four times a year. He or she would fast, and then just before sunrise go to his or her door barefoot and blindfolded. He or she would go to the doorpost and remove the blindfold. The first thing the frithir would look at would be considered a significant sign and be interpreted for oracle. Dr. Bluestone in *How to Read Signs and Omens in Everyday Life* offers a more modernized approach to the frithir ritual. Go to a quiet place outdoors where you will not be interrupted by noise or bothered by other people. Stand still with your eyes closed. With your eyes still closed, slowly turn around three times in a clockwise circle. Open your eyes and focus on the first object you see. Another similar method for seeing into the forest is as follows. Allow your eyes to go unfocused and slowly look around you. What is the first thing your eyes focus in on? Is it something moving? Is it something otherworldly? Do you feel an important message from what you witnessed?

Water Scrying

Scrying is the art of gazing into a reflective surface to receive divinatory messages. Most people are familiar with the image of someone using a dark mirror or crystal ball to gaze, but scrying can also be performed in nature as well. You can scry in the surface of water. Some people will suggest you find a calm body of water, and scry in the moonlight. Others may even suggest gazing into a bubbling brook with the sunlight sparkling on the surface. There is also an old belief that Druids would stand behind a waterfall and scry through the falling water. Experiment with whatever is not only most comfortable for you, but what is safest! Take time to stare into the surface of the water, letting your vision go fuzzy. When thoughts or outside distractions creep into your mind, let them wash away in the water. What do you see? How do you feel? Some people say that they see things in the scrying surface, while others feel things or hear things. If anything, enjoy it as a soothing opportunity to meditate and connect with the element of water.

Floromancy

Floromancy is divination using flowers, and from looking at various resources, it appears that many of the divinations using flowers tend to be folkloric in style. For example, there is the old tradition of pulling petals from a daisy and saying "He loves me, he loves me not," to determine if your love is requited. It is believed that the first wildflower you see in the spring can give an outlook on the coming year. Seeing a daffodil is considered unlucky. Seeing a rose suggests upcoming love. Having hiked in my particular Appalachian neck of the woods at spring, I can extend this list with my own offerings for first spring flowers. Seeing bloodroot first shows that your year will be one that develops courage and passion, as you will focus on what you love the most. Seeing dandelion first means that you must focus your intent on manifesting wishes into reality. If the first flower you see is trillium, your year will be focused on feminine divine, Goddess teachings, and good luck. If the first flower you see is jack-in-the-pulpit, your year will be focused on the masculine divine, Green Man energy, and primal desires.

Casting of Lots

It is important to remember that if you are in public woods it is often not allowed to remove or disturb any of the plant life or wildlife. If you are on private land and have permission to do so, collect small items such as empty snail shells, dried juniper berries, acorns, special stones, pine cones, seeds, leaves, and so on. Give an interpretation to each item, and cast the items to give divination. For example, acorns are symbols of wisdom and are sacred to Druids. Pine cones can be symbols of protection and purification. Create interpretations based on what is best for you from your own research and intuition. If you are familiar with runes, you may want to take a walk through nature and see which runes you naturally come across. Sometimes sticks will be laid out in the path in front of you laid in the perfect position of a runic message.

BELTANE CHAPTER NOTES

[1] Marquis, Melanie. Beltane: *Rituals, Recipes and Lore for May Day*. Llewellyn Publications: Woodbury, MN, 2015. P. 29.

[2] Nock, Judy Ann. *The Provenance Press Guide to the Wiccan Year*. Provenance Press: Avon, MA, 2007. P. 14.

[3] Nock, Judy Ann. *The Provenance Press Guide to the Wiccan Year*. Provenance Press: Avon, MA, 2007. P. 23.

[4] Montley, Patricia. *In Nature's Honor: Myths and Rituals Celebrating the Earth*. Skinner House Books: Boston, 2005. P. 139.

[5] Varner, Gary R. *The Mythic Forest, The Green Man, and the Spirit of Nature*. New York: Algora Publishing, 2006. P. 7.

[6] Varner, Gary R. *The Mythic Forest, The Green Man, and the Spirit of Nature*. New York: Algora Publishing, 2006. P. 130.

[7] Leeming, David Adams. *The World of Myth: An Anthology*. Oxford University Press, 1990. P. 188.

[8] Palin, Poppy. *Craft of the Wild Witch: Green Spirituality and Natural Enchantment*. St. Paul, MN: Llewellyn Publications, 2004. P. 27.

[9] Green, Miranda. *Symbol and Image in Celtic Religious Art*. New York: Routledge Publishing, 1989. P. 87.

[10] Draco, Melusine. *Traditional Witchcraft for the Woods and Forests*. Winchester, UK: Moon Books, 2012. P. 19.

[11] Webster, Richard: *Flower and Tree Magic: Discover the Natural Enchantment Around You*. Woodbury, MN: Llewellyn Publications, 2008. P. 10.

CHAPTER SIX:
LITHA

OVERVIEW, MAGIC, ACTIVITIES, AND CORRESPONDENCES

Litha is celebrated at the Summer Solstice, which is the longest day of the year. If seeds were planted at Beltane they have begun to sprout under the strong sun. Love is in the air, and the fruits of our labor are beginning to show at this time.

History of Litha

The Summer Solstice has been celebrated by cultures around the world since ancient times. It is a holiday when we celebrate the blessings of sunshine, imagination, growth, and love. The Celts felt the Summer Solstice was a time to connect with the Otherworld. Germanic tribes lit bonfires to celebrate the sun's power. In India, the Summer Solstice was a primary holiday.

The Saxons called the month of June *Aerra Litha*, meaning "before Litha," and the month of July *Aeftera Litha*, meaning "After Litha." The word *Litha* translates to "light" or "moon." Author J.R.R. Tolkien used the term in his writing to describe Midsummer festivals,

and many modern Pagans and Wiccans use Litha as the name of the sabbat. The Summer Solstice, or the sabbat of Litha, is the best time of the year to get outdoors and celebrate the abundance of life while the sun is high in the sky, and moods are equally as bright. It is also a fortunate time to perform divination, connect with faeries, and reflect on the power of love.

Celebrate Sunshine

At the Summer Solstice in the Northern Hemisphere, the Earth's tilt is towards the sun, creating the longest day of the year. The sun has been worshipped for bringing warmth and growth to the world around us, but it is beneficial for our bodies as well. Vitamin D is produced in the skin from sunlight exposure. Sunlight can boost serotonin levels, making you feel more alert and optimistic. Enjoying sunlight in the early hours of the day can help regulate melatonin production, which combats seasonal affective disorder and

insomnia. Soak up some rays this Litha and know that the sunshine will help you heal and feel happier. The power of sunlight can be used to cleanse and purify the energies of stones and crystals: simply let your crystals soak up sunshine on Litha. You can also energize drinking water in the sun as well, or steep a Summer Solstice Sweet Tea with black tea, honey, and orange and lemon slices.

Celebrate Imagination

Did you know that Litha is the perfect time of the year to see faeries? It's been said that they come out to play on the longest day of the year. There's something mystical in the air at Litha: perhaps it's the illumination of fireflies flickering in the humid night air or the electrifying feeling of a passing thunderstorm. The presence of faeries at Litha indicates a special attribute worth honoring at this time of the year: imagination. This is the perfect time to begin a dream journal, as dreams at this time of year are said to be prophetic. Or, use the day to meditate on ideas, wishes, and goals you've been holding onto in your mind. They deserve intention and direction at Litha: use this day as a time to manifest your dreams into reality.

Celebrate Community

It appears that today we have translated our ancient rites of June into massive modern festivals like Bonnaroo. However, Druids host a more ancient ritual at Stonehenge at sunrise on the morning of the Summer Solstice. Thousands of people gather at Stonehenge to watch the appearance of the sun through the mysterious stones at dawn. In Scandinavia, the celebration of Midsummer is marked with feasts and games that run late into the still bright night. While the sun is out late and we have heightened energy, reflect on your connections with those around you and the communities you belong to and depend on. Celebrate with friends and family at bonfires and late night feasts.

Celebrate Growth

In ancient cultures the Summer Solstice was seen as a powerful point in the year. Gardens are fertile and in full growth, and young animals are growing stronger as well. Greens would be a welcome sight in the summer meal. June is also known for its fantastic strawberries. Enjoy sweet treats for Litha. To honor the sun's power and to get into the spirit of summer, share some sangria or berry wine with a side of ice cream or honey cake. Litha is said to be the perfect day to collect herbs and flowers, so if you are a gardener, get outdoors to collect sun-seasoned flowers and herbs for teas, tinctures, folk remedies, and magic.

Celebrate Love

The ancient Romans named the month of June after Juno, the goddess of marriage and childbirth. June has long been a favored month for brides who have used the fine weather for the perfect outdoor wedding. Make the time to spend with your romantic partner. And as important: take time to work on growing a relationship with yourself.

Rose Water

Rose water is a wonderful thing to have on hand for skincare as well as magic. Rose water makes a gentle toner, can reduce skin redness, and helps keep skin clear. Rose water can be used as a hair rinse, keeping your hair shiny and your scalp moisturized. It can also be used in spells for love, romance, beauty, friendship, and faery work. And it's very easy to make at home! Add 1 cup of fresh, cleaned rose petals (if you can pick roses from your garden in the morning, this is when they are the most fragrant) into a large pot. Pour two cups of distilled water over the petals, and bring the water to a boil. Stir, lower the heat, and let the petals simmer for about thirty minutes. Run the petals through a strainer, and store the water in a glass container. It's best to keep the rose water the refrigerator, and if you have a spray bottle, it would be a refreshing splash in the summer heat.

Lucid Dreaming and Dream Journaling

Lucid Dreaming is the ability to control what you do while you are dreaming. Some people can do this really easily, while others have to practice at it. People who can lucid dream say that there are some waking life benefits to it. It allows you to sleep better, fight insomnia, and work through problems that may be causing you anxiety.

The Maiden asks the Moon to help her.

There are a couple suggested techniques for lucid dreaming. The first is to give yourself "reality checks" during the waking day. It is believed that by checking in during your waking hours make it easier to check in while dreaming. With that in mind, it is believed that while dreaming you may think to yourself "I'm dreaming right now. I can manage this." Another method for lucid dreaming is to set your alarm clock to go off around 4am or 5am, when most people are normally in a deep mode of sleep. It is thought that when you go back to sleep you have a better chance to remember your dream and even take control in it.

I am not the greatest lucid dreamer, but this is what I've found most effective for me. When I wake up from a dream that is halfway done, I will close my eyes and try to complete the dream. Even if I am still partially awake, I attempt to go back into the dream and resolve it. Sometimes I will fall back asleep while this is happening, and when I do I can lucid dream.

Dream journaling is a great way to reflect on messages and signs you receive in dreams. For some, dreams can be fascinating experiences with vivid images and multi-layered lessons. I have found personally that the more I journal my dreams, the more I am able to recall from them. Here are some questions you may want to consider writing about to help you remember important points in the dream:

- What time of the day is it? What is the weather like?
- What colors do you see? Were there numbers you recall from the dream?
- How do you feel?
- Do you see anyone you know?
- Are there conversations in the dreams you remember?

There are dream dictionaries available that will list interpretations for images and events; however, I would recommend that you reflect on your own feelings towards a symbol you see in a dream. For example, a cat may be good luck to one person while someone who is allergic to animal fur may look at a cat in a dream as a completely different omen. Create your own interpretations based on your own experiences and reactions.

Get Outside

If there is one thing you do in the spirit of Litha, take a moment to wander outdoors. Visit a flower garden and admire the bumble bees as they hop from flower to flower to collect pollen. Lay in the grass and look upwards to make shapes out of the clouds. Watch the sunrise and feel the awe of the burning colors in the early dawn sky.

Litha is all about recognizing that the growing world around you contains magic and intrigue, even in the most gentle and simple observations.

Journaling for Litha
- What are your favorite childhood summer memories?
- What is something fun you plan to do this summer?
- What developments have recently happened in your life? What work is there still to be done?
- What is the most vivid dream you still remember?
- Do you believe in faeries? If so, have you ever had an encounter?

Correspondences
- Names: Litha, Midsummer, Alban Hefin, Festival of Baldur, Thing-Tide
- Date of Celebration: Summer Solstice, typically between June 20 and 23
- Deities Honored: Apollo, Dagda, Puck
- Magical Focus: Dreams, Faery magic, love magic
- Activities: bonfires, camping, decorating a fir tree with ribbons, dream work, divination, faery magic, gardening, going to the beach, handfastings and weddings, harvesting magical and holistic plants, hiking, performing abundance and love spells, picnics, watching the sunrise, weddings
- Altar Decorations: faery figurines, sea shells, summer flowers, summer fruits
- Food and Beverages: blackberries, cherries, cucumber, green beans, grilled meats and vegetables, honey, lemonade, lemons, mead, peppers, oranges, spinach, strawberries, summer squash, sun tea, wine
- Plants, Herbs, Incense: basil, calendula, carnation, chamomile, fennel, heliotrope, honeysuckle, lavender, lilac, marigold, mint, orchids, Queen Anne's Lace, rose, rue, saffron, sandalwood, St. John's Wort, thyme, vervain, yarrow
- Crystals: agate, citrine, fluorite, lapis lazuli, tiger's eye, topaz
- Colors: Gold, Green, Red, Yellow

SUMMERTIME FAERY ENCHANTMENT

There is a legend that says on May Eve the trooping faeries of Ireland leave their winter homes and migrate to their summer homes. If you were wandering the forest at just the right time it was believed that you may catch a glimpse of their procession or hear their enchanting music. It is at Beltane and with their migration that we transition into the light half of the year: we celebrate outdoors under the strong sun, gardens grow and nurture us, and the faeries take the center stage. The Summer Solstice is an excellent time to contemplate the enchanting realm of Faery, when it is believed they come out of hiding to celebrate the longest day of the year with us. Perhaps Shakespeare helped to inspire a faery-filled Midsummer festival with his play *A Midsummer Night's Dream*, or perhaps we are wishing the faeries to bestow good fortune on nature at its greenest time of the year. Here we will look at a brief guide for connecting with faeries during the summer.

Who are the Faeries?

Faeries are an exciting topic: we love to contemplate the idea of an ancient, mystical race with endless magic and wisdom. Many have written about faeries, and more recent authors have explored the idea of having interaction with faeries. Faeries have been defined a number of ways by a number of researchers.

In *Faery Craft*, Emily Carding describes Faery as an umbrella term to cover a range of creatures: "It encompasses the spirits of place and nature and otherworldly beings of the entire globe, which can vary in size and appearance as much as the landscape of the world itself—from the small yet potent to beings of almost unfathomable size."[1]

In *The Faery Teachings*, Orion Foxwood describes them as people from a realm of enchantment: "In tradition, they are both feared and revered, as were their human counterpart seers and magic workers."[2]

There are many theories about who faeries are. They have been called banished angels who fell from heaven but landed on Earth instead of in Hell. There are even claims that faeries are aliens, with theorist pointing out that historical accounts of faery abductions are quite similar to alien abductions. Faeries have also been connected to spirits of the dead. In Celtic mythology, there is no separation between the world of the dead and the world of the Faery. Consequently, faeries also play a role in the tradition and folklore of Halloween.

Some theorize that the Tuatha de Danaan, or the Children of Danu, are the ancient and divine ancestors of the Faery. The Tuatha de Danaan were early settlers of Ireland, and according to Irish legend, they were accomplished magicians and prophets. When they arrived in Ireland from the west, notably the direction of the Underworld, they arrived in a magical mist. They brought with them four magical treasures: the Stone of Destiny, Lugh's spear, Nauda's sword, and Dagda's cauldron. The Tuatha de Danaan were not the only inhabitants of Ireland, which was already inhabited by the giant race of the Fir Bolgs. Though they were able to take over the land from the Fir Bolgs, they were defeated by the Milesians, a wandering people from Spain. After they were defeated in battle by the Milesians, the Tuatha de Daanan moved to the hill mounds underground to live.

From my own interactions and research, I believe faeries are creatures connected to and devoted to Earth. The Fae are ancient, their nature can be mystical, wise, and healing. They are of a different dimension than our own: their dimension appears to be more fluid and magical than ours. However, they can visit our realm as we can learn to visit theirs. Some wish to share with us their knowledge, while others see our presence as a threat to the fragile habitat of our shared home planet. Some are kind in their actions, while others are mischievous, and others still are downright nasty. We are both curious of each other, and through respectful activity and mindfulness, we can connect with benevolent forces.

It also seems that the deeper a researcher gets into the world of the Fae, the more difficult it is to describe them with words. Every experience with the Fae seems personal and unique, sometimes so much so that it is difficult to explain or even awkward to share. It is almost as if the only way to talk about them is to say, "They are who they are and you just had to be there!"

Types of Faeries

Categorizing the Fae is a challenging and lengthy procedure. Encyclopedias have been written with thousands of entries on the different types of faeries that are said to exist. Some have said that they take on the form or shape that we believe we should see. We have divided and categorized them for our own simplification. Ultimately, it is important to remember that faeries are classified in a variety of ways, and that faeries have diverse and varied features and personalities, just like humans. Some are playful or mischievous, while others are ancient and wise. Some are kind and caring, while others are cruel and malicious. Some are curious about humans and wish to interact with them in a mutually beneficial relationship, while others would prefer to have nothing to do with humans.

There seem to be major classes of faeries, within which there have been different "subclasses": domesticated or wild, solitary or group, trooping or stationary. Domesticated faeries live in the household while wild faeries are only found within the untouched corners of nature. Solitary faeries live alone while groups of faeries are large families or gatherings. Trooping faeries are nomadic and can roam to various locations while stationary faeries are connected to (or limited to) a specific location. However, for the pleasure of this chapter, we will examine some of the more "common" types of faeries, ones which we tend to enjoy discussing.

- *Sidhe:* The Sidhe are considered to be the descendents of the Tuatha de Danaan and are a beautiful and noble race who live underground in the mounds and caves of Ireland. This, however, could be symbolic of the Sidhe being inhabitants of the Underworld. In *The Sidhe: Wisdom from the Celtic Otherworld*, John Matthews writes of his conversations with a member of the Sidhe. This communicator tells Matthews that they are an ancient race who have lived on Earth much longer than humans.

- *Seelie and Unseelie Courts:* In Scottish lore, faeries are divided into two courts: the benevolent Seelie Court and the nasty Unseelie Court. The Seelie Court, or the Blessed Court, are said to be a kind and beautiful court of faeries who will approach humans when they wish to aid them. They are said to be kind and fond of feasting and dancing. On the other hand, the Unseelie Court is an ugly, corrupt, and cruel court. It is believed they were once members of the Seelie Court, but fell from grace. They are fond of harming humans and abducting humans to greaten their numbers.

- *Banshees:* Banshees are infamous faeries from Scotland and Ireland who attach themselves to old families. The dreadful wailing of a banshee can be heard as an omen for the death of someone within that family. They are said to have red hair and red eyes from constantly crying. Though rarely seen, the banshee is sometimes spotted on the banks of a river, cleaning death shrouds in the water. The banshees have been known to follow their families to the New World as well.

- *Elves:* Early on, the Anglo-Saxon word for elf was used to describe all types of faeries. However, elves progressed to being a specific type of Faery. In the Scandinavian mythology, elves were divided into two groups: dark elves and light elves. Many people in modern day Iceland believe in elves. There

145

was even an instance when the construction of a highway was diverted around a boulder which was believed to be the home of an elf.

- *Brownies:* Brownies are household spirits from English and Scottish folklore. They are said to be small creatures who wear brown clothing and assist in household chores. Thanking them with food is well appreciated, but to thank them with new clothing is an insult. They are solitary and said to live in dark corners of the home, such as under the stairs. Yet, even though they are solitary, they like to be included in family celebrations. They can bring blessings and protection to the household.

- *Pixies:* Pixies are said to be mischievous faeries with turned up noses and pointed ears. They are small in size, sometimes wearing a foxglove flower as a cap. They have the ability shapeshift to change their size and appearance.

- *Dryads:* Dryads are spirits of the trees, groves, and woods. They are connected to Greek and Roman tradition, the word *drys* meaning oak in Greek. Tree spirits in general are found in many cultures around the world, and they are universally wise, primitive, and magnificent.

Building a Faery Fellowship

Seeing, hearing, or sensing the faeries in our own world is a magical and personal experience. While some people are happy to share their tales of encounters, others keep their experiences private. Just because you wish to have an encounter with Faery does not mean that it will happen or that it will happen as you expect it to. There is debate that some faeries are harmful, not just mischievous, towards humans. Historical accounts of faery encounters are not all pleasant and romantic. There are tales of people disappearing into the world of Faery only to reappear decades later. Faeries have been accused of stealing babies in the middle of the night and exchanging them with faery babies. Some even say they curse humans, causing terrible illness and in some cases death.

So the question has to be asked: are we truly supposed to be in contact with the realm of the Faery? It is a spiritually expanding experiences for those who have studied and approached them with reverence and caution. Teachers such as R.J. Stewart, Orion

Foxwood, and John Matthews, and Raven Grimassi have all done work communicating with the Fae and have not been cursed or abducted. They have also said that the work is not fun and playful at all times. In an interview, John Matthews warned: "Be wary of all kinds of strangeness and wonder. Your whole life can be turned upside down by these beings, who can be every bit as cruel as they are kind."[3]

If you are interested in having contact with faeries, the first thing you must contemplate is why you want to have contact with them. What is your interest in communicating in faeries? Why would it be a mutually beneficial relationship? Stepping forward into the world of the Fae requires honesty, knowledge, respect, and confidence, but also respect and purity. Faery contact is not meant to be a benefit for just one party, but a mutual exchange. Being honest about your intentions will help in your journeys with the Fae. Being protective of your own psychic shield is also a benefit to your well-being. Having manners is equally as important when embarking on a fellowship with the Fae. It is not polite to command them of anything or ask for favors. Stand your ground, be kind and courteous, ask questions, and say please and thank you.

- *Mindful Walks and Nature Connection:* Imagine it is twilight on a June evening. The heat of the day has broken, although the air still holds its summertime humidity. You go outside to enjoy the comfort of the late evening: there are fireflies in the air, frogs are croaking from a nearby pond, and moths flutter by the porchlight of your home. You step out into the backyard, as though you have a craving to touch the grass. You take off your shoes and tiptoe through the grass of your backyard, convening amongst the fireflies, remembering how when you were a child you would try and catch them with your hands. You hear a branch in the tree above you shake and you look up to see the silhouette of an owl. The owl is still but watches you, you observe each other with curiosity and hold the stare until you look away for just a second. You look back upwards to see the owl must have flown away.

Connecting with nature is one of the most valuable keys to building a fellowship with Faery. Within the magical observances of nature, the innocent curiosity of the creatures, and the mindful effort to feel the present sensations, you can open the gateway between yourself and the otherworld. In-between places, such as shores, islands, arches, and caves may be natural entryways to the world of the Fae.

Next time you are on a walk in the woods, try to experience nature in the very present moment. Leave your phone in the car, take the walk alone, and give yourself ample time to enjoy nature and not rush. Before entering the woods make a statement in spirit to the spirit of the woods that you are a friend of nature and wish to interact with the Good Folk. Slowly walk the woods, noticing the present sensations. Do you hear or see any animals? How does the earth smell? How does the ground feel beneath you? When you look around, notice the variety of life. Take a moment to find a tree, stone, flower, leaf, or animal you are drawn to.

Ask the Fae for signs of their presence. It may come in a variety of forms. Perhaps you will see an animal that takes extra curiosity in you. You may feel the tickle of a spider web run across your face when there is no spider thread in sight. Or, you may receive a gift such as a feather or four leaf clover. You may smell sweet honeysuckle or roses even when there is no blossom in sight. Or, you may have an even more mystical encounter, seeing something inexplicable from the corner of your eye, or hearing enchanting music play amongst the rustling of leaves in the wind.

- *Creating an Inviting Space:* There are many ways to create an inviting space for attracting faeries. Consider creating an altar for faeries in a special place in your home. Keep the altar cleaned, and do not put iron items on it. A garden is an ideal place to welcome faeries to your homestead. Foxglove, chamomile, pansies, lily of the valley, sage, bluebells, thyme, lilac, lavender, honeysuckle, rosemary, calendula, and roses are flowers said to attract faeries. Faeries are also said to reside where oak, ash and hawthorn trees grow together. Rings of mushrooms are said to be meeting places for faeries. If you are creative, build Faery ring with a boundary of stone or flowers where you can meditate or leave offerings.
- *Offerings:* It customary to leave offerings for faeries as a way to show companionship. Some traditional offerings left for faeries include fresh cream, berries, honey, cake, bread, and

148

ale. Try to be consistent with leaving offerings. Any offerings that remain the following day should be buried or burned, and should never be left to spoil. You could create an offering of an original poem or song. Burning natural incense or oils with sweet and floral fragrances may also attract faeries as well.

- *Midsummer Faery Tea Dreams:* On Midsummer, you can ask the Fae to come visit you in your dreams with this tea spell. First, find a meaningful offering you would like to share with the Fae. You may wish to bake a honey cake, share a trinket of personal value, or create a cup of tea for the Fae as well. For the tea you will need to make a sweet tea, such as jasmine green tea, milk oolong, or hibiscus. Add a 1/2 teaspoon calendula, 1/2 teaspoon lavender, and 1/2 teaspoon rosebuds. Steep for five minutes and add honey and cream to taste. When it is time for bed, drink the tea and recite the following: "I drink this tea on Midsummer Eve to open my eyes to the Fae. May the Good Folk come in kind spirit during my dreams to play. I give to you this bowl of honey and cream, so we may be companions during this fine Midsummer dream."

- *Thyme and Shiny Dimes:* You will need dried thyme and shiny dimes. Go outside into a place of nature (preferably at dusk on Beltane or Midsummer) and hold the thyme and dimes in your hand. Recite "I call on you who fly and flit to talk with me for just a bit and in return, I'll give you this thyme and this shimmering, silvery dime." After they have visited you, throw the thyme and dime into the wind.[4]

- *Protective Precautions:* If faery contact does not sound like something you wish to incorporate into your life, there are methods of protection as well. Hang a cast iron pot in your kitchen to keep faeries away. Utilize other protective amulets in your home, such as hanging a besom or hiding a protective spell bottle. Line your property or house with sea salt or black salt borders. It is also believed that tomatoes grown in a garden will keep faeries away.

Deepening Our Understanding of Faery

It shows great honor to the Fae to deepen your understanding of their mythology as well as connect with nature. During the summer months, take the time to curl up with a wonderful book on faeries to deepen your understanding of their world. Meditate in nature and show reverence for the flourishing green world of abundance around you. Be open to the ancient wisdom of the Fae and consider any encounters as affirmations that there is hope, magic, and enchantment available for us.

CURIOUS MODERN-DAY FAERY SIGHTINGS

Faery sightings are not so out of the ordinary after all. Tales of real life encounters with faeries intrigue us, pulling us away from our electronic world to awaken our imagination and give us hope that this universe still holds mysteries. The exploration of what faeries are and how faeries interact with us has been a topic for many authors and researchers. Faeries have been linked to ancient gods, fallen angels, transformed spirits of the dead, and even demons. Some tales say that faeries are an immortal, wise and beautiful ancient race. Other tales describe faeries as malevolent creatures who steal babies in the middle of the night. Others still say that faeries take the shape of animals to visit and observe us.

Encounters with the Fae

Many researchers have collected volumes of information on the relationship between faeries and humans. One thorough collection, and perhaps one of the more famous is *The Fairy Faith in Celtic Countries* by W.Y. Evans-Wentz. In this collection of tales, Wentz recounts hundreds of witness stories across the Celtic Nations. Examples of the tales include the sound of hearing pipes at the sacred Hill of Tara and King Arthur's spirit visiting his birthplace of Tintagel in the guise of a blackbird with red feet and a red beak.

The Fairy Investigation Society, which was founded in the late 1920s in Britain, had meetings to discuss faery phenomenon and collect data on faery encounters. In the 1950s, the secretary of FIS, Marjorie Johnson, carried out a "fairy census" in which she collected 20th century faery sightings. One of the most peculiar from the collection happened in Wollaton Park, Nottingham, where a group of children claimed to have been chased by gnomes driving little cars.

Ms. Johnson's research was finally published last year in a book called *Seeing Fairies*. You can visit the FIS website for an extended list of recent faery sightings: http://www.fairyist.com/fairy-investigation-society/

In today's metaphysical and modern pagan revivals, people have warmed up to faeries and their reputation has thawed. Modern authors such as R.J. Stewart, Orion Foxwood, and Emily Carding have written books outlining methods for interacting with faeries in a beneficial manner. In *The Sidhe: Wisdom from the Celtic Otherworld*, John Matthews shares his encounters of speaking with a member of the Sidhe, the Irish ancient faery race connected to the divine Tuatha de Danann. He was able to communicate with the Sidhe by meditating with a spiral glyph he saw in an Irish hillmound chamber.

A friend of mine within the Pagan community also has encounters with faeries. She shared her story with me about how they would often hide her things: "The Fae are great borrowers of things they find fascinating or useful. They can also be wickedly clever tricksters. Back when I was still waiting tables, I came home from my day job to change for my server job. I laid my work apron and my server book on a chair, and then went to the bedroom to change. When I returned to collect the apron and book, the book was gone. After an exhaustive search, I lost my temper. I demanded the Fae return my book or I would salt the entire house and surrounding property. I went back in the bedroom, counted to ten and then returned to find my book exactly where I had left it."

I had my own faery encounter during high school. I resided with my family in Connecticut, a walk away from a state forest that was rumored to have ghosts, midnight coven meetings, and men in black appearances. At that point in my life I was already reading about about faeries. I used to leave out small dishes of berries, cream, and honey in my backyard as offerings to the faeries I believed resided on such supernaturally charged land. One midsummer evening I woke up to the distinctive feeling of the bottom of my feet getting tickled. Stirring from slumber I shifted awake when I heard the most unusual thing: the sound of what I could only describe as a chorus of tiny voices giggling. I sprung up in bed and turned on the lights to an empty room.

Modern fantasy novels have also created beautiful, immortal, magical faeries, perhaps sparking the idea that faeries did indeed have their merits. Were they misunderstood for thousands of years? Do we now have access to benevolent forces through practicing mindfulness, meditation, and connecting with nature? One theme that seems to link all modern faery encounters together is the connection to nature and the awareness that there is divine spirit in all living beings on earth. By touching the world of faery we open ourselves up to magic, fantasy, and an ancient wisdom that is connected to the natural world around us.

FAERY HOTSPOTS

If you ask ten different people what a faery is you'll likely get ten different answers. There may, however, be similarities in each description of faeries. Faeries seem to be ancient spirits of nature with supernatural abilities. Some see them as wise and divine, though the more benevolent view of faeries seems to be a modern one. Historical accounts of faeries tend to be more negative, showing their mischievous and sometimes malicious nature. Faeries appear to inhabit a dimension parallel to our own in a beautiful and magical place known as the "Otherworld" or "Faery Land." Some contend that faeries once lived in our world, while others believe we can go back and forth between our world and theirs. Some believe they are physical creatures while others believe they are supernatural, much like ghosts or angels. However you may define faeries, humans have encountered them both in ancient and modern times. While this is by no means a complete listing, as faeries are seen around the world and by many cultures, the following examines places that seem to have a good deal of faery activity.

Newgrange, Ireland

Wherever you wander in Ireland there is likely a tale of banshees, leprechauns, and the Kind Folk. There is no shortage of faery tales in Ireland, probably because oldest legends speak of the ancient faery race Tuatha de Danaan. The Tuatha de Danaan were said to be divine and magical faeries who lived in Ireland prior than humans. After battling other tribes in Ireland, they moved underground to earthworks all over Ireland. The Megalithic tomb Newgrange is one of the most stunning and well preserved ancient sites in Ireland. Although it is most well-known for the illumination of light through the tomb on the Winter Solstice, it also has a connection to the faeries. It is believed to be one of the places the Tuatha de Danaan relocated to. Legends said it was built by the god Dagda. There are also tales of people seeing faeries moving in and out of the site at night.

Doon Hill, Scotland

In the 1600s, Robert Kirk was a minister at a monastery in Aberdoyle, Scotland. He wrote a book in 1691 called *The Secret Commonwealth of Elves, Fauns, and Fairies*, which explored the folklore of faeries in the region. Doon Hill was near his monastery, and Kirk often visited there, claiming that he had faery encounters. One day he hiked to the top of Doon Hill, where he collapsed and died. According to legend, he visited a family member from beyond the grave to inform him that he was not dead, but was actually taken to the land of faeries. It is believed that he may even still be held captive by them, his spirit imprisoned in a pine tree at Doon Hill known as Minister's Tree.

Cumbria, England

Like all of Ireland and the United Kingdom, there is no shortage of stories of faeries in England. Known as *Tylwyth Teg*, or "The Fair Ones," faeries in northwestern Cumbria seem to be especially active. Elva Hill, which happens to be located near an ancient stone circle, is said to be a gateway to the faery world. Carved within limestone rock in Beetham are a flight of stairs known as the "Fairy Steps;" legend says that if you can climb the steps without touching the rock sides the faeries would grant you a wish. St. Cuthbert's Well in Edenhall are remnants of a now demolished mansion; a glass vase family heirloom that doubled as a good luck charm was said to have been made by the faeries who lived in the garden surrounding the well.

Hafnarfjordur, Iceland

In Iceland it is said that over 50% of the population believes in the existence of elves, where they are known as *Huldufolk* or "hidden folk." They believe the elves live in natural areas of Iceland, but it also appears that humans are intruding on elf territory. A 50-ton boulder said to be a sacred elf church recently halted the construction of a highway. Luckily, the bolder was safely relocated and the elves are okay with their move. The town of Hafnarfjordur is said to be an especially active place for elf activity. Some say that elf royalty lives in the lava park in town, and the town hosts regular elf tours.

Southern Appalachia, United States of America

The Cherokee Native Americans had their own series of tales of an enchanted faery race. The *Yunwi Tsunsdi,* or "Little People," are a spirit race that are small in stature but have hair down to the floor. They are believed to live in caves, mountains, and rocks. Cherokee hunters tell stories of finding small footprints in the snow. At Fort Mountain in Georgia, the Cherokee said that a tribe known as the Moon-Eyed people lived there before they did. The Moon-Eyed people were described as being tall, with light hair and pale eyes. The unusual thing about the Moon-Eyed People was that they would only come out at night, some believing they worshipped the moon. They were eventually driven out of their land and into the mountains, a fate strikingly similar to that of the Tuatha de Danaan in Ireland.

In 1891, a professor witnessed people floating around on Chimney Rock Mountain. In Dunn, North Carolina, a farmer in the 1960s went out to one of his fields and came across a small man walking towards him. The small man was dressed in black boots, blue pants, and an impeccable white tie. When he noticed the farmer looking at him he darted off in the opposite direction. There is also the unexplained phenomenon of floating lights at Brown Mountain in North Carolina, which is seen by many who visit the overlooks. The floating lights are reminiscent of tales of the Will O'Wisps, faery spirits said to float through forests.

Mount Shasta, United States of America

Mount Shasta in Northern California is a place revered by Native Americans and visited by metaphysical tourists looking to raise their vibrations at a variety of retreats for meditation, sweat lodges, and yoga. Mount Shasta has a plethora of supernatural events. One metaphysical visitor recounted a faery encounter she had while meditating at Mount Shasta. Her solitude was interrupted by the sound of delicate song playing. She then witnessed small, blue, winged faeries floating around a tree. There is a belief that a strange race lives at the top of Mount Shasta. Some say Lemurians relocated there after their island was destroyed, and there are also legends of Little People living there, as well. There are reports of Bigfoot lurking around Mount Shasta. Bigfoot resides deep in the forest, and it could be argued that even he is a creature of the Otherworld and a protector of natural habitats.

Atacama Desert, Chile

The Atacama Region has witness accounts of UFO sightings, ghosts in abandoned mining towns, and encounters with Little People. In 2013 an unusual skeleton was found in the Atacama Desert of Northern Chile. This skeleton has been called a "Fairy Skeleton" because of its six-inch size and bizarre, elongated skull. This region of Chile is both isolated and supernatural in nature, so much so, that it caught the attention of the paranormal television show *Destination Truth*, which visited the region to explore claims of Little People. While investigating an abandoned mine shaft, they found another very weird skeleton and had a rock thrown at them.

Your Neighborhood

There are those in modern Pagan and metaphysical paths who believe you can communicate with faeries anywhere in the world. Before searching high and low for the Wee Folk, take time to deeply study their mythology and folklore. If you've had an encounter with faeries I would love to hear your story. If you know of a special place associated with faeries please contact me at kiki.dombrowski@gmail.com. I believe that it is worth cataloging faery encounters that happen worldwide and I am happy to examine and research your personal stories. Perhaps your neighborhood will be discussed in the next edition of Faerie Hotspots!

DIVINATION HIGHLIGHT: SEEING AURAS

Litha is a time of year that is wrapped in fantasy: the world around us is lush, there is love in the air, the weather lets us explore the Otherworldly forest. So at this dreamy time of year, let's explore our sixth sense and that special, curious, and fascinating ability to tap into things beyond our five senses. This divination highlight honors psychic development by working on being able to see auras.

Auras are said to be the natural energy our bodies give off: they are colors that surround our body, reflecting our moods, our physical health, and our personalities. Some people see auras naturally, while others can train to see them in the right settings. Auras are said to surround the body, emanating as far outwards as ten feet, though some claim their auras can press further out. Auras are not a new age exploration: the energy emitting from bodies has been studied for centuries, from ancient Sanskrit texts to painting saints with halos.

In *How To See and Read the Aura*, Ted Andrews says that auras are comprised of energies which come from the physical body, including: light, electrical, heat/thermal, sound, magnetic, and electromagnetic energy. Rosalyn Bruyere describes the aura as a metaphor for life in her book *Wheels of Life*, saying: "A person's energy field or the individual aura around the body, which is created and controlled by the chakras, reflects how one's life is actually lived; it mirrors the flow of that life."

With meditation, practice, and patience, anyone can learn to read auras. We are already engaging with each other's energy, so reading auras is a chance to better connect with yourself and those around you.

Meditation for Colorful Visualization

It is believed that auras are connected with the energy of chakras, which radiates outwards into our auric space. While chakras are said to be energy points that are situated in specific locations, auras are energy fields that radiate from the body and can change, shift, and evolve. Both are associated with colors, making them both powerful visual experiences. Visual meditations can help you work within a deeply relaxed state as well as let you practice seeing vivid images with your mind's eye. In *Power of the Witch*, Laurie Cabot has a vivid and visual meditation that allows you to not only work on seeing colors with your mind's eye, but also allows you to pass into a deep trance-like meditation. This meditation is called the "Crystal Countdown Meditation," which is a countdown from 7 to 1, using the numbers and colors associated with the seven chakras.

Begin this meditation by seating yourself in a comfortable manner. Close your eyes and take a few deep breaths, paying attention only to the feeling of the breath moving in and out of your body. In your mind's eye, visualize a red number seven. See the number seven manifest in a bright red color. If you need help seeing the color, imagine items that are traditionally that color, so for the red imagine strawberries, a fire truck, or something else that reminds you of what red looks like. Hold the red seven in your mind's eye for a few seconds, and then allow it to disappear. Now replace the vision in your mind's eye with an orange number six. If you need to imagine the color orange, think of the orange fruit or the sun. Hold the orange six in your mind's eye for a few seconds, and then allow it to disappear. Repeating this process, visualize a yellow number five. Next, visualize a green number four. Then, visualize a blue number three. Still counting down, visualize an indigo number two. Finally, visualize a lilac or lavender number one.

This meditation can be used to initiate deeper meditations, such as guided meditations or psychic work. If you wish to continue the meditation, slowly count down from ten to one, feeling heavier and more relaxed with each number. Before I complete the meditation I like to visualize all of my chakras spinning gently and smoothly, bright and balanced. Or, when you are finished with the meditation, slowly count from one to ten, feeling lighter, more awake and aware with each number.

Seeing and Feeling Auras with the Hands

Some of the first steps in working with auras can be solitary practice and include some easy and interesting exercises. Take your index fingers and put them together. Stare at them for about 10 to 20 seconds, keeping them touching while you stare. Then, slowly pull them apart. Do you see a thread of light? Do you feel a thread of energy between your two fingers? Next try this exercise in front of a white or cream colored piece of paper. Do you see any colors around between the two fingers? These threads of energy are part of your aura.

157

Rub your hands together and move your hands over the different chakra points on your body. Do you get any feelings or intuitive sensations when you move over different areas? What colors do you see? You can also try and rub your hands together and then hold them up in front of a white or cream colored wall. Stare softly at the outline of your hands and see if you see any light or color coming off of them, thus expanding the spectrum of your own aura that you are examining. Some people will then further this exercise by standing in front of a mirror and trying to self-examine the aura by staring into the mirror's reflection.

Learning to Read Other People's Auras

Seeing the auras around other people can be a fascinating study into a person's personality and mood. With a partner's permission, ask her or him to stand in front of a white or cream colored wall. Make sure there is gentle lighting. Softly stare or gaze beyond your partner, as if you are looking at a point behind her or his head. Take your time staring, your eyes may go out of focus, and gently breathe through the process. You may begin to see a light cloud or haze around your partner's body: congratulations, you are seeing an aura! It may take a little time to start seeing many colors in an aura this way. Many people say they see white, yellow, and blue first, as those are apparently easier colors to pick up on. Over time and with practice, you can develop the ability to see various colors in another person's aura.

Reading auras doesn't necessarily mean just being able to see them. You may feel them as well, and may have already sensed interacting with other peoples' auras. Do you get certain "vibes" when you are around someone? For example, do you feel inspired with certain people, while with other people you feel relaxed? Have you met someone you automatically liked, or automatically disliked? You may be interacting with auras already!

Interpreting Aura Colors

Colors of auras can be interpreted to better understand the personality, character, and mood of a person. There are some psychics, intuitives, and healers who believe that these interpretations are too generalized; therefore, be mindful of your own intuitive feelings and interpretations of colors. Take notes about the colors you see and your interpretations.

- Red: Red can show high energy, passion, and activity. In some cases red can show stress, aggression, and frustration. Dark red could indicate a conservative person. You may feel excited or anxious around someone with a lot of red in his or her aura.
- Orange: Orange in an aura shows high energy, sexuality, and ambition. People with a great deal of orange in their auras can be optimistic, social, and creative. You may feel artistic and inspired around someone with a lot of orange in his or her aura.
- Yellow: Yellow in an aura shows intellectualism. People who have yellow in their auras are focused on studying, research, and philosophy. You may feel like having deep conversations with someone who has a lot of yellow in his or her aura.
- Green: Green in an aura can indicate a phase of growth and change. Green can sometimes indicate a teacher, while blue-green can indicate a healer. Green may also show someone who is compassionate and has a strong bond with nature. You may feel comfortable and at ease around someone with a lot of green in his or her aura.
- Blue: Blue in an aura shows idealism and care. People who have blue in their auras care for those around them. Blue can show sincerity and intuition. You may feel supported, understood, and listened to when around someone with a lot of blue in his or her aura.
- Purple: Purple in an aura shows spirituality. People who have purple are profound and engage in deeply spiritual practices. A deep purple or indigo aura can show psychic abilities. You may feel intrigued by people with purple in their auras, as if they have old souls and deep wisdom.
- Pink: Pink in an aura shows love and affection. This is a common energy to see around expecting mothers and in auras of affectionate couples. You may feel happy and hopeful around someone with a lot of pink in his or her aura.
- White: White tends to show up to show spirit guardians and divine energy.
- Brown: There is less agreement on what brown means: some say brown indicates illness and imbalance, while others say brown

indicates being grounded in the world. Perhaps see where brown lies in the aura and if there are other colors that surround it.

- Black: Black is not a common color to see, though some believe that a black aura can show evil, addiction, or even looming death. Many aura readers advise against believing this is the only way to read black in an aura. It could also mean illness, exhaustion, emotional blockages, and protective boundaries. You may feel uncomfortable or uneasy around someone with black in his or her aura.

Extra Information about Auras

- If an aura seems small it could mean feeling frail, tired, and/or weak. It could indicate a need for self-care.
- If an aura seems too large it could mean the person is influential at best, overpowering at worst.
- The left side of a person's aura is said to be the receptive, feminine side.
- The right side of a person's aura is said to be the proactive, masculine side.
- The brighter and more vibrant the colors in an aura, the better. If they appear dull or gloomy in color it may be an indication of imbalance or challenges.
- The aura is said to be shaped like an egg. When you get a picture of your aura taken with a Kirlian camera, it only reveals the aura around the chest and head.
- The aura is said to be in different layers. Colors closer to the body indicate physical conditions while outer layers indicate emotional and spiritual feelings. If you are interested in deepening your interpretations and studies of auras, research the seven layers of auras.

Benefits of Reading Auras

Reading auras is an opportunity to deepen your connection with and understanding about yourself and the people around you. By reading your aura you can examine your level of wellness and discover where energetic imbalances may reside. Not only this, you have the opportunity to develop your psychic abilities and bond with others while practicing reading auras. Most importantly: you connect on a deeper level to yourself, others, and divinity through reading auras.

LITHA CHAPTER NOTES

[1] Carding, Emily. *Faery Craft: Weaving Connections with the Enchanted Realm*. Llewellyn Publications: Woodbury, MN, 2012.

[2] Foxwood, Orion. *The Faery Teachings*. R.J. Stewart Books: Arcata, CA, 2007. P. 3.

[3] Carding, Emily. *Faery Craft: Weaving Connections with the Enchanted Realm*. Woodbury, MN: Llewellyn Publications, 2012. P. 25.

[4] This was shared with me by someone who passed away over ten years ago and I am not sure where she got this from. If this passage is familiar to you, please pass along to me where you have heard it before.

CHAPTER SEVEN:
LUGHNASADH

OVERVIEW, MAGIC, ACTIVITIES, AND CORRESPONDENCES

On Lughnasadh we celebrate the bounty of life: we are seeing rewards in the garden as vegetables and fruits ripen, offering up some of the sweetest and most delectable treats of the year. Also known as First Harvest, Lughnasadh celebrates the harvest of crops, both in the literal and metaphorical sense. We give thanks to Earth and living creatures that are sacrificed for our survival and well-being. We also look forward to and prepare for coming harvests and gather for colder seasons.

Lugh and Harvest Festivals

Lughnasadh is named after the Celtic God Lugh, who has taken on the role of a Sun King, though he is known as a master of all human skills. His name means "the Shining One," and he is said to be a clever magician, wise poet, masterful warrior, skilled blacksmith, and king of the Tuatha de Danaan. This holiday is as much about Lugh's adoptive mother Tailtiu, who in legend, clears the plains that will serve as agricultural land in Ireland. She dies as a result of exhaustion from her challenging chores, but her sacrifice allows for others to sustain. Lugh was said to have introduced the celebrations of Lughnasadh in honor of Tailtiu.

At this time of the year many festivals were held to celebrate sports, compete in games, and enjoy contests. In some places these harvest celebrations started in mid-July and went through mid-August. In Ireland, bonfires would be lit and outdoor feasts would take place. Rituals and sacrifices would be held to ensure bountiful harvest. The retelling of Lugh's tales would be shared and sporting competitions would be held. This is a time of the year associated with the practice of a trial marriage, where a couple would devise a contract to stay together for a year and a day. In the Scottish Highlands, rites were performed at this time to bring protection to animals and homes. Races were held and sports were played. Wells were visited on the Isle of Man because they were said to have increased healing powers at that time of year. British Lammas was an important holiday through medieval times when festivals were held, elections took place, and bills were paid. In the spirit of ancient August festivals, many pagans enjoy celebrating outdoors with sports, races, games, and fun competitions. Some great games to play for Lughnasadh include archery, capture the flag, kickball, horseshoes, bocce, or cornhole.

Harvest festivals were not exclusive to Britain and Ireland. Native American tribes celebrated the harvest of corn at this time with festivals, song, dance, and the settlement of arguments. In West Africa, the harvest of yam was celebrated at this time of the year. In Eastern Europe and Russia, this time of year welcomed helpful nature spirits. The arrival of the Dog Star, Sirius, in the night sky was charted and revered in ancient civilizations from Greece to Rome, from Mesopotamia to Egypt. In Egypt the star marked the beginning and celebration of rising flood waters in the Nile. This is a great time of year to go stargazing, especially with the annual Perseid meteor shower during August.

The First Harvest and Kitchen Celebrations

Because of the holiday's connection to first harvest, one way to honor the spirit of the day is by spending time in the kitchen. Even though it is one of the warmest times of the year, we begin prepping and storing extra food for fall and beyond. If you have never tried canning and making preserves, Lughnasadh is an excellent time to practice this fairly easy way of preserving food. At this time of year my favorite jam to make consists of wild blackberries from local woods and locally sourced peaches. Fresh figs are also available in some supermarkets this time of year, and a fig and strawberry jam is a unique jam to try out, as well. Another fun activity is cooking with family and friends. Share family recipes or create new dishes and bond over fun in the kitchen. Grape harvest is also at this time, so enjoy some little sangria or red wine in honor of the Old Ways!

There are some great dishes to consider cooking up with in-season food as well. For main courses, consider barley soup, baked fish, or chicken pot pie. For side dishes consider cornbread, potato salad, tomato and basil salad, or squash casserole. For desserts perhaps consider oatmeal cookies, blackberry or peach pie. Tea brewed in the sun, sweetened with honey, and decorated with circular slices of orange to represent the sun makes a great beverage for the day as well. Cooking isn't your thing? Why not celebrate with a potluck, and invite friends to come over and share their favorite dishes with everyone while enjoying board games at the kitchen table? How else do you use the kitchen? Oftentimes it becomes a space where people love to gather and talk. In honor of storytelling perhaps play word games, share poetry, or host a writing workshop.

Lughnasadh Abundance Magic

The first harvest is the perfect time to reflect on the abundance in your life. It is also an excellent time to ask for continual abundance and think about which projects still need completing. At the time of harvest, consider cooking magical dishes associated with prosperity.

In *Lammas: Celebrating the Fruits of the First Harvest* authors Anna Franklin and Paul Mason suggest: "Make a loaf of bread at Lammas, and before you put the loaf into the oven, dip a paintbrush in milk and write on the crust what you most desire. Bake the bread, and then eat it while it's still warm."[1]

Empowerment Magic

At a time of the year when we honor warriors and heroes in competition and game, this is an excellent time to rediscover your own inner warrior and hero/heroine by working with courage and personal power spells.

Offerings at Lughnasadh

As a time of thanks and gratitude, consider giving offerings to the gods, goddesses, spirits, or nature. Which deities do you work with and what are the appropriate offerings to share with them? Or, do you wish to show gratitude to nature? You can take time to pick up litter or volunteer time with a beautification or environmental group. Or, do you wish to show gratitude to your friends and family? Send a personal letter, make a date to catch up in person, or share a gift (magical or otherwise) with someone you are grateful to have in your life.

Protection Magic

This is a traditional time of the year to protect your home with magic. Traditionally, houses were marked with crosses. In honor of this, use amulets and crystals to protect your homestead, or research and paint traditional Pennsylvania Dutch Barn Hex signs/symbols.

Journaling for Lughnasadh

Although Lughnasadh is frequently an active holiday, there is plenty to reflect upon at this time of year. If you are so inclined, contemplate, meditate, draw, or write about the following questions for Lughnasadh:

- What do you hope will come into fruition by the end of the harvest season?
- What abundances are in your life?
- In what areas in your life do you need courage?
- For what are you thankful? For whom?

- How do you thank divinity? Nature? People? Yourself?
- What does the planet provide for you with ease?
- What did you learn from working towards completing your goals?
- What still needs preparation for growth and harvest?
- What in your life needs to be sacrificed?

Correspondences:
- Names: Lugh's Day, Lughnasa, Lammas, First Harvest, Feast of First Fruits, Harvest Home, Freyfaxi
- Date of Celebration: August 1st, or around the first week of August
- Deities Honored: Adonis, Ceres, Demeter, Green Man (as John Barleycorn), Isis, Lugh, Persephone, Tailtui
- Magical Focus: banishment, continued abundance, offerings of gratitude, protection, renewal
- Activities: baking, berry and fruit picking, bonfires, canning, cleaning, contests and games, dancing, feasting, giving thanks, going to fairs, picnics, singing and storytelling, star gazing, swimming in a lake or ocean, visiting farmers markets
- Altar Decorations: bread, corn, shafts of wheat and grain
- Food and Beverages: blackberries, blueberries, bread, cherries, corn, fish, oats, peaches, plums, peppers, potatoes, poultry, summer squash, tomatoes
- Plants, Herbs, Incense: basil, cornflower, daisy, dill, heather, passion flower, sunflower
- Crystals: amber, tiger's eye
- Colors: burgundy, brown, dark green, gold, yellow

RECLAIMING THE PASSION FLOWER

One of the greatest pleasures of hiking through Tennessee forests in July and August is seeing the return of the exotic and beautiful passion flowers. Species of passion flower are found in regions of North America, South America, Asia, and Australia. In the United States, Purple passion flower can be found from Pennsylvania to Florida, from the east coast all the way to Texas, and in Tennessee it is the state wildflower. Also known as May-pops or Passion Vine, passion flower is a beautiful purple or white flower that can be used for attractions spells, peace, and femininity.

Peace and Calming

Passion flower has actually been used as a sedative holistic remedy to help in calming nerves and reducing stress. The tincture can be commonly found at health food stores, and it can be taken to help with reducing anxiety, aiding in sleep, soothing PMS symptoms, and assisting in relieving PTSD symptoms. Holistic remedies aside, you can bring passion flower into a home to bring in peaceful energy, calm tempers, and diffuse tension. If you put passion flower under your pillow or by your bedside it will help you rest well and can also be used in dream magick. Decorate a sacred space with amethyst and passion flower to welcome in calm dreams, transformation, and soothing divine downloads during meditation or creative work.

Attraction

Passion flower is said to be a flower helping in attraction work, especially when it comes to attracting friends and allies. Carry passion flower to attract friends and help enhance your popularity. Consider carrying passion flower in an amulet bag with carnelian, rhodochrosite, and/or rose quartz to attract happy and caring relationships into your life. You can bathe in passion flower-infused water to attract a potential romantic interest. Sirona Knight in *Faery Magick* suggests that passion flower can attract more than

friends. According to her, you can leave passion flowers at your door to welcome in protective and happy faeries. She also suggests you can tie together passion flowers with pink and red ribbons to attract the one you love into your bedroom.

Associations with Venus

Passion flower corresponds with the planet Venus. The Venus aspect of the passion flower connects the beautiful plant to goddesses of the heaven: Inanna, Aphrodite, Isis, Bast, Freya, Lakshmi, Venus, Branwen, Astarte, and Ishtar. All of these goddesses connect with beauty, love, sensuality, femininity, and divine creation magick. Venus also links passion flower to female sexuality, marriage, relationships, love, leisure, art, happiness, kindness, and creativity. Consider a blend of Venus essential oils such as rose geranium, gardenia, bergamot with passion flower petals and pure water that has been left out to absorb light from the bright, rising planet of Venus.

Reclaiming the Pentacle

It is claimed that the a Jesuit priest gave the passion flower its name when he discovered it in the 1600s. He named it so because he associated the flower's shape and parts to Christ's crucifixion. Although the shape of the Passionflower has traditionally been connected to Christianity, I would like to reinterpret it from a Pagan perspective and hopefully add some more insight into how magical of a flower it can be for Pagans and witches. The five anthers create a shape of a star, and it is encompassed within a circle of wispy corona filaments, making the shape of a pentacle. It has ten exterior petals and sepals, five of each. According to Shirley B. Lawrence in *Exploring Numerology*, 55 is a master number of intelligence and reaching perfection. Oftentimes in numerology 10 is reduced to 1, and in this case could indicate new beginnings. The three stigmata represent the three phases of the goddess: maiden, mother, and crone. The central, chalice shaped ovary is a culmination of all of the goddess and sensual symbolism in the passion flower: the chalice is connected to the healing Holy Grail or Cauldron, as well as the container for the element of water and tarot suit of the cups.

Reviewing all of these elements from the eye of the witch can show the true, magical nature of the passion flower: it is an empowering flower for women who need healing of all kinds (emotional, psychic, sexual). It can brighten confidence and self-esteem through perfected qualities and awareness of collected intelligence as well as divine wisdom. The spirals of the plant's winding vines can be connected to the spiral dance and the ritual circle. The pentacle shape within the flower shows it is a flower of the witch: one of protection, power, and connection to the feminine divine. It is a wonderful wildflower that in many places (on private property as well) can be found in abundance. Save and dry the flowers to use in magical incenses for Lughnasadh and Mabon. Enjoy passion flower for its ability to be soothing and loving, but also encourage joy, sensuality, empowerment, and inspiration.

THERE'S NO PLACE LIKE HOME: WITCHCRAFT FOR THE KITCHEN, HEARTH, AND GARDEN

Even in the heat of August we begin our harvest and preparations for the fall and winter months. Lughnasadh marks the first harvest, and so it is a fitting time to begin reflecting on the various types of witchcraft and magic that can take place in the kitchen, hearth, and garden. You can use your homestead and the objects in and around your homestead to nourish, enhance, and support your spiritual practices.

Different Types of Homestead Witchcraft

There are many terms to describe the magic and witchcraft practiced around the homestead, with many of their practices and lore overlapping. Here we focus on witchcraft that connects with the magic at the homestead.

- Kitchen Witchcraft: A kitchen witch is someone who honors the domestic realm, instilling magic into the daily tasks in the homestead. Cooking is part of kitchen witchcraft, and learning how to use magic and love in food preparation is part of being a kitchen witch. Creating a sacred space in the kitchen is equally as important. A kitchen witch may also take interest in the medicinal and holistic properties of herbs and foods, serving as both a mystic and a healer.

- Green Witchcraft: A green witch is someone who uses herbs, plants, and all things natural to tap into a diverse world of magical energies. Green witches feel a great connection with nature, the elements, and faeries. They enjoy spells with nature, healing, and teaching. There is more information on Green Witchcraft in the Beltane chapter.

- Hedge Witchcraft: A hedge witch is someone who combines the elements of witchcraft with shamanism, practicing rituals and magic in rural and wild areas. The hedge refers to the boundary in a metaphysical sense, symbolizing a boundary between our world and the otherworld. Hedge witches are said to be able to traverse the boundary, being able to link their healing and magic to that of the Otherworld. A hedgewitch studies nature, healing lore, herbalism, and homestead crafts. She may have a garden, but also celebrates all things that grow wild.

Witchcraft in the Hearth

"Hearth" is defined as the brick or stone-lined space at the base of a chimney where a fire can be built and cooking could take place. The hearth represents a central location in the homestead, a focal point where cooking and company meet, where there is warmth and hope. It is the heart of the home. What is the spiritual center in your home?

Goddesses of the Hearth and Kitchen

- Brigid: Celtic triple goddess of smithcrafting, healing, and poetry.
- Cerridwen: Celtic goddess of the cauldron and transformation.
- Frigga: Norse domestic goddess who is Odin's wife. She is the goddess of marriage, love, fertility, motherhood, and domestic skills.
- Hestia: Greek goddess of the hearth who is associated with baking and cooking. She preserves the sacred home and spiritual renewal.
- Okitsu-Hime: Japanese goddess of food and the kitchen.

Food Magic for Lughnasadh

Foods and beverages contain magical energies that can be used for spiritual and spell work as well. Kitchen witchcraft considers the magical components of food while creating a meal. Some meals are given a magical boost in the way they are prepared. At the first harvest of Lughnasadh farmers markets are thriving and gardens are in full bloom. I love to can at this time of year and make it part of my Lughnasadh tradition. I make a jam from blackberries from a neighborhood park (I get the blackberries with the Naturalist's permission) and peaches from a local orchard. If you enjoy the idea of making food infused with magic, I highly recommend you visit the blog Gather Victoria. This is a gorgeous blog with recipes that tie into folklore and magic. If you would like traditional recipes for the seasons try *Witch in the Kitchen* by Cait Johnson and *Celtic Folklore Cooking* by Joanne Asala.

Spiritual Hearth Meditation

Begin by picturing your ideal home. What does it look like? Where is it located? Take a moment to create the ideal homestead, its decorations, its gardens, and its location.

Close your eyes and get comfortably seated. Take a deep breath, hold the breath, and release. Feel the breath enter, expand your chest and belly, and release. When you breathe in, visualize a white light coming from your heart chakra, comforting and healing you. As you breathe deeper and deeper, this ball of white light expands to surround you and protect you.

Now visualize yourself sitting in your ideal home. What do you see around you? What do you smell? What are you seated on? Who lives there with you? Do you have any animals?

In your ideal home move towards the window. Where is your house located?

As you gaze out the window you see a beautiful garden outside. This is a special garden. Go walk outside to visit it.

Know that this garden contains flowers and herbs that symbolize your spiritual path and magical practice. Take a moment to walk around your garden and hold to your memory the flowers and herbs that you see in the garden.

Before you go back to your home think about something you would like to manifest in your life. Is it prosperity? Good health? Romance? Creative success? Gather items from your garden to make a magical spell bottle and return to your kitchen.

What does your kitchen look like? Is there food cooking? Do you have a pot of tea or coffee brewing? What are the decorations here? Know that you can return to this kitchen to regain focus and clarity, and find what you need for growth and healing in your life.

You will find an empty bottle on your counter for making a spell bottle. Lay all of your garden items on the counter and review them. In your kitchen find the magical utensils you need to blend these items. Is it a wooden spoon? A cast iron pot? A mortar and pestle? Find the utensils and begin to blend your herbs and flowers. How do they feel? What is the smell? As you blend the herbs and flowers they begin to glow a brilliant golden light as they are infused with your magic. Place the items into the empty bottle and bring them to the room where your hearth or fireplace is.

You walk into the central part of your house: the heart of your home, reflecting the love in your own life. There are paintings and decorations that show images of what you are hopeful for in your life. What do you see in these decorations?

A warming fire is burning in the hearth, and you know you can come to this room to center yourself and connect with the feelings of inspiration and hope. You have an altar by or above your fireplace. There is a special crystal on the altar to add to the spell bottle you are creating. Hold to your memory what crystal this is. This crystal would be a powerful amulet to you in your waking life to carry with you and offer you healing energy.

There is also a small trinket to add to the spell bottle. This trinket offers a message of guidance and will assist you in manifesting your magical spell. What is the trinket and what does it symbolize to you?

Place all the items in the spell bottle and seal it shut. Hold the bottle and visualize the most benevolent outcome that results from your magic. Anytime you need to remember your spiritual practice, recharge your energy, or connect with hope and healing, know that you can visit this spiritual homestead. It will bring you comfort and reveal messages to you about the path you can take to bring all you wish into creation. You can always close your eyes and visualize your magical spell bottle to empower you as you move towards succeeding in your goals.

KITCHEN AND GARDEN GRIMOIRE

This brief grimoire contains herbs and flowers that can be obtained at grocery stores, herbal specialty shops, or grown in a garden.

- **Allspice**: Allspice is used for money and luck magic. It is a one-herb incense for good luck, money, and providing energy.

- **Angelica**: Angelica is used for healing, purification, and protection. You can grow it in your garden for protection. Carry the roots as a good luck amulet or burn in an incense to promote healing.
- **Basil**: Use basil for love, prosperity, and business success. Grow basil and then gift the basil plant to someone you love. Sprinkle basil in the corners of your home to bring happiness and love into your life. Steep basil in water and use the water to clean a new home for good fortune, purification, and protection.
- **Bay**: Use bay for clairvoyance, wisdom, and prophetic dreams. It can also be worn or carried to ward off evil and negative energy. Bay is said to attract love into your life.
- **Blackberry**: Blackberry is connected to Brigid. The leaves and berries can be used to attract wealth and healing.
- **Calendula**: Calendula (or Pot Marigold) is used for psychic abilities, prophetic dreams, protection, and legal matters. In incense it can be used for divination. In tea it can be used to enhance psychic abilities, intuition, and meditation.
- **Cardamom**: Use cardamom for love and lust spells. Carry the seeds to attract love into your life, or carry on a first date to ensure a great connection. The fragrance is said to attract passion into your life.
- **Catnip**: Add catnip to simmering potpourris to promote peace and happiness. Combine with rose petals in love sachets. Feed to your cat for an entertaining show.
- **Chamomile**: Chamomile can be used in teas to help with meditation, relaxation, and sleep. The sun-yellow bud is often associated with sun magic, and can be used in love potions, money spells, and sprinkled around the house for protection. Wash money in chamomile-infused water to keep the flow of money and abundance moving into your life.
- **Cilantro**: Also known as coriander. Cilantro is used in peace and love spells. It is said you can add cilantro to wine to make a love potion. It also releases you from the pain of difficult past relationships.
- **Cinnamon**: Used for astral projection, courage, divination, energy, healing, love, lust, money, projection, psychic awareness, purification, and spirituality. Add a cinnamon stick to a money spell bottle or honey jar to attract prosperity. Cinnamon can be

burned in spiritual incense to enhance clairvoyant abilities. Drink cinnamon in tea before bed to have vivid dreams.

- **Cinquefoil**: Cinquefoil can be used for wealth, protection, and prophetic dreams. The five points of the leaf are said to represent love, money, health, power, and wisdom. Carrying cinquefoil is said to grant these things.

- **Clove**: Clove can be used for abundance, love, protection, and psychic abilities. Cloves can be carried to attract love or burned to protect a home. They will stop gossip from entering your home as well. Add cloves to a money spell bag or honey jar to attract abundance. You can stick cloves into an orange or lime to make a protection amulet for your home.

- **Dandelion**: It's not an unwanted sight in your garden! Dandelion is a wonderful flower to have around for both magical and holistic purposes. Dandelion can be used for divination and psychic abilities. Burn with peppermint oil to enhance psychic abilities. Dandelion leaf contains iron, potassium, beta-carotene, and vitamin C. Cleaned leaves can be added to salads and dried roots can be a substitute for coffee.

- **Dill**: Dill is used for money, mental clarity, protection, and blessings. Plant dill in your garden to attract money into your home. Sprinkle dill in a bath before a date to ensure a romantic connection. Burn dill in an incense to awaken mental prowess and wisdom.

- **Fennel**: Used for healing, fertility, protection, and purification spells. Fennel can be used in incense to awaken mental powers. Romans used to chew fennel seeds before battle. Carry fennel to help you feel courage and confidence. Fennel is said to be best gathered at Midsummer. Decorate houses with St. John's Wort and fennel at Midsummer to protect your home against mischievous spirits.

- **Garlic**: Use garlic for protection spells and warrior energy. The scent is said to help clear away negative thoughts. Hang in your home to keep away evil. Paul Beryl in *The Master Book of Herbalism* suggests that garlic can be used to invoke Hecate if left as an offering at crossroads on a pile of stones.

- **Ginger**: Ginger is used for love, lust, money, and courage. Put in love and lust spells. In simmering potpourris ginger can promote confidence and abundance. The root is said to be a lusty aphrodisiac.

- **Honeysuckle**: Although an invasive species in many yards, there are magical properties of honeysuckle that can be used. It is used for healing, money, protection, psychic awareness, and spirituality. Place honeysuckle flowers around a purple candle to strengthen psychic abilities. The flowers are said to attract money. Place honeysuckle flowers in a vase to attract money into your home. I collected honeysuckle petals one Beltane and soaked them in carrier oil, thinking it would be a wonderful fragrance to add to oil blends. The fragrance did not translate well in this method, but the magic did. I used this oil in a fast money blend with great success.
- **Lavender**: Lavender is used for balance, happiness, love, protection, enhancing intelligence, centering the spirit and mind, and purification. The fragrance is soothing, calming, and can help a person relax and rest. Soak in a lavender bath for healing and purification. Add to sachets and spell bottles to attract love. It is also said to be an inviting garden herb for faeries. Throw lavender in Midsummer bonfires as offerings to Divinity and summer gods.
- **Lemon Balm**: Lemon Balm is used for love, success, and healing. It can be used to attract love and romance in your life.
- **Lilac**: Lilac is an otherworldly flower, said to be connected to the faery realm.
- **Mugwort**: Mugwort is used for psychic powers, protection, prophetic dreams, healing, and astral projection. An evening tea with mugwort and induce psychic dreams. Steep in water and use the water to cleanse scrying and divination tools.
- **Nutmeg**: Nutmeg is used for luck, money, prosperity, clairvoyance, and psychic awareness. It can also be used in moon and sea magic. Nutmeg can intensify dreams. Carry the nut to strengthen clairvoyant abilities. A whole nutmeg can also be used as a good luck charm. Draw a sigil on the nut for money and carry to attract prosperity and abundance.
- **Oregano**: Use for love, peace, rest, happiness, and healing. Oregano can be used for love and creating long term, permanent relationships. It was a symbol of happiness to the Ancient Greeks

and Romans. In a simmering potpourri, the fragrance is said to soothe depression and grief.

- **Parsley**: Parsley is used for fertility, lust, protection, and purification spells. The fragrance of parsley is said to uplift moods and purify the air. Parsley was a decoration on Ancient Greek and Roman graves; therefore, it could be connected to otherworldly magic. According to Rachel Patterson in *A Kitchen Witch's World of Magical Plants and Herbs*, you can rub parsley on your forehead, temples, then heart chakra "with the intent of happiness and joy."[2]

- **Patchouli**: I had the fortune of finding a Patchouli plant at a Whole Foods one summer. It grew during the summer months in my Tennessee garden very well. Patchouli is a natural insect repellant, so it has a great place in the garden for keeping unwanted critters away. Patchouli is used for earth magick, luck, money, manifestation, lust, love, and riches. Dried leaves can be put into wallets to attract money.

- **Pepper**: Use black pepper for banishment and protection spells. It can also be used to remove jealousy, gossip, and negative energy from a home. Mix black pepper with salt to create a protective boundary that no evil can cross.

- **Peppermint**: Peppermint is used for purification, sleep, healing, love, and psychic abilities. Use in a dream pillow for peaceful sleep and dreams. Use in a tea for healing. Burn peppermint as incense in the home during the winter for purification.

- **Raspberry Leaf**: Raspberries are ruled by Venus, and raspberry leaf has loving and protective energies. Raspberry leaf can be carried by pregnant women to alleviate pregnancy and childbirth pains.

- **Rose**: Rose is used for love, luck, sex, harmony, protection, divination, and psychic awareness. The fragrance is said to enhance compassion, and promote inner beauty. Roses growing around a home attract high spiritual vibrations, love, and calmness.

- **Rosemary**: Rosemary is used to uplift moods, enhance concentration and creativity, and aid in healing and purification magic. It is wonderful to combine in homemade smudge sticks, especially when combined with juniper berries. Drink rosemary tea before an exam to promote powerful mind function and to stimulate creativity. The tea is also said to help ease depression. Use rosemary in love spells to increase loyalty.

- **Sage**: Although garden sage is different from white sage, they have similar uses. Use sage for wisdom, mental clarity, healing, and money spells. Use sage to manifest wishes and attract money. Add to healing and prosperity incenses, sachets, and amulets.
- **Scullcap**: Scullcap is used for love, fidelity, and peace. Carry it with you to maintain a peaceful and relaxed feeling. It is an herb used in marriage and handfasting festivals.
- **St. John's Wort**: St. John's Wort is used for protection and happiness.
- **Star Anise**: Used for luck, purification, psychic abilities, and protection. Place star anise under your pillow or in a pillowcase for prophetic dreams. Or, place star anise in each corner of your home to draw good luck into the home.
- **Thyme**: Thyme is used for purification, healing, psychic abilities, love, courage, health, and clairvoyance. Thyme in a dream pillow is said to aid in restful sleep and ease nightmares. Use in sachets to relieve depression and enhance healing. Ancient Romans washed their faces with thyme-infused water to enhance their attractiveness. Thyme is said to assist in seeing faeries.
- **Vanilla**: Vanilla can be used in love and lust spells. Carry a vanilla bean to attract love, or add to love potions and spells. Blend vanilla bean into a bowl of sugar to draw in loving energy into your home.
- **Yarrow**: Yarrow is used for love, courage, and psychic abilities. It is an excellent addition in love spells, but can also be used to attract friendship. It can also be used in psychic and divination incense. Added to tea, yarrow is said to improve psychic powers.

DIVINATION HIGHLIGHT: KITCHEN DIVINATION

Tarot, palmistry, astrology, runes: these are a few of my favorite things! When we think about divination, these are the types most often thought of: they are accessible, both in research and in practice. However, there are other forms of divination that are ancient, fascinating, and unusual. There are means and methods for predicting the future in almost every aspect of life. When we celebrate the wonders of the kitchen at Lughnasadh, let's explore divination in one of the most loved rooms of the home: the kitchen.

Divination of Wine

As we learned in the Samhain chapter, scrying is the ancient art of the gaze. By gazing into a dark, reflective surface, the oracle may see visions. But did you know that you can combine the pleasure of a glass of wine with scrying? Oinomancy is divination using wine. Pour a glass of red wine into a clear glass. Place a candle behind the glass. Sitting in front of the glass, gaze into the illuminated wine to scry and search for symbols and omens to appear. Another potential way to read wine is to read the residue left in the bottom of the glass, or read the way the wine swirls, splashes, or moves against the side of the glass.

Divination of Cheese

Tiromancy, the divination of cheese, was apparently at its peak in popularity during the Middle Ages. The shape of the holes in cheese; for example, a heart shape would indicate love and letters would be searched out to indicate initials. The aging process of cheese may have been read, as well as the quantity and shapes of mold. One other method with cheese that may have been used was to assign slices of cheese to specific people or outcomes. The cheese would then be fed to rodents, and the first piece to be eaten entirely would indicate the answer. Since it would be a shame to let a good Brie turn moldy, or a little gross to collect rodents for cheese-eating races, tiromany lost its popularity to other forms of divination. Perhaps you will feel adventurous enough to divine the shapes of the holes in a slice of Swiss or create a new method altogether for reading cheese.

Divination of Oil

Ancient Babylonians were devoted to their divination. They practiced astrology, they read smoke for messages, and they performed lecanomancy, which is the divination of oil and water. To try this out for yourself, you will need olive oil and a bowl of warm water. Pour a very small amount of oil into the water. If the oil forms an unbroken ring, the answer is positive. If the oil covers the entire surface of the water in the bowl there is trouble ahead. Many small, unconnected droplets signify money. A crescent or star shape is a good fortune, though if the oil divides into two sections there is a negative answer.

Divination of Fruits and Vegetables

The produce section also offers an array of oracular options. As mentioned in the Samhain chapter, apples are a common fruit used for divination. You can also use an orange to receive a simple yes or no answer. While eating an orange, consider a question you would like answered, saving all of your seeds. Count the number of seeds in the orange: an even number of seeds means the answer is no, an odd number of seeds mean the answer is yes. Cromnyomancy is the divination of onions. One method of reading onions involves carving the initials of potential suitors into the onion skins. The first onion to sprout would be the chosen love.

Divination of Salt and Flour

Halomancy is the divination of salt and the patterns it makes after being poured onto a surface. To try this out you will need coarse sea salt and a tray or dish that you can pour salt onto. Take a small handful of salt and consider a question you have in mind. Pour it onto the surface and interpret the shapes the salt makes. You may also wish to pour an even layer of fine salt onto a dish or tray. Close your eyes and allow your finger to draw freely in the surface. Interpret the shapes and designs you drew in the salt. Aleuromancy is the divination of flour and is linked to the fantastic fortune cookie. In Ancient Greece priest would write wise and inspiring messages on small pieces of paper that were baked into cakes. Another method of divining with flour would be to interpret shapes in a water mixture. Mix flour and water in a bowl and interpret the shapes that the mixture takes on.

Divination with Tea Leaves

Tea leaf readings can be an intricate and extensive form of divination. Known as tasseography, this is a well-loved and old technique of divination by reading the shapes and patterns of tea leaves in the bottom of a tea cup. You will need a traditional teacup -- the less of an angle on the sides, the better. In other words: you do not want a coffee mug, but instead a cup with plenty of surface for the leaves to remain on the sides as well as the bottom of the cup.

Begin by placing a teaspoon of loose leaf tea in the cup and pour water on it. While sipping the tea, either discuss your question (if you are reading for someone else), or contemplate your question (if you are reading for yourself). One the tea is nearly gone, take the cup in your left hand and slowly turn it around three times in a counterclockwise direction. Then, place a napkin on the top of the cup and turn the cup upside down on the napkin. Keep the handle towards you, turn the cup over and begin reading the shapes inside of the cup.

Interpretations for shapes in the tea cup can be found in a variety of books and through a quick online search. However, you may find

that certain shapes symbolize something special to you that go beyond the traditional interpretations. Not to mention, the tea leaves can almost feel like an inkblot test: you may see one shape in the leaves, while someone sees something different. It takes time to feel comfortable reading tea leaves, so take time to write and reflect on what you see, thinking about what it could mean to you without turning to a list of ready-made messages. To just get started, here are some simple interpretations to keep in mind for tea leaf readings:

- Look for letters and numbers in the patterns and determine if they have any significance to the reading.
- Look for common shapes like squares, circles, arrows, triangles, and stars.
- Look for animals, people, or nature images (i.e. mountains, waves, trees).

Creating Your Own Divination

If you are so inspired, consider creating your own kitchen divination system. Perhaps you assign a special meaning to the first snack you pick from a handful of trail mix. Maybe the M&M signifies a positive answer, the nut signifies prosperity, and the raisin signifies a negative answer. Maybe when water boils over and spills onto the stove top that signifies an omen of some kind to you (or maybe it just indicates that you need to watch your pots more closely). Maybe you want to divine an omelet, combining the forces of oomancy and tiromancy to see what shapes you get as everything cooks in the pan. However you divine in the kitchen, discover methods that are not only fun but meaningful ways for receiving omens and fortunes.

LUGHNASADH CHAPTER NOTES

[1] Franklin, Anna and Paul Mason. *Lammas: Celebrating the Fruits of the First Harvest.* St. Paul, MN: Llelwellyn Publications, 2001. P. 99.

[2] Patterson, Rachel. *A Kitchen Witch's World of Magical Plants and Herbs.* Hants, UK: Moon Books, 2014.

CHAPTER EIGHT: MABON

OVERVIEW, MAGIC, ACTIVITIES, AND CORRESPONDENCES

At the Autumn Equinox we begin to feel the transition of nature into the darker half of the year. While the First Harvest at Lughnasadh feels like an outgoing celebration of games, fairs, and parties, the Second Harvest at the Autumn Equinox feels like a more reserved and mellow day. At this point we take a pause to rest, relax, and reflect on the bounty of the growing season. We enjoy the final weeks of comfortable outdoor weather. On the Autumn Equinox the day and night are equal in length, and the nights will grow longer until Yule. It is a time of giving thanks: we reflect on the abundance and growth of the spring and summer, contemplating what changes and opportunities can be mastered during the fall and winter. It is a holiday of balance, reflection, gratitude, and preparing to move indoors and inwards.

Pagan's Thanksgiving

Mabon is often referred to as the Pagan's Thanksgiving or the Witch's Thanksgiving, and for many it is a holiday of gratitude and feasting. Consider hosting a dinner for your friends, asking everyone to share a homemade dish, perhaps utilizing foods associated with

Mabon and in-season vegetables. At each place setting for pagan Thanksgiving have a blank thank you card labeled with the guest's name on it. During dinner discuss the successes you've had through the summer months. After dinner pass around the cards and ask everyone to write a personalized compliment, words of encouragement, or a special thank you in each of the cards. Consider having a bonfire and raising energy with a drum circle or sharing a ritual to offer thanks to nature and the elements for another growing season.

Mabon ap Modron

Mabon is a particularly new name for the Autumn Equinox which was created by Aidan Kelly around 1971. Mabon is a Welsh God of harvest whose name means "The Son of the Divine Mother." Mabon's legend is found in the *Mabinogion*'s "Tale of Culhwch and Olwen," which features supernatural and mystical symbolism, ancient Celtic deities, the brave hero Culhwch, and his first cousin King Arthur. Mabon's mother Modron, is an early mother goddess, and Mabon is known as her divine son. Mabon possibly be linked to Maponus or Apollo, the god of poetry and hunting. Maponos was mostly worshipped in Gaul and Northern England, especially near Hadrian's Wall. In *The Book of Celtic Magic*, Kristopher Hughes argues that offerings for Maponos near Hadrian's Wall suggest that he was a god who had attributes useful for those in the military.[1]

The most well-known story Mabon comes from the Mabinogion, where he is kidnapped soon after being born. The hero Culhwch and his cousin King Arthur go on a quest to find Mabon, being led by animals through the forest. They talk with a blackbird, who leads them to a stag. The stag sends them to find an owl, and the owl sends them off to find an eagle. The eagle then tells them to speak with a salmon. The salmon then leads them to the prison where Culhwch is being held captive. With the knowledge of the animals, Mabon is freed from his imprisonment.

This story may seem like madness to modern day readers, but it is filled with mystical symbolism that show Mabon's divine nature and the Otherworldly powers of animals the Celtic people held in high regard. John Matthews argues that the animals are "extensions of the Mabon's soul and also represent those of the animal kingdom who recognize the young god."[2] The argument has also been made that there is a link between Persephone and Mabon, both young deities who are abducted from their mothers. In response, their mothers mourn and the earth goes into a barren state. Even though I see similarities in this sense, the god and the goddess both have different outcomes. Persephone was abducted and force to wed (and bed) Hades, to whom she returned to every year. Mabon on the other hand, remained free, once Culhwch and King Arthur came to his rescue.

Balancing Reiki and Yoga

Before we transition into longer nights and shorter days, the Autumn Equinox is a valuable time to check in with yourself to restore physical and spiritual balance in your life. What does the word balance mean to you? What does it feel like to be in balance? What does it feel like to be out of balance? How do you restore balance? These are questions that may be easily answered with self-care and self-maintenance. Taking time to make yourself a priority is not selfish, but a valuable practice that can help you feel rested, aware, and healthy.

A simple Reiki exercise for self-healing and balance is known as the "Three Diamonds Meditation." To do this, lie on your back in a comfortable position. Place one hand on your forehead/3rd Eye Chakra and place your other hand on your heart/Heart Chakra. Hold this position for at least five minutes. Next move the hand that was on your forehead to your Earth Center/Sacral Chakra (just below the naval). Hold this position for at least five minutes. Finally, move the hand that was on your heart to your forehead.

There are also some easy yoga poses to try out for physical and spiritual balance. I recommend meeting with a certified yoga instructor to gain the best understanding of doing these poses correctly, as these are brief descriptions to consider. The Mountain Pose, or Tadasana, is a simple pose where you firmly plant your feet in the ground and stand up straight. The hands are held out by the hips, and sometimes then the palms are held together over the heart or stretched over the head. The Tree Pose, or Vriksasana, is another common pose that helps with balance and can be transitioned into after the Mountain Pose. This position is done by taking your foot and placing it on the inside of your thigh (or for modification at the inside of your ankle).

Sacred Spaces at the Autumnal Equinox

Sure, it may be a little cliché to drive around to gawk at foliage, but getting into the woods can be a peaceful and magical place to reflect on the changing of the seasons. Cool nights allow for incredible camping and bonfires, while day hikes allow to chance to see the transition of nature into autumn. The woods and apple orchards close to home (or to your heart) are perfect sacred spaces for visiting at this time of year. Oak and Apple groves were considered magickal and sacred spaces. Decorate your altar with apples and acorns at the Autumnal Equinox to access the magick and wisdom of the Otherworld and Avalon.

During the fall, acorns begin to drop from oak trees. The acorn is a powerful symbol of strength and wisdom. Carry an acorn for protection or use in charms to connect with sacred ancestral energy. According to Gerina Dunwich, there is a simple divination you can perform to predict the outcome of a romance. Take two acorns and put your initials on one, and your fiancé's initials on the other. Place the two acorns into a cauldron or bowl of water. If the acorns drift towards each other it is a sign that there is a positive outcome for a wedding/relationship. If the two acorns drift apart it is not a good sign that the relationship will make it to the wedding.

Psychic Enhancement for Divination Tools

Mabon is traditionally a time to work on psychic enhancement magic. This candle spell will help to enhance your psychic abilities and your divination tool's powers. You will need three purple candles, which you can anoint with a psychic oil (such as jasmine or sandalwood). You will need a loose incense blend for psychic abilities (the blend I use is equal parts Arabic gum, mugwort, benzoin resin, and cinnamon). Set up the purple candles in a triangle and put your divination tool in the middle of them. Light a charcoal briquette in a fire safe container, and then light the candles. Put your hands over your divination tool – visualize indigo or violet light coming from your hands and being saturated into your divination tool. Recite the following three times: "Claircognizance, clairvoyance, clairaudience: I know, I see, and I hear with psychic clarity. Enchanted divination in this tool is gained: wisdom, guidance, and truth are obtained." Put some of the incense on the charcoal, and run your divination tool through its smoke three times.

Witchcraft and Magic with Late Season Wildflowers

Even though the wildflower season is winding down, there are still many flowers growing in nature that can be incorporated into Mabon/Autumn Equinox magic.

- Aster: Also known as Michaelmas Daisy or Starwort. There are many varieties that come in blue, purple, pink, and white. Use aster for love magic. Share a bouquet of aster with someone you love, or place it on your altar at the Autumn Equinox to draw love energies into your life.
- Goldenrod: Goldenrod can be used for prosperity and divination magic. Place goldenrod in a vase on your Autumn Equinox altar to draw prosperity into your life, or use dried flowers in a prosperity incense. The plant was said to be used as a dowsing rod that would point to treasure.
- Evening Primrose: The yellow evening primrose grows most of summer and into early fall and is also known as night willowherb, night candle, and tree primrose. Evening Primrose is used for love magic, faerie magic, and moon rituals.
- Jewelweed: Another late summer and fall flower, this pretty orange flower is also known as orange jewelweed, spotted touch-me-not, and orange balsam. The juice from the stem would be used by Native Americans as a remedy for poison ivy. Jewelweed is associated with the planet Venus. Because of its bright orange color, use jewelweed to assist in love communication, helping you discover what you desire, and awakening creative interests.
- Thistle: Also known as Blessed Thistle, or Lady's Thistle, this common wildflower is used for protection, strength, and energy. Keep thistle nearby to drive away evil and protect you from mischievous faeries. According to Scott Cunningham you can place thistle in boiling water to communicate with spirits. Remove the water from the heat and listen for spirits to speak to you as the steam rises. He also suggests that if men carry thistle they will become better lovers. At the Autumn Equinox (carefully) gather thistle to encourage strength and the continuation of projects as the harvest season comes to a close.

Journaling at the Autumn Equinox

This time of year we begin to reflect on what has grown in our lives. We can take stock of what we have and give thanks for the abundance in our lives. Additionally, we look ahead to the darker season: nights now grow longer and we move indoors and inwards. Use the month of September to reflect on nature's transitions as well as your own.

- What has blossomed in your life over the past year?
- What aspects of yourself have grown? What have you developed?
- How do you show gratitude?
- When can you change "I'm sorry" to "Thank you"?
- When in your life do you feel you had to descend into the Underworld and explore your shadow side?
- How do you respond physically to autumn weather?
- How do you respond psychically to autumn weather?

Correspondences
- Names: Second Harvest, Mabon, Wine Harvest, Feast of Avalon, Alban Efed, Winter Finding
- Date of Celebration: Autumnal Equinox (falls between September 19th and 23rd)
- Deities Honored: Bacchus, Demeter, Dionysus, Gaia, Inanna, Mabon, Modron, Persephone, Pomona, Thor
- Magical Focus: Abundance, intellectual strength, psychic enhancement, wand consecration
- Activities: Pagan Thanksgiving feast, wine making, yoga, meditation, reiki, hiking, visiting an apple orchard, cooking, creating a wand.
- Altar Decorations: Fall leaves and flowers, pine cones, seed pods, mum flowers, hazelnuts, acorns, apples, gourds, Indian corn, cornucopia, grapes, vines, antlers
- Food and Beverages: Apples, blackberries, bread, carrots, corn, cranberry, figs, grapes, nuts, onions, pears, plums, potato, smoked or roasted poultry, squash, tomato, turnip
- Plants, Herbs, Incense: Cinnamon, cloves, cypress, juniper, chives, sage, cedar, honeysuckle, marigold, rosemary, saffron, sage, thistle, yarrow, rue, sunflower, passionflower
- Crystals: Amber, citrine, tiger's eye, sapphire
- Colors: red, brown, bronze, orange, yellow

THE ISLE OF APPLES: EXPLORING AVALON AND ARTHURIAN LOCATIONS

Avalon is a magical place that is part of the legends of Arthurian legend. Some have linked it to the Celtic mythology of the Otherworld, were the immortal reside, magic persists, and only joy and peace are present. The name itself is linked to the words "Place of Apples." It is believed that this is the place where Morgan le Fay and Merlin learned their crafts, and it is where Arthur was taken after his final battle. After being mortally wounded by Mordred, Morgan le Fay and Priestess of the Isle took him to Avalon where they could heal him; and there he waits, until he is ready to return again as king. Many have speculated an actual location for Avalon, most believing it could either be Glastonbury, England or Bardsey Island, off the coast of Wales. Some people also believe the gateway to Avalon resides at locations of great spiritual importance, such as Faerie Mounds and stone circles. Some have described visiting Avalon in dreams and meditation, while others have connected to its powers through past life regressions and Shamanic experiences. In this section we are going to explore some of the speculated locations linked to Avalon, locations in Britain connected to Arthurian legend, and then conclude with a fun personality quiz and a mediation.

Bardsey Island

This remote island bears the influence of Celtic, Norse, and Christian life. The Welsh name for the island is "Ynys Enlli," meaning "island of great current," or "island of the tides." Celts visited the island to pray and often to die on this most western isle as they followed the setting sun. This became a very important religious center and a holy burial place. In the fifth century it was a refuge for persecuted Christians and monks. Many pilgrims remained on the island for their entire lives. After so many were buried there, Barsey became known as "the Isle of Twenty Thousand Saints." It was believed that three pilgrimages to Bardsey Island was equal to one pilgrimage to Rome.

Avalon means "Place of Apples," and we see that apple orchards were once prevalent on the island. Monks tended to an apple orchard on Bardsey over 1000 years ago. Only one tree survives now, and experts believe this strain of apple is unique only to Bardsey. This tree grows on the side of one of the island's few houses, Plas Bach. Uniquely, the tree is free of disease, which is a very rare occurrence in the climate of northern Wales. Today, between 8 and 13 people live on the island, including a farmer, a warden, and bird watchers.

Glastonbury Tor and Chalice Well, Glastonbury, England

Glastonbury Tor is located atop the 518 foot high Glastonbury Hill, which is speculated by some to have been the specific location of the Isle of Avalon. Archaeologists have suggested that at one time, floods from the marshes in the surrounding lands of Glastonbury would have risen around the hill, giving it the appearance of an island in the mist. At the top of the hill are the remains of a Norman stronghold-turned-monastery. According to Welsh legend, Gwyn, lord of the Underworld, used this tor as the entranceway to his otherworldly kingdom. It's also been told that Glastonbury Tor was the stronghold for Melwas, the king of the Summer Country who abducted Guinevere. Many enjoy the hike up the hill, and see it as a shamanic experience in itself due the spiral path towards the summit. The man-cut terraces on the climb up give the shape of rings. Many have wondered why these rings have been cut into the mountain; some speculate that it was meant to be a three dimensional labyrinth, a cavalry mount, or even the steps to a pyramid.

Chalice Well contains the remnants of a natural spring that ran between Glastonbury Hill and Chalice Hill. In *Le Morte D'Arthur*, Lancelot retires to a valley between the hills of Glastonbury, thus suggesting the location of the Chalice Well. Many legends center around the well, but the most famous is the one about Joseph of Arimathea hiding the Holy Grail within the well. The well itself is in a peaceful garden, and visitors are welcome to collect water from the well if they wish. The red, iron rich water, is said to have miraculous healing powers, by both Pagans and Christians. The lid of the well depicts the Bleeding Lance, the holy lance which pierced Christ, and the connection of the Visible and Invisible worlds. Others say that the symbolism is in the shape of Excalibur and Vesica Pisces. The shape of the vesica pisces is derived from the intersection of two circles, the Pythagorean "measure of the fish" that was a mystical symbol of the intersection of the world of the divine with the world of matter and the beginning of creation. As such, it is also a doorway or portal between worlds, and symbolizes the intersection between the heavens and the material plane.

Stonehenge

Located on Salisbury Plain, Stonehenge is the most popular and well known stone circle. According to Geoffrey of Monmouth, Merlin transported the stones from Ireland (by floating them) and assembled them into Stonehenge as a monument for the Kings of Britain. These are supposedly lines of natural energy, that seem to link ancient monuments, megaliths, hill mounds, hill forts, castles, churches, water, crossroads and standing stones. It is theorized that ley lines are spirit pathways, paths for funeral processions, astronomical alignments, or earth's natural magnetic fields. They tend to be places of significant spiritual importance. Stonehenge is on a ley line that forms a right triangle with Avebury Stone Circle and Glastonbury. So what was Stonehenge used for? Some say ritual, some say sacrifice, some see it as an astronomical observatory. The most current postulation is that it was a place of burial for royalty.

South Cadbury Hill

Certainly not a tourist attraction, nor a place where much meets the eye, South Cadbury Hill is a place where visitors must connect with an invisible yet very present Otherworldly Britain: one of Camelot, faery tales and hidden secrets from ancient civilizations. From the top of the hill you can see Glastonbury Tor.

South Cadbury Hill dates back to 3500 BCE. Bracelets, rings, and pottery have been excavated from the site, suggesting that the location may have had religious significance. Archaeological evidence also suggests that during the period of Arthur, 400 AD to 600 AD, this was a place of significant political importance. Timber and cobblestone were used to build up the fort. The people who occupied this fort used the Celtic methods of masonry, as opposed to the Roman. So we have to question: did a patriotic chieftain of Britain reside here? Did a Celtic political leader reside here? No one is sure, but many have speculated that this is the location of Camelot.

Those who visit, yes even muggles, say that there is a heightened energy at the site. Some envision that within the surrounding forests are spirits of knights riding on horseback or that one could witness faeries sing as etheric balls of light playfully float through the air. Some say this occurs every June 20th, when a door opens every seven years within the hills, so Arthur and his company can leave Camelot to feed their horses. Coincidentally, the date of June 20th is synonymous with Midsummer, a time when legends say that the veil between our world and the world of fairies is said to be open.

Tintagel, Cornwall

In Tintagel you will find the ruins of Tintagel Castle, which according to Arthurian tales is the scene where Merlin used sorcery and shapeshifting and King Arthur was born. During the time of Roman occupation in Britain, Tintagel was most likely a Celtic Chieftain stronghold turned monastery, and was probably a place which served as a trading post between Ireland, Brittany, and Wales. It is also believed people here were allowed to hold onto their Celtic lifestyles. What remains on the site now are the ruins of a Norman castle, which are a stunning site indeed. Not far from the ruins is Merlin's

Cave, another supposed residence of Merlin's while Arthur was at Tintagel.

Northumberland National Park and Hadrian's Wall

The old wall once believed to have kept the wild Picts out of civilized Roman society, Hadrian's Wall is Britain's longest monument and spans the length of more than 70 miles across the northern regions of England. Not only is it a spectacular sight, it also offers a glimpse into the masterful building skills of the Roman Empire, which ruled the land of Britain over 2000 years ago. North of Hadrian's wall lies the great span of Northumberland National Park, once land to Celtic nations, and now a place of preserved nature and archaeological beauty. In the northern region of Northumberland National Park lies another hillfort, similar to the fort in South Cadbury, known as Yeavering Bell. Here, Anglo Saxons and kings of Northumbria presided, and prior to that, Neolithic people had a temple, and Bronze Age communities buried their dead here. Although described as having a "stark" landscape, one has to again extend imagination and see that the earth holds many stories and mysteries in this old land. It is speculated this area may have been where the Green Knight from *Sir Gawain and the Green Knight* resided. Also dotting the Northumbrian landscape are various rock carvings dating from Neolithic and Early Bronze Age. The common motif for the carvings is spiral in design, showing a reverence for the cyclical nature of life in regions that exhibit extraordinary beauty in nature.

Orkney Islands, Scotland

The archipelago of Orkney in the North Sea, Scotland is so far north, you'll feel like you've left Europe altogether. Since it is so far away, one would think that the only people who visit would be academic scholars, Viking aficionados, and pagan nomads who may potentially have gotten on the wrong ferry. But in reality, the Orkney Islands are a very popular tourist location, and although a bit of a trek from London or Edinburgh, the sites and activities available there are distinctive only to the Orkney Islands. A place for the adventurous, a place for the nomad and the hermit alike, a place for those who have a passion for Viking history and monolithic stone circles, iron age hill mounds and stunning coastal towns, the Orkney Islands is a true treasure of the north.

I have always found that the Orkney Islands is a place that truly satisfies the desire and dream for an actual Avalonian location. The journey alone could have been considered a shamanic trial for ancient peoples, who would have had to travel to it by boat as well as deal with difficult weather in the northern regions of Scotland. Additionally, the immense number of sacred sites on the islands, combined with the fact that both ancient Celts and Scandinavians resided here, truly exhibit the culmination of a mystical and magical past. Kirkland is the central city in Orkney, and from there, four fascinating ancient monuments can easily be reached: Maeshowe, Skara Brae, Ring of Brodgar, and the Standing Stones of Stenness.

Maeshowe has been called the Egypt of the north and an architectural achievement of prehistoric peoples in Scotland. It is a chambered cairn that is dated to approximately 2700 BCE, and appears as a large, grassy mound. No bodies were found in here, but Vikings did indeed break into Maeshowe 3000 years after its creation, leaving behind so much graffiti on the walls that it is the largest collection of runic inscriptions outside of Scandinavia. For the visitor with the ability to interpret the runes, you may blush at the language that these Vikings left behind, or get a good chuckle depending on your sense of humor. The Ring of Brodgar is the third largest stone circle in the British Isles. Coincidentally (or maybe not so coincidentally), the Brodgar Ring is the same exact size as Avebury's two inner rings. Although only 24 stones of the original 60 remain, the Ring of Brodgar exhibits cryptic runic inscriptions known as twig runes, which still are up to interpretation by scholars. Legend has it that the Ring of Brodgar was known as the "Temple of the Sun," while the Standing Stones of Stenness were known as the "Temple of the Moon."

Skara Brae is a large, stone-built Neolithic settlement, which was occupied between 3180 BCE and 2500 BCE. Due to its proximity to the ocean, time covered it with coastal sand, leaving the eight dwellings of Skara Brae as some of the best preserved relics of a faraway past. Archaeological finds include pottery, bone pins, and even fungi which were most likely used for medicine. Some have even reported seeing ghostly balls of light, or will o'wisps appear at Skara Brae.

Gwynedd Region and the Snowdonian Mountains

Gwynedd is the northwest region of Wales and encompasses a majority of the Snowdonian Mountains as well as touches the Irish Sea. Gwynned is a massive area to cover, but is worthy of time and exploration, as the Snowdonian Mountain Range is a beautiful landscape where it's easy to get lost in fantastical thoughts. Hillfort Dinas Emrys and Lake Llyn Dinas are located near the town of Beddgelert, and here we find a scene connected with Arthurian Legend. In Geoffrey of Monmouth's *History of the Kings of Britain*, King Vortigern summons Merlin to his castle at Dinas Emrys, where two sleeping dragons slept underneath the fortification. Archaeological evidence does show that the fort dates back to about 400 AD. For those seeking inspiration, you can travel south of Snowdon to Cader Idris, another mountain peak in the Snowdonian Mountains. In past traditions, bards would sleep at Cader Idris, hoping to become inspired by it. And, today, it is believed that anyone who sleeps on the slopes of Cader Idris alone will wake up either a poet or a madman. It's a risk I'm willing to take, as this place is also said to be the residence of faeries.

Quiz: Which Arthurian Place Should You Visit?

1. What is your number one priority in life?
   a. Taking care of those you love through protection and loyalty.
   b. Being one with nature and understanding its cycles.
   c. Being spiritually attuned to gain success and prosper.
   d. To counsel others through alchemy, knowledge, and psychic premonitions.
   e. To always challenge yourself at succeeding at what you're passionate about.

2. How would you spend an ideal vacation?
   a. Learning about the history and lore of the sea.
   b. Navigating different forest trails to find old archeological sites.
   c. Going to a place where I can find spiritual relaxation.
   d. Visiting a world-famous place with mysteries and legend.
   e. Hiking, camping, and seeing the world from great heights.

3. Your favorite fragrance:
> a. The ocean water
> b. Patchouli or Vetivert
> c. Apples
> d. Sandalwood
> e. Lavender

4. Your ideal environment is:
> a. By the shore
> b. The forest
> c. On an island
> d. In a field with geometric ley lines
> e. In the mountains

5. Who is your favorite Arthurian Character?
> a. King Arthur
> b. The Green Knight
> c. Lady of the Lake
> d. Merlin
> e. Any of the dragons, faeries, or giants

6. What is your favorite theme in Arthurian Legend?
> a. Heroes
> b. Quests
> c. Magic
> d. Prophecy
> e. Battles

7. What is your favorite type of spiritual work?
> a. Shapeshifting
> b. Green witchcraft
> c. Spellwork
> d. Divination
> e. Meditation and Astral Projection

8. What is most important to you in your relationships with your friends?
> a. Being loyal and helping those I love.
> b. Helping others understand themselves on a deeper level.

c. Offering your friends magickal and spiritual solutions.

d. Giving advice and counsel to your friends.

e. Sticking up for your friends and fighting for what is right.

9. What would be the perfect home for you?

a. A beautiful, fortified, home on the waterfront.

b. An otherworldly home with a strong connection to nature.

c. A sanctuary with plenty of agriculture.

d. A highly secluded but spiritually and supernaturally charged location.

e. A place where they say the land is inhabited by faeries and dragons.

If you pick mostly A's: Tintagel: You are a beach baby, someone who longs to feel the comfort of the ocean breeze. Family heritage is important to you and you feel a strong connection to ancestral spirits. You are loyal to your family and friends.

If you pick mostly B's: Northumbria: You love to be in the forest, where you feel at peace with nature. You sense that there is an Otherworldly element in the woods and long to deepen your connection with it.

If you pick mostly C's: Bardsey Island/Glastonbury: You are devoted to better understanding yourself and others through spirituality and spiritual practices. You are always looking for opportunities to learn more about philosophy and religion.

If you pick mostly D's: Stonehenge: You are fascinated by the ancient magic of mythology and folklore. You believe that there are omens and signs all around us, guiding us to the most benevolent outcome. The wisdom you share with others helps them heal and move along their paths of spiritual evolution.

If you pick mostly E's: Dinas Emrys/Snowdonian Mountains: You are ambitious and curious about seeing things from different perspectives. You are willing to take on a challenge if you believe it will make you a better person.

Meditation: A Journey to Avalon

Find a path in your favorite place in nature, or make one up. This path is going to lead you to a shore of an ocean or an enormous lake. Look out and observe the vastness of the body of water. Is it day or night? Warm or cold? Sunny or grey?

At the shore, you will find a beautiful boat waiting to bring you to Avalon. This boat is beautifully carved and adorned with jewels. What do you like about this boat? There is a guide in the boat, there to assist you. Thank him for your help, as he rows the boat to Avalon.

You are going across the body of water. The water is calm, and all is calm around you. What sounds do you hear? Perhaps the lapping of the water against the boat or birds flying above. There is a very thick mist around you. This mist is so thick and heavy; you can't see much in front of you. You can feel the moisture of the mist on your skin. Your boat travels onwards, and you begin to see signs of land. You see lights the shore. You smell the inviting fragrance of apples. You are approaching the mystical isle of Avalon.

Your boat reaches the shore. Bid your farewell to the guide in the boat, and make your way to land.

You are now on the Isle of Avalon. What do you notice about your surroundings? What is the weather like? Observe the layout of the island, and remember how it looks to you, how it sounds, how it smells, how it feels. How do you feel on the island? Do you feel you have magical gifts here that you may not have anywhere else?

Walk along the shore until you find a small dirt path leading you deep into the island. This path leads you upwards, towards a summit in the center of the island. Continue up this hill towards the summit. Keep climbing the path. Observe your surroundings. Is the forest thick around you, or do you see green fields? Observe all the greens of nature and the smell of apples, perhaps even a hint of sage or sandalwood incense burning. What animals do you hear in the forest? What else do you notice as you go up this path?

You finally reach the summit point. What does it look like? Are there trees? Do you see a cave, or perhaps a bonfire? Or, perhaps you are in front of a glorious stone circle? Whatever you see, you know this is one of the most beautiful and magical locations you have ever seen. You feel at complete peace here.

Look around and see if anyone is at the summit with you. If don't see anyone, that is okay as well. If you wish to meet with someone, call out, asking for someone to come and visit with you.

If you find that you are in the presence of someone else, introduce yourself warmly. Let them know that you are a follower of the Old Religion, and you come in peace to gain knowledge and show reverence for the Old Religion. If you have questions about Avalon, or need guidance about your own life, feel free to ask, knowing that you may gain some wisdom from this interaction. Ask for advice on how to better your life.

Or, perhaps you find that you want to convene with nature on your own, or in the presence of animals. Who visits you? What magical abilities do you find you are most successful with in this sacred space?

It is now time to bid your new friend farewell. Thank them very much for speaking with you. Ask them if it would be okay to visit them again. Thank them and say goodbye. Or, if you were alone, it is now time to thank the land for allowing you the opportunity for spiritual pilgrimage. Know that you can always visit this place for serenity, inspiration, and magic.

Go swiftly back down the path. Walk along the shore to the boat, and get onto the boat again. Feel the mist as you ride along the water. Watch the isle of Avalon as it falls further and further into the mist. You've learned a lot on your journey here, and you feel at a place of great peace and joy.

Your boat lands to the shore where you started, and you are back at the path where you began the journey. You are happy to see your favorite place in nature again.

CRANBERRIES AND COOL WEATHER MAGIC

For many, cranberries become a part of the meal between Samhain and Yule. Prior to Samhain, fresh cranberries are harvested from northern bogs and available for many autumn dishes. At Thanksgiving, stuffing is sweetened with a heaping spoonful of delicious cranberry chutney. And at Yule, many enjoy the fragrant smell of cranberry cooking in dessert dishes or in its perfume smell by the hearth with cranberry-scented candles. The cranberry's deep red color is admirable, exotic, and comforting. It's unique tale of growth in bog and harvest in water, it's lavish mythical lore, and even its long list of health benefits make it a berry worthy of examining for magical qualities.

Cranberry Growth

Cranberries are one of only three berries native to North America (the other two being the blueberry and concord grape) . They grow on low-level vines and flourish in bogs (that is to say: they need acidic peat soil and fresh water to grow) . Cranberries are also a berry of the north, commonly growing in Massachusetts, New Jersey, Oregon, Washington, Wisconsin, and Canada. A smaller variety of the cranberry also grows in Scandinavia. Oftentimes when we see commercials on television with cranberry gardeners knee-high in cranberry-filled water, we assume that the cranberries actually grow in water. However, this is an image of a specific farming technique known as "water harvesting." In this process, the cranberry vine-filled bogs are flooded with water. Special farming equipment known as watering reels turn and stir the water in the flooded bogs, loosening the berries from the vine. Because the cranberries contain pockets of air inside them, they float to the surface, which then makes it easy to corral and harvest. Cranberries can also be harvested the old fashion way. "Dry harvesting" is the simple method of plucking the berry from the dry vines during the fall.

The Cranberry in History, Lore and Mythology

The bog is the home of the cranberry, but was also the sacrificial stomping ground of ancient societies in Northern Europe. Consider all of the archeological findings that have been discovered in bogs in Denmark, Scotland, England, Sweden, and Northern Germany: daggers, swords, shields, spears, javelins, drinking vessels, sickles, y-shaped dowsing rods, and jewelry have all be recovered from bogs. Also recovered from a bog was the famous Gundestrup Cauldron, a silver cauldron of Celtic origin, which had mythological narratives associated with it. Even more shockingly, excellently preserved human bodies, which appear to have been victims of sacrifice, have been discovered in bogs. It appears that to ancient society, the watery bog was a place of significant importance, where sacrifices and treasures were willingly deposited.

Some researchers and academics have suggested that the bog deposits were offerings for protection, or rituals to bring fertility to the land and well-being to the land's inhabitants. One cannot avoid the idea of a spooky, dank bog on a cold, dark night, either. Perhaps it is the fact that the unstable, marshy territory could lead to hazardous falls and injuries. Legend has it that the murky, watery parts of a bog were bottomless, so to step in one meant imminent doom. Hans Christian Andersen shared many stories of the bog, most of which involved witches, elves, and fairies. And in English and Welsh folklore, Will-o-the-wisps are said to be glowing lights that would float above the bog. Some believed that they were benevolent fairy or nature spirits that acted as guides to lost travelers; on the other hand, some saw the Will-'o-the-Wisps as ill spirited fairies, dark elves, or spirits connected to the devil.

It's also interesting to note that the cranberry has a special place in the hearts of the Finnish and students and admirers of ancient Lapland mythology. *The Kalevala*, epic legend of Finland and reputed inspiration for J.R.R. Tolkien's *Lord of the Rings*, is a compiled collection of Finnish oral stories that have been sung by Lapland bards for centuries. In the final passage, or Rune, of *The Kalevala*, we hear of the tale of a virgin Goddess' encounter with the cranberry. Described as a beautiful maiden, Marjatta is a Goddess who is chaste, yet connected with her Northland home. While roaming the forests, she hears the singing of the cranberry, which begs her to eat him. Because of her maidenhood, she couldn't pluck the berry, but instead used a charm to have the berry rise from the vine and into her mouth. After she ate the berry, she was impregnated. When her family found out of her pregnancy, they did not believe her story of the cranberry and they shunned her. Similar to the story of Christ's birth, Marjatta gave birth to her son in a stable in a forest. The heroic god of *The Kalevala*, Väinämöinen, is summoned to decide the destiny of the baby. When it is told that the child's father is a cranberry, Väinämöinen sentences the baby to banishment in the forest and seals his death. However, when the baby pleads for his life by pointing out Väinämöinen's unfair judgement, he is saved. Väinämöinen also recognizes that the son of the cranberry would grow to be his successor: a royal king and mighty ruler.

Some of the American history and lore of cranberries is fascinating as well. Native Americans were very familiar with the cranberry, and used it frequently as food, medicine, and dye. They used the berry to flavor meats, in a poultice to heal wounds and lower inflammation, and as a dye to make deep burgundy rugs. When Dutch and German settlers came to America, they named the berry "Crane Berry." This name was inspired by the berry's pink spring blossoms, which were said to resemble the head and bill of a Sandhill Crane.

The Cranberry's Astounding Health Benefits

There are so many health benefits of cranberries that after seeing how they can help your general health, you may consider keeping cranberry juice, tea, or supplements in stock in your kitchen. Cranberries are very effective in the healing and relief of urinary tract infections. Cranberries are chock-full of antioxidants, which could mean that cranberries could have anti-aging qualities. The juice is said to prevent peptic ulcers, while eating the berry is said to cut back dental plaque. Recent research has suggested that cranberries can reduce the development of kidney stones and the risk of cancer and heart disease. Cranberries contain no cholesterol, trace amounts of fat, and minimal sodium. They have a hearty amount of Vitamin C and fiber, and historically were taken to sea by mariners who wished to fight scurvy.

Cranberry Recipes

There are countless recipes for cranberries available. If you have not indulged in the tart, yet sweet taste of cranberries, autumn and winter are the seasons to incorporate them into your meals, as they will usually be in stock between September and December. Cranberries can be frozen, so they can last in the freezer for a long period of time. And, they are a "Prepper" and "Homesteader" friendly food, as they can be purchased canned, or be made into a preserve. Keep in mind as well: cranberries were used as a form of barter amongst Native American tribes!

Cranberry's Magickal Components

Oftentimes, the cranberry's beautiful red color has associated it with the planet Mars, and as a result, its magical correspondences are similar to that of Mars. Because of this, cranberry can be used for protection, positive energy, courage, passion, determination, goals, and action. Consider having Cranberry Sauce as part of a protective meal, or drinking cranberry juice or tea while doing magic for anything associated with Mars.

If color were considered as a way of marking the cranberry's magical associations, it would be foolish to not highlight the deep, sensual and erotic red color as corresponding to love and lust magic. If you are cooking a meal for a loved one, consider incorporating cranberry into the meal. There is actually cranberry wine available, which fermenters of homemade wines and meads would find easy to brew.[3]

In *Magick Potions: How to Prepare and Use Homemade Incense, Oils, Aphrodisiacs and Much More*, Gerina Dunwich supplies a recipe for "Lovers' Meditation Blend."[4] In the context of her book, she suggests using this while working with the Lovers Tarot Card. You may also want to sip this tea while performing love magic. Simply add two teaspoons cherry juice to 1-cup hot cranberry tea. Stir it with a cinnamon stick clockwise. There is something incredibly comforting and warming about Cranberry, so to show your love and appreciation for your family and friends, consider adding Cranberry sauce or chutney to a dinner. It will bring a feeling of peace, comfort, warmth, good health, and love to those who enjoy it.

The Tale of Marjatta reminds us of the nutritional value of the cranberry- so fertile and powerful is the cranberry, that it is the vehicle for immaculate conception. Since it is tied to immaculate conception, and the birth of a child who will replace the old King, it can be linked to rejuvenation, reincarnation, and the themes of Yule and Christmas. Cranberry also has clear links to fertility magic in this context. Spell work aside, the nutritional benefits of the cranberry are worthy enough to be incorporated into a routine diet, as it will aid in overall health and well-being.

Finally, it is important to not forget the magic of the bog, the motherland of cranberry. Here, we see cranberry's tie to the supernatural, mystical, and ancient. In a place where humans and precious objects were sacrificed, there was much value put on the mystical powers of the bog. It is a place where the protection of people and armies, the fertility of land and nature, and the well-being of those who visit it, could be determined and sought after through ritual and sacrifice. Perhaps you will include a bowl of cranberries next to your pomegranate on your Samhain altar to show thanks to the supernatural powers of the bog. Or simply, while cooking cranberries during the colder season or enjoying its fragrance in oil or a candle, you can reflect on the mystical, protective, and fertile powers of the deep red berry.

DIVINATION HIGHLIGHT: THE OGHAM

The Ogham has a complex and long history, one that has been researched and reinterpreted by modern-day Druids, witches, academics, historians, and mythologists. The origin of the Ogham is unknown, though there are various theories about its origins. One of the theories is that the Ogham was created, much like the Nordic runes, as a method of writing after coming in contact with Latin.

There are about 370 stone inscriptions that show the Ogham, and it appears they were in use between 300 and 600 CE. None of these are magical in nature and tend to be place markers for locations in Ireland, Scotland, Wales, the Isle of Man, and England. Inscriptions were usually in Old Irish, Old Welsh, and Latin, often on stone or wood. Much of our knowledge about the Ogham comes from a book that was compiled in 1391 called *The Book of Ballymote*, though its contents is a compilation of documents that date back to 9th century.

According to Sandra Kynes in *Whispers from the Woods*, the Ogham could have been ways to pass along valuable information: "Rather than being an alphabet that was written and read like Latin and Greek, the cryptic characters of the Ogham were abstract symbols – "keys" to a wealth of information. If you have tried using the Ogham, you will have found that the letters are not practical for writing more than simple instructions."[5] Some have even suggested that the simple lines of the Ogham alphabet are pictorial representations of a sign language.

The Ogham Alphabet

The Ogham alphabet originally had twenty characters with an additional five characters added later. The original twenty characters are simple lines while the five added characters were more complex to accommodate Greek and Latin letters. The original twenty characters are called *feda*, the additional five letters are called *forfeda*. The characters are divided into groups of five, each called *aicme*. Ogham are written down a middle or stem line called a *druim*. When written horizontally the Ogham is read from left to write. When written vertically, the Ogham is read from bottom to top. Please keep in mind when reviewing the meanings of the Ogham that there are variations on which trees some practitioners associate with certain feda.

While there may always be a debate on the Ogham's origin and a continued reevaluation of their uses, modern-day users and students of the Ogham revere them for their symbolic wisdom. The trees they represent, and the Celtic mythology and Druidic history they are a part of, make them a valuable tool for witches, Druids, and practitioners of divination. Nigel Pennick in *Magical Alphabets* offers the following wisdom for modern explorers of the Ogham: "We should not fall into the trap of imagining that the older a system is, then the more 'pure' it must be…Although we study the past, we should remember that it is the repository of errors as well as truths, and enlightened people of the present day can make a contribution to the understanding of divination through alphabets as well as many a practitioner of former times."[6]

How to use Ogham in Divination

Historically there are not many accounts of Ogham being used as divination. However, they have been incorporated into modern studies as a means of examining a situation. Ogham is not a simple or straightforward form of divination; instead, it offers insight, messages, and wisdom through the knowledge and myths woven into the trees and symbols connected to the various *feda*. The common method of using Ogham as divination is to use small sticks with the characters carved into the sticks. There are also cards with the Ogham on them as well. Some people only use the original twenty feda, while others like to incorporate the added five forfeda as well.

An easy way to begin working with Ogham as divination is to pull one stick from a bag and study its divination and symbolism. Become familiar with the tree, journaling and take notes about how it has been used in history and stories. In *Celtic Tree Magic*, Danu Forest suggests pulling three sticks for a reading. The first stick, in the bottom position, represents the lower world and the roots of your situation. The second stick, in the middle position, represents the middle world and all circumstances that surround the present situation. The third stick, in the top position, represents the upper world and your connection to divinity and the most benevolent outcome of a situation.

Meaning of each of the Ogham
Aicme Beith:

B – Beith – Birch: Beginnings, release, change. Sacred to Mother Goddess and a tree that shows the first signs of spring. Time to clear away old to make way for new. Generally a sign of good fortune.

L – Luis – Rowan: Insight, dedication, courage, protection. A need to create psychic boundaries around oneself. Overcoming difficulties with imaginative solutions. Needing to stay grounded and practice healing.

F – Fearn – Alder: Foundation and evolving spirit. Move forward with confidence to face challenges. Defend yourself in mind, body, and spirit. Consider how music and poetry play a role in your life.

S – Saille – Willow: Intuition, harmony, inspiration, flexibility, knowledge, relationships. Gently flowing events. Moon magic. Pay attention to dreams and messages from the Otherworld. Practice compassion and listen to your intuition.

N – Nuin – Ash: Transitions, strength, creativity, connection. A time when focus and determination are needed. Take action when you are feeling spiritually inspired.

Aicme Hauath:

H – Huath – Hawthorn: Challenge, hope, healing. A need for strength, facing a test of some kind. Challenges that make you feel stronger and transformed. Self-sacrifice and protection.

D – Duir – Oak: Strength, confidence, fate. Answers will be received by going inwards. Growth and opportunities of all kinds. Practicing mindfulness to be in the present moment.

T – Tinne – Holly: Hearth and home, energy, courage. A need for balance and unity. This may be a time of tests.

C – Coll – Hazel: Wisdom, knowledge of secrets, creativity. Discovery of information and divine inspiration.

Q – Quert – Apple: Love, faithfulness, happiness, rebirth. Being kind to yourself and others to feel a sense of wholeness. Things coming to fruition.

Aicme Mauin:

M – Muin – Blackberry or Vine: Inward journey, learning lessons, harvest. The completion of plans. Bounty, yearning to achieve goals and understand the cycle of planning, growing, and harvesting.

G – Gort – Ivy: Growth, development, confronting the mystical. Changes are necessary for growth and transformation. Seeking out a support system. Pay attention for red flags and warnings.

 **Ng – Ngetal – Reed or Fern**: Healing, preservation, gathering, adaptation, written communication. A need for independence, being resourceful, and thinking outside of the box. Further work needed.

 **St – Straif – Blackthorn**: Authority, control, magical power, initiation. A sudden change. Liberation and rebirth.

 **R – Ruis – Elder**: Maturity, self-examination, awareness, transition. A need for sacrifice and facing your shadow side. Corrections of mistakes and missteps.

Aicme Ailm:

A – Ailm – Elm or Scots Pine: Rising above, regeneration, healing. A time of peace and pause to gain perspective and contemplate next steps.

O – Onn – Gorse: Hope, fertility. Resurgence of new ideas and inspiration. A bright time of pride and power. Increase in material possessions.

U – Ur – Heather: Passion, generosity, good luck. Reconnecting with loved ones. A time to trust spirit and the natural flow of the universe.

E – Edadh – Aspen or White Poplar: Communication, success, courage, animation. Connect with others and get the ball rolling. Spiritual success, need to remain humble.

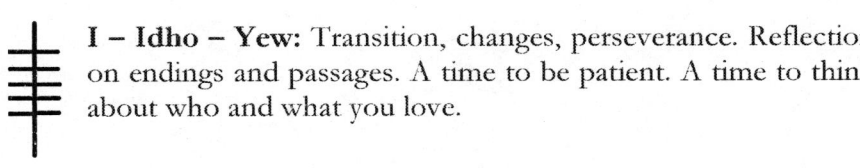

I – Idho – Yew: Transition, changes, perseverance. Reflection on endings and passages. A time to be patient. A time to think about who and what you love.

Aicme Eabhadh/ The Forfeda:

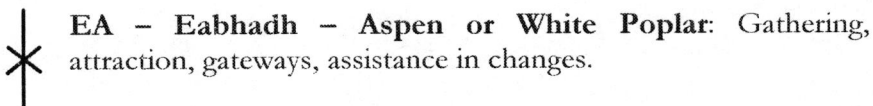

EA – Eabhadh – Aspen or White Poplar: Gathering, attraction, gateways, assistance in changes.

OI – Oir – Spindle tree: Creativity, inspiration, abundant resources.

UI – Uinllean – Honeysuckle: Manifestation, magic, resistance. Learning unconditional love as a means of healing.

IO – Ifin – Gooseberry: Clarity, psychism, ancestral wisdom, visions.

AE – Phagos – Witch hazel: Cleansing, purification, crossing over.

MABON CHAPTER NOTES

[1] Hughes, Christopher. *The Book of Celtic Magic: Transformative Teachings from the Cauldron of Awen.* Llewellyn Publications: Woodbury, MN, 2014. P. 72.

[2] Matthews, John. *The Winter Solstice: The Sacred Traditions of Christmas.* Wheaton, IL: The Theosophical Publishing House, 2003. P. 57.

[3] "How to Make Cranberry Wine" http://www.ehow.com/how_2123157_make-cranberry-wine.html

[4] Dunwich, Gerina. Magick Potions: *How to Prepare and Use Homemade Incense, Oils, Aphrodisiacs and Much More.* New York: Citadel Press, 1998.

[5] Kynes, Sandra. *Whispers from the Woods: The Lore and Magic of Trees.* Woodbury, MN: Llewellyn Publications, 2006. P. 43.

[6] Pennick, Nigel. *Magical Alphabets.* Boston: Weister Books, 1992. P. 127-128.

A special thank you to Lindsay Grey for her assistance on helping me find some information on the Ogham. You can connect with Lindsay Gray at www.lindsaygrey.com.

CONCLUSION

With each passing season we acquire more wisdom through experiences, friendships, celebrations, and study. I want to thank you for reading this book and being part of this magical journey with me. It has taken years of research, practice, reflection, and writing to compile the information shared in this book. I am happy to finally extend it to a greater audience. My hope is that you found information that has left you feeling inspired and excited for the holidays. Additionally, I hope you feel you have collected a little more mythological knowledge and spiritual wisdom. I hope you have the opportunity to reflect, bring more joy into your life, and celebrate the traditions of the seasons.

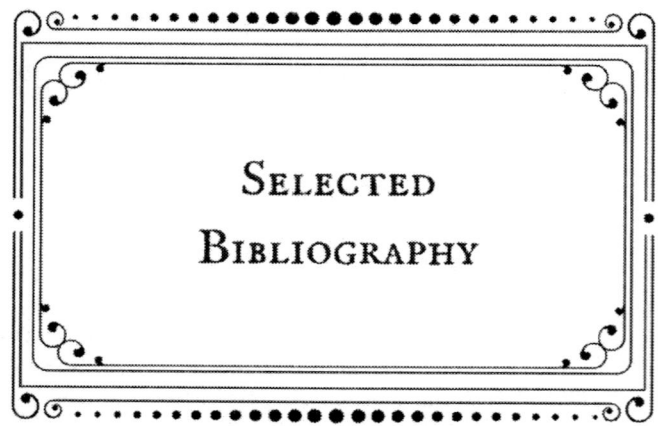

SELECTED
BIBLIOGRAPHY

Andrews, Ted. *Crystal Balls and Crystal Bowls: Tools for Ancient Scrying and Modern Seership*. St. Paul, MN: Llewellyn Publications, 2004.

Andrews, Ted. *How To See and Read the Aura*. Woodbury, MN: Llewellyn Publications, 2010.

Aniera, Crystal. *Herbal Riot*. Blog: http://www.herbalriot.tumblr.com.

Asala, Joanne. *Celtic Folklore Cooking*. St. Paul, MN: Llewellyn Publications, 2004.

Aswynn, Freya. *Northern Mysteries: Runes & Feminine Powers*. St. Paul, MN: Llewellyn Publications, 2002.

Bane, A.R. *The Secret of Mistletoe*. Self-Published, 2011.

Barrette, Elizabeth. "Ostara: The Blossoming Time." *Llewellyn's 2016 Sabbats Almanac: Samhain 2015 to Mabon 2016*. Woodbury, MN: Llewellyn Publications, 2015.

Baumgartner, Becki. "The Reiki Three Diamonds Meditation – Self Healing Made Easy." *LuminEarth*. 5 Jul. 2016. http://www.luminearth.com.

Behrendt, Greg. *He's Just Not That Into You: The No-Excuses Truth to Understanding Guys*. New York: Simon and Schuster, 2004.

Benson, Kristina. *Potions, Herbs, Oils, and Brews*. Equality Press, 2008.

Beryl, Paul. *The Master Book of Herbalism*. Blaine, WA: Phoenix Publishing, Inc., 1984.

Bird, Stephanie Rose. Sticks, *Stones, Roots & Bones: Hoodoo, Mojo, and Conjuring with Herbs*. St. Paul, MN: Llewellyn Publications, 2004.

Blamires, Steve. *Celtic Tree Mysteries: Practical Druid Magic and Divination*. Woodbury, MN: Llewellyn Publications, 1997.

Bluestone, Sarvananda. *How to Read Signs and Omens in Everyday Life*. Rochester, VT: Destiny Books, 2002.

Bonser, Wilfrid. "The Magic Birth 'Motif' in The Kalevala." *Man* 18 (1918) : 20-22. http://www.jstor.org/stable/2787792.

Bord, Janet. *Fairies: Real Encounters with Little People*. New York: Dell Publishing, 1997.

Briggs, Katharine. *The Vanishing People: Fairy Lore and Legends*. New York: Pantheon Books, 1978.

Brown, Colette. *How to Read an Egg: Divination for the Easily Bored*. Hants, UK: Dodona Books, 2014.

Bruyere, Rosalyn. *Wheels of Light: Chakras, Auras, and the Healing Energy of the Body.* New York: Fireside, 1994.

Buckland, Raymond. *The Fortune-Telling Book: The Encyclopedia of Divination and Soothsaying.* Canton, MI: Visible Ink Press, 2004.

Cabot, Laurie and Tom Cowan. *Power of the Witch.* New York: Delta Books, 1989.

Carding, Emily. *Faery Craft: Weaving Connections with the Enchanted Realm.* Woodbury, MN: Llewellyn Publications, 2012.

Cavendish, Lucy and Serene Conneely. *The Book of Faery Magic.* Newton, Australia: Blessed Bee, 2010.

Cielo, Astra. *Signs, Omens, and Superstitions.* New York: George Sully and Company Publishers, 1918.

Coffey, Timothy. *The History and Folklore of North American Wildflowers.* New York: Houghton Mifflin Company, 1993.

Columbie, Charles A. "The Fairy Skeleton of the Chilean Desert." 12 May 2013. *Taki's Magazine.*

Connor, Kerri. Ostara: *Rituals, Recipes, and Lore for the Spring Equinox.* Woodbury, MN: Llewellyn Publications, 2015.

Cunningham, Scott. *Cunningham's Encyclopedia of Crystal, Gem and Metal Magic.* St. Paul, MN: Llewellyn Publications, 1996.

Cunningham, Scott. *Cunningham's Encyclopedia of Magical Herbs.* St. Paul, MN: Llewellyn Publications, 1987.

Cunningham, Scott. *Earth Power: Techniques of Natural Magic*. Woodbury, MN: Llewellyn Publications, 2008.

Cunningham, Scott. *The Complete Book of Incense, Oils, and Brews*. St. Paul, MN: Llewellyn Publications, 1997.

Cunningham, Scott. *The Art of Divination*. Freedom, CA: The Crossing Press, 1993.

Cunningham, Scott. *Wicca in the Kitchen*. Woodbury, MN: Llewellyn Publications, 2003.

Cymraes, Winter. "Blodeuwedd." *Druidry*. www.druidry.org.

Dacey-Foundelius, Elizabeth. "Easter in Sweden: when the witches come out to play." The Local. 21 Apr. 2011. www.thelocal.se.

Daimler, Morgan. *Pagan Portals Brigid: Meeting the Celtic Goddess of Poetry, Forge, and Healing Well*. Hants, UK: Moon Books, 2015.

Daniel, Marilyn F. *Kitchen Witchery*. Weiser Books: Boston, MA, 2002.

Draco, Melusine. *Traditional Witchcraft for the Woods and Forests*. Winchester, UK: Moon Books, 2012.

Dugan, Ellen. *Cottage Witchery: Natural Magick for the Hearth and Home*. Woodbury, MN: Llewellyn Publications, 2005.

Dugan, Ellen. *Natural Witchery: Intuitive, Personal, and Practical Magick*. Woodbury, MN: Llewellyn Publications, 2007.

Dunwich, Gerina. *A Witch's Halloween: A Complete Guide to the Magick, Incantations,*

Recipes, Spells, and Lore. Avon, MA: Provenance Press, 2007.

Dunwich, Gerina. *Dunwich's Guide to Gemstone Sorcery: Using Stones for Spells, Amulets, and Divination.* Franklin Lakes, NJ: Career Press, 2003.

Dunwich, Gerina. *Herbal Magick: A Witch's Guide to Herbal Folklore and Enchantments.* Franklin Lakes, NJ: New Page Books, 2002.

Dunwich, Gerina. *Magick Potions: How To Prepare and Use Homemade Incense, Oil, Aphrodisiacs and More.* New York: Citadel Press Books, 1998.

Dunwich, Gerina. *The Wicca Garden.* New York: Citadel Press Books, 1996.

Eason, Cassandra. *A Complete Guide to Faeries and Magical Beings.* Boston: Weiser Books, 2002.

Eason, Cassandra. *Scrying the Secrets of the Future.* Franklin, NJ: New Page Books, 2007.

Eastwood, Luke. *The Druid's Primer.* Hants, UK: Moon Books, 2012.

Eilthireach, "Deeper into Lughnasadh." *The Order of Bards, Ovates, and Druids.* druidry.org.

Ellis, Peter Berresford. *A Brief History of the Druids.* New York: Carroll & Graf Publishers,1994.

Forest, Danu. *Celtic Tree Magic: Ogham Lore and Druid Mysteries.* Woodbury, MN: Llewellyn Publications, 2014.

Forest, Danu. "The Cailleach, the old woman of winter." *Danu Forest.* Nov. 2009. www.danuforest.co.uk.

Forest, Danu. *The Magic of the Autumn Equinox*. London: Watkins Media Limited, 2015.

Forest, Danu. *The Magic of the Spring Equinox*. London: Wakins Media Limited, 2016.

Forest, Danu. *The Magic of the Winter Solstice*. Watkins Publishing: London, 2015.

Fox, Selena. "Riding with Holda." *Beliefnet*. http://www.beliefnet.com.

Foxwood, Orion. *The Faery Teachings*. Arcata, CA: R.J. Stewart Books, 2007.

Franklin, Anna. *Midsummer: Magical Celebrations of the Summer Solstice*. St. Paul, MN: Llewellyn Publications, 2004.

Franklin, Anna and Paul Mason. *Lammas: Celebrating the Fruits of the First Harvest*. St. Paul, MN: Llewellyn Publications, 2001.

Friedlander, John and Gloria Hemsher. *Basic Psychic Development*. San Francisco, California: Weiser Books, 2012.

Froud, Brian and Alan Lee. *Faeries*. New York: Harry N. Abrams, Inc., 1978.

Green, Miranda J. *Dictionary of Celtic Myth and Legend*. London: Thames and Hudson, 1992.

Green, Miranda. *Symbol and Image in Celtic Religious Art*. New York: Routledge Publishing, 1989.

Green, Susie. *Animal Messages: Seek Inspiration from your Animal Guides*. London: Cico Publishing, 2005.

Greer, John Michael. *Encyclopedia of Natural Magic*. Woodbury, MN: Llewellyn
   Publications, 2000.

Grimassi, Raven. *Beltane: Springtime Rituals, Lore, and Celebration*. St. Paul, MN:
   Llewellyn Publications, 2001.

Halvorsen, Ingred. *Runes: Alphabet of Mystery*. 2014.
   http://www.sunnyway.com/runes/index.html

Hamilton, Edith. *Mythology: Timeless Tales of Gods and Heroes*. New York: Grand
   Central Publishing, 1942.

Harper, Clive. "The Witches' Flying-Ointment." *Folklore*. Vol. 88, No. 1, 1977.
   http://www.jstor.org/stable/1259606.

Haughton, Brian. *Hidden History: Lost Civilizations, Secret Knowledge, and Ancient
   Mysteries*. Franklin Lakes, NJ: New Page Books, 2007.

Heaney, Marie. *Over Nine Waves: A Book of Irish Legends*. London: Faber and Faber
   Limited, 1994.

Heldstab, Celeste Rayne. *Llewellyn's Complete Formulary of Magical Oils*. Woodbury,
   MN: Llewellyn Publications, 2012.

Holland, Eileen. *The Spellcaster's Reference: Magickal Timing for the Wheel of the Year*. San
   Francisco, CA: Weiser Books, 2009.

Hopman, Ellen Evert. *A Druid's Herbal for Sacred Earth Year*. Rochester, VT:
   Destiny Books,1995.

Hughes, Christopher. *The Book of Celtic Magic: Transformative Teachings from the
   Cauldron of Awen*. Llewellyn Publications: Woodbury, MN, 2014.

Illes, Judika. *Pure Magic: A Complete Source in Spellcasting*. San Francisco, CA: Weiser Books, 2007.

Jacobs, Ryan. "Why So Many Icelanders Still Believe in Invisible Elves." *The Atlantic*. 29 Oct. 2013.

Johnson, Marjorie T. *Seeing Fairies*. San Antonio, TX: Anomalist Books, 2014.

K., Amber and Azrael Arynn K. *Candlemas: Feast of Flames*. Woodbury, MN: Llewellyn Publications, 2012.

Kieckhefer, Richard. *Magic in the Middle Ages*. Cambridge University Press, 2000.

Knight, Sirona. *Faery Magick: Spells, Potions, and Lore from the Earth*. Franklin Lakes, NJ: New Page Books, 2003.

Kynes, Sandra. *Llewellyn's Complete Book of Correspondences*. Woodbury, MN: Llewellyn Publications, 2013.

Kynes, Sandra. *Whispers from the Woods: The Lore and Magic of Trees*. Woodbury, MN: Llewellyn Publications, 2006.

Lady Sabina. *The Witch's Master Grimoire: An Encyclopedia of Spells, Formulas, and Magical Rites*. Franklin Lakes, NJ: New Page Books, 2001.

Lambillion, Paul. *Auras and Colors: A Guide to Working with Subtle Energies*.

Larrington, Carolyne. *The Land of the Green Man: A Journey through the Supernatural Landscapes of the British Isles*. New York: I.B. Tauris & Co., 2015.

Larrington, Carolyne, trans. *The Poetic Edda*. Oxford University Press, 2014.

Lawless, Sarah Anne. "Pantry Folk Magic" *Sarah Anne Lawless*. 1 Aug. 2013. www.sarahannelawless.com.

Leeming, David Adams. *The World of Myth: An Anthology*. Oxford University Press, 1990.

Macdonald, Fiona. *Christmas: A Very Peculiar History*. Brighton, UK: The Salariya Book Company LTD. 2012.

MacLeod, Mindy and Bernard Mees. *Runic Amulets and Magic Objects*. New York: Boydell Press, 2006.

Madden, Kristin. *Mabon: Celebrating the Autumn Equinox*. St. Paul, MN: Llewellyn Publications, 2002.

Mager, Marcia Zina. *Believing in Faeries: A Manual for Grown Ups*. C.W. London: Daneil Company LTD, 1999.

Mann, Nicholas R. *The Isle of Avalon: Sacred Mysteries of Arthur and Glastonbury*. London: Green Magic, 2001.

McCoy, Edain. *Sabbats: A Witch's Approach to Living the Old Ways*. St. Paul, MN: Llewellyn Publications, 2001.

McLaren, Karla. *Your Aura and Your Chakras*. York Beach, ME: Samuel Weiser, Inc., 1998.

Mankey, Jason. "Eostre, Easter, Ostara, Eggs, and Bunnies." *Raise the Horns*. 12 Mar. 2013. www.patheos.com.

Marquis, Melanie. Beltane: *Rituals, Recipes and Lore for May Day*. Woodbury, MN:

Llewellyn Publications, 2015.

Marquis, Melanie. *Lughnasadh: Rituals, Recipes, and Lore for Lammas.* Woodbury, MN: Llewellyn Publications, 2015.

Martin, Laura C. *Wildflower Folklore.* New York: The East Woods Press, 1984.

Mason, Herbert, trans. *Gilgamesh: A Verse Narrative.* New York: First Mariner Books, 2013.

Matthews, Caitlin. *Celtic Visions: Seership, Omens and Dreams of the Otherworld.* London: Watkins Publishing, 2012.

Matthews, John. *The Sidhe: Wisdom from the Celtic Otherworld.* Issaquah, WA: The Lorian Association, 2004.

Matthews, John. *The Summer Solstice: Celebrating the Journey of the Sun from May Day to Harvest.* Wheaton, IL: Quest Books, 2002.

Matthews, John. *The Quest for the Green Man.* Wheaton, IL.: Quest Books, 2001.

Matthews, John. *The Winter Solstice: The Sacred Traditions of Christmas.* Wheaton, IL: The Theosophical Publishing House, 2003.

Matthews, John and Will Worthington. *The Green Man Tree Oracle: Ancient Wisdom from the Spirit of Nature.* New York: Metro Books, 2008.

McColman, Carl and Kathryn Hinds. *Magic of the Celtic Gods and Goddesses: A Guide to their Spiritual Power.* Franklin Lakes, NJ: New Page Books, 2005.

McCoy, Edain. *Ostara: Customs, Spells and Rituals for the Rites of Spring.* St. Paul, MN: Llewellyn Publications, 2002.

Millet, Deacon. *Hoodoo Honey and Sugar Spells*. Forestville, CA: Lucky Mojo Curio
    Company, 2013.

Mitchell, Mandy. *Hedgewitch Book of Days*. San Francisco, CA: Weiser Books, 2014.

Monaghan, Patricia. *The Encyclopedia of Celtic Mythology and Folklore*. New York: Facts
    on File, Inc., 2004.

Monaghan, Patricia. *The New Book of Goddesses and Heroines*. St. Paul, MN: Llewellyn
    Publications, 1997.

Montley, Patricia. *In Nature's Honor: Myths and Rituals Celebrating the Earth*. Boston:
    Skinner House Books, 2005.

Motz, Lotte. "The Winter Goddess: Percht, Holda, and Related Figures." *Folklore*.
    Volume 95 (1984): 151-166. http://www.jstor.org/stable/1260199.

Morgan, Adrian. *Toads and Toadstools: The Natural History, Folklore, and Culture Oddities
    of a Strange Association*. Berkeley, CA: Celestial Arts Publishing, 1995.

Morrison, Dorothy. *Yule: A Celebration of Warmth and Light*. St. Paul, MN: Llewellyn
    Publications, 2000.

Moura, Ann. *Grimoire for the Green Witch*. Llewellyn Publications: Woodbury, MN:
    Llewellyn Publications, 2004.

Murphy-Hiscock, Arin. *Birds: A Spiritual Field Guide*. Avon, MA: Adams Media,
    2011.

Murrell, Deborah. *Superstitions*. London: Amber Books, 2008.

Neal, Carl. *Imbolc: Rituals, Recipes, and Lore for Brigid's Day*. Woodbury, MN: Llewellyn Publications, 2015.

Nock, Judy Ann. *The Provenance Press Guide to the Wiccan Year*. Avon, MA: Provenance Press, 2007.

O'Gaea, Ashleen. *Celebrating the Seasons: Beltane to Mabon*. Franklin Lakes, NJ: New Page Books 2006.

Olsen, Brad. *Sacred Places Around the World: 108 Destinations*. San Francisco, CA: Consortium of Collective Consciousness, 2004.

Page, R.I. *Runes: Reading the Past*. University of California Press, 1987.

Palin, Poppy. *Craft of the Wild Witch: Green Spirituality and Natural Enchantment*. St. Paul, MN: Llewellyn Publications, 2004.

Patterson, Rachel. *A Kitchen Witch's World of Magical Food*. Hants, UK: Moon Books, 2015.
Patterson, Rachel. *The Cailleach*. Hants, UK: Moon Books, 2016.

Paxson, Diana. *Taking Up the Runes: A Complete Guide to Using Runes in Spells, Rituals, Divination, and Magic*. San Francisco, CA: Weiser Books, 2005.

Penczack, Christopher. *The Witch's Coin: Prosperity and Money Magick*. Woodbury, MN: Llewellyn Publications, 2009.

Pennick, Nigel. *Magical Alphabets*. Boston: Weister Books, 1992.

Pickover, Clifford A. *Dreaming of the Future: The Fantastic Story of Prediction*. Amherst, NY: Prometheus Books, 2001.

Pike, Signe. *Faery Tale: One Woman's Search for Enchantment in the Modern World*. New York: Perigee Books, 2010.

Plowright, Sweyn. *The Rune Primer A Down to Earth Guide to the Runes*. Sweyn Plowright, 2006.

Pollington, Stephen. *Rudiments of Runelore*. Anglo Saxon Books, 2008.

Powell, Shantell. *Toads, Magic, and Witchcraft*. http://www.shanmonster.com/witch/familiar/toad.html.

Pritchett, Jeffrey. "A Real Fairy Sighting in North Carolina." *Before It's News*. 23 May 2014.

Reese, M.R. "The Mysterious Stone Kingdom of Great Zimbabwe," *Ancient Origins*. 11 Oct. 14. http://www.ancient-origins.net.

Roberts, Sarah. "Homemade Chamomile Lavender Milk Bath." *Handmade Mood*. 30 Apr. 2015. http://www.handmademood.com.

Rose, Carol. *Spirits, Fairies, Gnomes and Goblins: An Encyclopedia of the Little People*. Santa Barbara, CA: ABC-CLIO, 1996.

Ruggles, Clive L.N. *Ancient Astronomy: An Encyclopedia of Cosmologies and Myth*. Santa Barbara, CA: ABC-CLIO, Inc., 2005.

Sach, Jacky. *Little Giant Encyclopedia: Tea Leaf Reading*. New York: Sterling Publishing, 2008.

Sanders, Jack. *Hedgemaids and Fairy Candles: The Lives and Lore of North American Wildflowers*. Camden, ME: Ragged Mountain Press, 1995.

Sanders, Jack. *The Secret of Wildflowers*. Guilford, CT: The Lyons Press, 2003.

Santino, Jack. *All Around the Year: Holidays and Celebrations in American Life*. University of Illinois Press, 1995.

Shaw, Judith. "Cailleach, The Queen of Winter." *Feminism and Religion*. 19 Dec. 2012. https://feminismandreligion.com.

Snyder, Christopher. *The World of King Arthur*. London: Thames and Hudson Ltd., 2011.

Stewart, R.J. *The Living World of Faery*. Lake Toxaway, NC: Mercury Publishing, 1999.

Stookey, Lorena Laura. *Thematic Guide to World Mythology*. Westport, CT: Greenwood Publishing Group, 2004.

Sturluson, Snorri. *Edda*. Trans. Anthony Faulkes. London: Everyman Library, 1995.

Summers, Montague. *History of Witchcraft and Demonology*. Kessinger Publishing, 2003.

Tainter, Frank H. "What Does Mistletoe Have to Do With Christmas?" *The American Phytopathological Society*. http://www.apsnet.org/publications/apsnetfeatures/pages/mistletoe.aspx.

Tate, Karen. *Sacred Places of the Goddess: 108 Destinations*. San Francisco, CA: Consortium of Collective Consciousness, 2006.

The Kalevala. Compiled by Elias Lönnrot. Trans. John John Marin Crawford. *Project Guttenberg*. 31 May 2002. http://www.gutenberg.org/.

The Mabinogion, trans. Gwyn Jones and Thomas Jones. London: Everyman Library, 1993.

Thorsson, Edred. *Runelore: A Handbook of Rune Magic*. York Beach, ME: Weiser Books, 1984.

Van Gelder, Dora. *The Real World of Fairies*. Wheaton, IL: Quest Books, 1977.

Varner, Gary R. *The Mythic Forest, The Green Man, and the Spirit of Nature*. New York: Algora Publishing, 2006.

Vedder-Shults, Nancy. "Egg Divinations." *MatriFocus: Cross Quarterly for the Goddess Women*, Vol. 6-3, May 2007.

Weber, Courtney. *Brigid: History, Mystery, and Magick of the Celtic Goddess*. San Francisco, CA: Weiser Books, 2015.

Webster, Richard: *Flower and Tree Magic: Discover the Natural Enchantment Around You*. Woodbury, MN: Llewellyn Publications, 2008.

Webster, Richard. *The Complete Book of Auras*. Woodbury, MN: Llewellyn Publications, 2010.

Whitehurst, Tess. *The Magic of Flowers: A Guide to Their Metaphysical Uses and Properties*. Woodbury, MN: Llewellyn Publications, 2015.

Wildwood, Rob. *Magical Places of Britain*. York, UK: Wyldwood Publishing, 2013.

Wimmer, Gary L. *Lithomancy: The Psychic Art of Reading Stones*. Self-Published, 2010.

ABOUT THE AUTHOR

Kiki Dombrowski lives in Nashville where is a tarot card reader, certified life coach, and workshop facilitator. Prior to her time in Tennessee, Kiki lived in Connecticut, Paris, and Nottingham, where she was an English and creative writing student. She received her Bachelor's Degree from Southern Connecticut State University and her Master's Degree from Nottingham University. Kiki's written work has been featured in *Witch Way Magazine*, *Green Egg Magazine*, *Witch Vox*, and *elephant journal*. For more information visit ***www.kikidombrowski.com***.

WITCH WAY MAGAZINE
Want to read more from Kiki? Visit
www.witchwaymagazine.com
for digital issues, special edition
paper copies, and more!